Commendations for
The Explorer's Guide to Judaism

'Whether Jew or Christian, anyone wishing to read an original and gripping introduction to Judaism that is well grounded and systematically constructed should go for this book. Christians interested in reform would be particularly happy with the courageous, constructive and sensitive way one of the best-known Reform Rabbis and representatives of Judaism presents his own major religion.'

Hans Küng

'Rabbi Jonathan Magonet performs the rare and impressive feat of writing an informative and critical interpretation of Judaism, while at the same time giving his non-Jewish readers an insider's understanding of what it feels like to be Jewish and why the religion continues to attract and appeal.'

Karen Armstrong

THE EXPLORER'S GUIDE TO

JUDAISM

JONATHAN MAGONET

Hodder & Stoughton
LONDON SYDNEY AUCKLAND

British Library Cataloguing in Publication Data
A record for this book is available from the British Library

ISBN 0 340 70984 7

Typeset by Avon Dataset Ltd, Bidford-on-Avon, Warks

Printed and bound in Great Britain by
Clays Ltd, St Ives plc

Hodder and Stoughton Ltd
A Division of Hodder Headline PLC
338 Euston Road
London NW1 3BH

Dedicated to the teachers, staff, students and graduates
of the Leo Baeck College.

For Doro, Gav and Avi.

Contents

Preface

When I was invited to contribute a book in this series and heard the brief, to describe Judaism as an 'insider' in a way that will help the reader engage with the issues it faces today, I welcomed the opportunity. Since Judaism is both a religion and the faith of a particular people, it has been a challenge to get the balance right between the personal and the informative, the spiritual and the sociological. Others must judge whether I have succeeded.

A book like this must inevitably be something of an apologia or defence of Judaism as well, even if unintentionally or unconsciously. For too much of our existence Jews have lived in exile, as a minority in the midst of other cultures and civilisations, absorbing much and giving in return, but transmuting much of what we have acquired into our own unique form. All too often that outer world was hostile, even life threatening, and we have been forced to justify our existence, holding our ground as long as we could, while keeping our suitcases packed. This leads to a kind of wariness in talking about our inner world to outsiders. And Jewish life is still overshadowed by the memory of the genocidal assault on the Jewish people in the heart of European civilisation in the middle of this century. It is not an easy legacy to inherit and must inevitably colour much of what will be described here.

But from interfaith dialogue I have learnt how important it is to be self-critical as well. Like any other community we have our good and our bad points. Revealing them may help demythologise some of the mystery that surrounds us and allow for a healthier encounter. I have always admired the insight that

Rabbi Dr Leo Baeck gave to Rabbi Lionel Blue which he in turn passed on to me: that Judaism should be your home, not your prison. So this book is written in the spirit of one who tries to live both within and without its walls, to make it a place where guests are welcome and to enjoy excursions elsewhere from time to time.

Writing a book like this has also been a terrible reminder of gaps in my knowledge that will never be adequately filled. Fortunately the early decision on how to structure the book gave it a framework even if I still have nightmares about discovering too late some essential topics that I forgot, or had no space to include. But if this book introduces people to Judaism, there are others to conduct them to more specialised areas and authorities.

My thanks are due to Dr Joanna Weinberg, lecturer in Rabbinics at Leo Baeck College, for looking through the manuscript – under strict instructions to find the howlers and restrain herself from commenting on the opinions expressed. She did this with admirable tact and restraint. (It was said of the compiler of a multivolume series on Judaism that all his facts were right but all his opinions wrong! I would be happy to follow in this honourable tradition.) Similarly Cesar Hamann kindly looked through the 'Time-line' and added a few essential dates. Rabbi Lee Wax read an earlier version of chapter 4 on the changing roles of Jewish women. The errors that remain are entirely my responsibility. Judith Longman has been a gracious editor, with the friendly spirit of Marcus Braybrook hovering somewhere in the background. They have allowed me to go where the spirit moved me and trusted the results.

I have dedicated the book to the teachers, staff, students and graduates of the Leo Baeck College. The College, in its modest way, strives to be the successor of the great pre-war Berlin Liberal Jewish seminary, the Hochschule für die Wissenschaft des Judentums, finally closed down by the Nazis in 1942. It has been my privilege to be part of the College as student, lecturer in Bible, and Principal, and to marvel at the quality of students and teachers it has managed to attract despite its few resources, and its imagination and sometimes courage in exploring the dimensions of a new Jewish life being born in Europe. I hope that the Judaism described in the following pages will be recognisable to my colleagues in this endeavour and worthy of the opportunity and responsibility we have inherited.

Jonathan Magonet
London
27th January 1998
29th Tevet 5758.

Introduction

When I started this book I knew where to begin even if I did not know where it was to go. And that brings to mind a Jewish story and another one in its train. So something about Judaism has already been evoked. Jews like telling stories.

It was in Madras. I had been invited as a last-minute participant in a conference on philosophy and religion. Come to think of it, the invitation came from Marcus Braybrooke who invited me to write this book, so the two events come neatly together. I was due to speak one afternoon and a polite young Indian man came up to me and told me that he was especially interested in my paper on Judaism. I was delighted at this recognition accorded to my own religion given that so many were represented here. Clearly he valued the particular quality of the Jewish faith that had somehow appealed to him even in this place so far from the Jewish world that I knew. 'Yes,' he added, 'I am very interested in the minor religions.' There was no irony intended in his remarks, nor any putdown. He was simply observing Judaism from his own particular perspective, and compared to the hundreds of millions of adherents to other faiths, the few million Jews on this planet were, if not insignificant, at least distinctly 'minor'. (At the same conference someone pointed out that from an Indian perspective, Britain is a small island off the European peninsula of the Afro-Asian land mass.)

It is for such a young man that I would like to write. Someone to whom Judaism is a curiosity, something heard about and vaguely puzzled over. In that way, perhaps, I can break through the 'knowingness' that so often attends presentations of Judaism.

If nothing can be assumed about the knowledge of my audience, I can take nothing for granted in the telling of my story, and that can only be for the good. Which having been said I must immediately add a rider. So much of Jewish tradition finds its origin in the Hebrew Bible (Christian 'Old Testament') that it is impossible to explain Judaism without constant reference to this. However, knowledge of the Bible is no longer something that can be taken for granted, so I will give the appropriate references when needed, but have to assume the reader can fill in that particular part of the background.

Which brings me to my story. An old Jew is on his way to synagogue when he is stopped by a policeman who asks him where he is going. 'I don't know,' replies the old Jew. So the policeman arrests him for loitering and he spends the night in prison. The next morning he is called up before the judge who asks the policeman why the old man had been arrested. 'Well,' says the policeman, 'I asked him where he was going and he said he didn't know.' 'Do you have anything to say in your defence?' asks the judge. 'Well, your honour,' he replies. 'You see, I am a religious man and I can never know what fate God has in store for me. So when this gentleman asked me where I was going, I could only tell him truthfully that I didn't know. And you see, I was quite right. I thought I was going to synagogue, but I ended up in prison!'

So we too can head off towards the synagogue, the Jewish place of worship, and see where we end up.

But this inevitably leads me to a second story to explain the first. (It is assumed that no Jew can tell a joke in the presence of another Jew. First because he or she has heard it before; and second, knows a funnier version; and anyway could tell it much better in the first place. This process may also occur within a single Jewish head as the above paragraph indicates. Hence the second story.) The Maggid of Dubno (Jacob ben Wolf Kranz), an itinerant preacher in eighteenth-century Poland, was famed for his ability to find exactly the right story to match the particular sermon he was giving. Once he was asked how he managed to find parables that fitted so well. Inevitably he explained with a parable: 'When you shoot arrows at a target, there are two ways of doing it. In the first way you find a wall, draw up a target, stand back and shoot. The other possibility is to find the wall, stand back and shoot, and afterwards draw the target.'

So did my story of the old man not knowing where he was going suggest the way I started this book, or did the way I wanted to start it lead to the story? Can you separate these two possibilities since both came out of the same head? This too is not an irrelevant discussion. Jews tend to see things from more than one side – a product perhaps of their experience as a minority in different cultures, together with the rigorous intellectual training that comes from the study of the Talmud (see chapter 6). It may lead to great sophistication – or paralysis when it comes to taking action. As yet another old Jewish joke would have it, 'There are always two possibilities.'

In the Hebrew Bible, God, speaking through an anonymous prophet, tells the Israelites in Babylon, defeated, exiled and demoralised, 'You are My witnesses, an oracle of the Eternal, and I am God!' (Isa. 43:12). To which a daring, but not exceptional, rabbinic comment is: 'When you are My witness, I am God, and when you are not My witnesses, I am, so to speak, not God!' (Midrash Psalms 123:2)

What arrogance! Or what a feeling of responsibility, to be witnesses to God in this world, whether the rest of the world is willing to listen or not. That is the self-proclaimed purpose of the Jewish people and it is one source of our extraordinary ability to survive as a tiny minority through remarkable changes of status and circumstances, horrendous vicissitudes and moments of awesome success and creativity. If the ultimate mystery of Jewish survival cannot be explained, or explained away, at least we can follow some of the features of the Jewish people and their religion, the stages in their journey across the centuries.

The Image of the Jew

Hath not a Jew eyes? Hath not a Jew hands, organs, dimensions, senses, affections, passions? fed with the same food, hurt with the same weapons, subject to the same diseases, healed by the same means, warmed and cooled by the same winter and summer, as a Christian is? If you prick us, do we not bleed? If you tickle us, do we not laugh? If you poison us, do we not die? And if you wrong us, shall we not revenge?

Shakespeare put this haunting series of questions into the mouth of Shylock in his *Merchant of Venice*, relishing the paradox of the despised money-lender asserting his humanity in the presence of the corrupt representatives of the supposedly higher humanity of Christianity.

I have no idea what lies behind this ploy of Shakespeare. It is certainly highly satisfying in dramatic terms, the irony not being lost on any open-minded audience. Is there a political reality behind it as well? I would not be surprised, because whatever else has been the fate of the Jewish people, time and time again we have been 'instrumentalised', used by others as bargaining chips in some third game.

It begins with the Gospel writer's attempt to reach a wider audience than just his own people. Thus in Mark 14 it is the disciples who sleep at a crucial time or who deny Jesus, while in 15:39 it is the Roman centurion who comments, 'Truly this man was the Son of God!' Sometimes such 'use' of the Jews is unconscious and out of sincere motives.

Ninety kilometers south of Berlin is Wittenberg, the Lutherstadt. Martin Luther came to teach at the university in 1508 and sparked off the Reformation in October 1517 with his ninety-five theses against the abuse of indulgences. In the middle of the town stands St Mary's Protestant Church, with the famous altar by Lucas Cranach, where Luther preached. It is located at number 35 Judenstrasse, Jews Street. In later life Luther published virulent anti-Semitic pamphlets. 'Concerning the Jews and their Lies' in 1543 advocated burning their synagogues to the ground and hiding all trace of their existence, destroying their homes, taking away their prayerbooks and Talmuds and preventing their rabbis from teaching. It comes as no surprise, though no less unpleasant for all that, to find high up on the outer wall of the church the figures of a pig, with children suckling it and someone standing behind it.

This is the notorious 'Judensau', the Jewish Sow, based on mediaeval Christian legends, commonly held in France and Germany, that assumed Jews suckled from a sow, despite, or probably because of, Jewish laws that considered the pig to be ritually unclean and forbidden. Such figures appeared in three-dimensional form within and on the doors of churches and town halls.[1] Above this fine example are the words *rabini*, presumably 'rabbi', and *schem hameforasch*. This latter is a transliteration of the Hebrew term for the divine name, made up in Hebrew of four letters (the tetragrammaton), the holiest designation of God which Jewish tradition has forbidden to be spoken aloud. There is a kind of grotesque irony in this, for it is as much a blaspheming of God for Christians as it is for Jews to treat the divine name in such a way. In one sense this strange juxtaposition symbolises the ambivalence about Judaism within Christianity itself, inheriting, and seeking at the same time to deny, the tradition from which it emerged.

But this particular location has an added dimension of irony because of a small plaque on the ground a couple of feet away from the base of the church. It commemorates the Jews of Wittenberg who were taken away and murdered during the Nazi period. This is not uncommon in different parts of Western Germany where Jewish communities were destroyed. But Wittenberg belonged to the former East German State where all such monuments were expressly forbidden. So how was it possible to place it here? Although the town belonged to the State, the ground immediately around the church belonged to the Church, and so within its 'territory' such an act of repentance and reconciliation was possible. However belatedly, the Church, or at least some people within it, had taken a symbolic stand for their former Jewish neighbours against the authority of a repressive State. But how far was this itself driven by political motives, in the struggle against a communist ideology and regime? If this is even partly the case 'the Jews' were still being 'instrumentalised' for other purposes, as had been in part the case with Luther. Anti-Semitism, and its peculiar alter ego, philo-Semitism, continue to retain their ambiguities.

Sometimes the treatment of Jews was simply the cynical manipulation of a subject people. A good example is the forcing of Jews into money-lending in the Middle Ages. In the wake of the First Crusade (1096–99), when Jewish communities in the Rhineland were destroyed by Crusaders on their way to the Holy Land (why wait to get to Palestine to destroy infidels when they could be found on one's doorstep?), Jews were unable to operate as merchants. They were not allowed to enter the guilds which dominated trade and crafts. The Church felt bound by the biblical laws against usury, except in cases where they could rationalise the law to their own benefit, which left the risky business of lending money on interest to individuals open to the Jews as their only available source of revenue. Risky because in many types of loan there were no guarantees of repayment, and when Jews tried to obtain their money they could find themselves under physical threat, trapped by economic as well as religious abuse. Thus the negative stereotype of the grasping Jew was established and it continues into our own times, reinforced by Nazi propaganda that survived into Soviet anti-Jewish activities and found a ready continuation in political anti-Zionism. (To see how pervasive this image is it is only necessary to look at the 1950 fourth edition of the *Concise Oxford Dictionary*:

Jew n. Person of Hebrew race; (transf., colloq.) extortionate usurer, driver of hard bargains; *rich as a–;* . . . v. t. (colloq.). Cheat, overreach.

No wonder someone has been running a campaign for years to get these definitions changed.)

All of which is to say that the 'image of the Jew' is a highly charged and often negative feature that distorts any account of the Jewish people.

But there is another factor that affects the image of the Jew. I encountered it when looking for illustrations for a series of prayerbooks I co-edited for the Reform Synagogues of Great Britain. We wanted to include pictures that would help those praying to identify with the prayers and feel at home within this particular spiritual ethos. But when we looked for illustrations, indeed whenever we asked people for materials to use, all we got was pictures of old men with beards, usually belonging to Chasidic communities, either praying solemnly or joyfully dancing. Which is not to say that there are not large numbers of old Jewish men with beards who pray and dance, but they represent a very small proportion of the Jewish world. Jewish women also pray. There are literally millions of Jews who belong to Liberal, Reform and Conservative synagogues who simply look like 'normal' everyday people, with no distinguishing dress or appearance, who also pray. That is to say, the 'image' of the Jew is totally coloured by a few limited stereotypes, that actually affect our own self-understanding as much as they affect the perceptions of outsiders. Old men with beards are 'authentic' Jews, and others are not!

So it comes as an enormous shock for many today when they come across the phenomenon of women rabbis, for, as a rule, they do not dress in black, and most certainly do not have beards. Their struggle to have their authority recognised and accepted is also very much tied to such 'folk-images' of what an 'authentic' Jew looks like. Of course alongside the 'religious Jew' there emerged in the 1950s and 1960s a new image, the picture of the 'Israeli pioneer', a much more youthful, often blonde, man, seen on his tractor, draining swamps and gazing meaningfully into the distance, or a raven-haired woman in shorts, dancing in a circle with her equally athletic girlfriends after a hard day on the kibbutz, the collective farm. It was a very positive image, at least till the Six Day War. Today it has been replaced yet again with a negative one of Israeli soldiers in riot gear facing down stone-throwing Palestinian children. The reality is always more complex. But it is the image that determines attitudes.

If we move away from actual pictures a different kind of perception of the Jew emerges. Here we come across the 'great men' image. Freud and Einstein are prominently there, and, even though both of his parents had converted to Christianity, so too is Karl Marx to complete the triumvirate. This is the Jew as disturber of conventions and shaper of modernity, in the sciences, arts and humanities, as well as in trade. And rightly so, in the sense that the achievements of Jews in these areas have been extraordinary in the past few centuries. It is as if energies and intelligence, pent up inside ghetto walls, exploded into creativity after the Emancipation, when Jews were allowed to become full citizens of their nation. But here there is another irony, for most of those Jews who 'made it' did so at the expense of their Jewish identity, either denying it entirely, or putting it on to some kind of back burner. Certainly few of them were 'practising' Jews in the sense of operating within the framework of normative Jewish religious life. In this they were no different from the majority of Jews similarly finding their way in this new world. The only problem is that it created yet another stereotype of the Jew as 'cosmopolitan, intellectual', brilliant yet contro-versial, the outsider, thus ignoring the vast majority of Jews who lead very humdrum lives and are no better nor worse than their middle-class neighbours, whose values they share. In short Jews find ourselves as bewildered as anyone else about who exactly we are.

Such a description would be incomplete without one more image that continues to haunt the Western imagination. The Jew as victim of the Holocaust or Shoah (destruction), to use the term preferred in Jewish circles. The pictures of the extermination camps, the story of the selection, concentration and murder of one-third of the Jewish people this century cannot but affect anyone who seeks to understand the Jewish people today. Fifty years after the end of the war, we are beginning more and more to examine the root causes of the Holocaust and in particular the social underpinnings that allowed it to happen – alongside the extermination of the mentally retarded, gipsies, homosexuals and indeed anyone who did not conform to a narrow perception of 'permitted humanity'. The appearance of memorials and Holocaust 'museums' both address the issues and spark further controversies in their wake, because questions about basic flaws and potential sources of disintegration in Western civilisation are still with us and cannot be ignored.

But to return to the implications of this within the Jewish world, we too find ourselves inextricably bound up with that past experience, for good and for bad. I will explore something of this in the final chapter, but here would only point to the hideous irony that Jews are seemingly forever bound to images of the Nazis, the murderers and their victims hopelessly intertwined. For decades it was only necessary to introduce into your detective or spy novel, or movie, a Jewish survivor or an ex-Nazi villain to guarantee a *frisson* of excitement and an obvious plot development about missing treasure or bloody revenge. Alongside the sincere attempts at historical evaluation, or the painfully written memoirs of survivors, there is an often obscene yet recurrent pairing of Jew and Nazi. Sometimes other games are played whereby roles are reversed, something often done with regard to modern Israel and the Palestinians. This grotesque and tragic past continues to invade a different present.

In a further twist, the language of 'Holocaust' or 'genocide' has entered the vocabulary of the media to be applied sometimes legitimately, but often indiscriminately, in many other conflict situations, and even with regard to animal welfare. This in turn leads to painful questions about whether the genocide of the Jews by the Nazis and their collaborators is to be considered a unique event or not, as if there was some hierarchy of suffering with points to be awarded. If the 'Shoah' is a Jewish tragedy to be remembered and struggled with, the 'Holocaust' is a terrifying question to the whole of our human civilisation.

I am sorry to intrude at such an early stage these difficult and disturbing issues, but they remain very present in Jewish life. All too often Jewish identity is assumed to start and end with that experience of being the victims of others. We too instrumentalise the Shoah for perceived Jewish needs – fund-raising, supporting the State of Israel, creating a Jewish identity when little of the tradition seems to appeal. It will take generations before we can separate ourselves from the direct effects of the Shoah and the long-term physical and psychological impact and begin to see what being Jewish means out of our own inner resources. Suffice it to say that questions surrounding the 'image of the Jew' in the outside world, and the exploration of the nature and content of 'Jewish identity' within the Jewish world, are central issues today.

Who Knows One?

When thinking about this book I wanted some sort of structure, if only to help with deciding what to include and where. And then I remembered a song, 'Who Knows One', that is sung in Jewish homes towards the end of the Passover celebration. Like other songs in that festival liturgy it builds on repeated phrases, which allows everyone to join in, and indeed to compete in how fast the list can be sung as it grows ever longer. By the time you have reached the thirteenth verse of this song (each verse appears as the title of a different chapter of this book), it is a daunting exercise in breath control, mastery of Hebrew pronunciation and singular dedication. It is also a great way to show off at the end of the evening. The listing covers many of the key elements of Judaism, conveniently based on numbers. I do recall seeing a version where the 'nine months to childbirth' were replaced by 'nine candles on the Chanukah menorah' (with a footnote explaining that the ninth was for the *shamash*, the extra candle used to light the others) in a Liberal version of the Haggadah, since superseded. (I am not sure whether it was out of distaste for such a biological element or the desire to cram in a more ideological note.)

Unfortunately the list does not really cover all the issues that one might want to address in a book like this, and some of the verses really overlap. So I have taken a number of liberties, looking for themes under the surface of the title. If this makes the book a little less systematic than it might otherwise be, I can always hide behind the unsystematic reality of Jewish life today. In any event this book cannot pretend to be comprehensive and the bibliographies point the way to more systematic reading on selected topics. Instead it feels appropriate that this song which belongs to the family life of the Jewish people, and is intended both to teach and entertain, should provide the framework for a book that seeks to enter the world of the Jewish people rather than look at it from without. That the song begins and ends with God, or, because of the way that it is sung, ends and begins with God, is also right.

Who knows One? I know One.
One is our God in heaven and earth.

1

One is our God in heaven and earth
God and the Jewish people

If nothing else can be said about Judaism as a religious system, one thing is utterly certain and fundamental – the belief in the One God. We need look no further than the central affirmation of Jewish belief, the *Shema*, stated several times a day in Jewish prayer, and traditionally recited on one's deathbed: *shema yisrael adonai eloheinu adonai ehad*, 'Hear O Israel, the Eternal our God, the Eternal is One' (Deut. 6:4). As if to reinforce this affirmation, it is introduced once during the daily prayers by a blessing that concludes with our task as Jews 'to unify God's name', which presumably means to acknowledge the unity of God and to bring the knowledge of this unity into the wider world.

The origins of this concept of God are quite uncertain. The Hebrew Bible itself seems to take this assumption for granted, at least on the surface. The magisterial opening of Genesis shows this One God, merely speaking a word, for that word to be transformed into tangible reality. 'Let there be light, and there was light' (Gen. 1:3) captures the idea but not the extraordinary brevity and power of the Hebrew that encapsulates this in two words that are simply repeated with a single consonant added: *yehee or vayehee or*. It requires no more than a simple expulsion of breath. For the One God, creation was that effortless.

Nevertheless even in Genesis there is a question mark to be raised about whom God is addressing when asserting: 'Let us make man . . .' (Gen. 1:26). Is this the royal 'we'? Or is God addressing some kind of semi-divine beings that belong to the

11

royal court – beings that turn up quite openly in Isaiah 6 and 1 Kings 22:19ff.? Are these the remnants of mythological figures that pre-existed Israel's concept of God – the gods and powers of Near Eastern legend? Are there traces elsewhere in the Bible of the gods of Egypt, that other great centre of culture? The ten plagues which 'smote the Egyptians' may also be intended to show God's judgments on Egypt 'and their gods' (Num. 33:4). Hence it is the Nile that is first 'attacked' by Moses when its waters turn to blood, and the other manifestations of the plagues may directly or indirectly involve Egyptian deities.

What are we to make of the various different names by which God is known in these early stories? We will look in more detail at the special name for God that Israel is never to pronounce, the one made up of four Hebrew letters, *yod-hey-vav-hey* (Y H W H), known as the 'tetragrammaton'.

Perhaps a word is needed already about how to deal with this name. It seems that in an earlier period the name was pronounced with its proper vowels, but after the destruction of the first Temple a substitute word *adonai*, meaning 'Lord', was used. Only the High Priest on the Day of Atonement when he entered the Holy of Holies in the Temple would pronounce the name in its correct form (Mishnah Yoma 6:2).

The Hebrew text of the Bible consists of consonants only, so each word could theoretically be pronounced in a variety of ways and have different meanings as a result. In fact Jewish commentators on the text made full use of this flexibility in their interpretations over the centuries. However a system of vowel signs was introduced, based on traditional understandings of the text, so as to help with the reading. In some cases the rabbis wished to substitute another word for the one that appears in the Hebrew text – occasionally they preferred to read a euphemism for a particularly harsh word, or change a word where they were aware that it had become corrupted in the transmission. In such cases, under the consonants they would place the vowels of the substituted word, and the reader, knowing the system, would read accordingly. One of the commonest examples of this is the case of the four-letter name of God. Beneath the letters *yod-hey-vav-hey*, they inserted the vowels of the word *adonai*. However in the Middle Ages, Christians studying the Hebrew Bible, and unaware of this practice, assumed the vowels simply showed the correct pronunciation and thus was created the hybrid name 'Jehovah'.

Jews became increasingly sensitive to the possible misuse of the divine name and substituted *ha-shem*, 'the Name', for *adonai* when using it in other than liturgical contexts. A tradition arose, based on Deuteronomy 12:4, that the name of God should not be obliterated once it had been written down, so great care was taken to preserve texts where the name appeared. Old prayer-books or documents containing the name of God would be stored in a special part of the synagogue, the Geniza, or buried in the ground. Thus when writing the name of God for some purpose, only one of the letters would be used, such as the letter *hey*, with an apostrophe following, to indicate what was intended. This practice of caution with the use of the written name even extended to the vernacular, and pious Jews will write 'G-D', though most religious authorities have seen no need for this.

But what does the name mean? The form 'Yah', exists, utilising the first two letters of the divine name, and may have originated in a kind of shout. But the usual text that is studied for an understanding of the name is the famous story of 'the burning bush' in Exodus 3, where Moses first encountered God. When he asks God for the divine name, God is evasive – knowing someone's name in the biblical world implied some measure of control over the person. God's answer 'I am that I am' (Exod. 3:14) effectively means 'that remains My business!' The Hebrew phrase *ehyeh asher ehyeh* is based on the 'imperfect' form of the verb *hayah* meaning 'to be'. Since *ehyeh* could mean 'I am', 'I will be', 'I shall be', 'I might be', 'I could be' or any other of the modalities, it is easy to see how difficulties arise in interpreting this phrase. However what does emerge is that the name Y H W H is related, at least in this folk etymology, to the verb 'to be'.

Those seeking to translate the name in the modern period, and to get away from the substitute name 'Lord', have explored the theme of 'being' in different ways. Moses Mendelssohn (1729–86) introduced the term 'der Ewiger', 'the Eternal', in his German translation of the Bible (1780–83), based on his philosophical understanding of God as the absolutely perfect being. In their German translation of the Hebrew Bible, which began to appear in the 1930s, Martin Buber and Franz Rosenzweig preferred a more 'existential' understanding of being – 'He who is present', and instead of using a name simply substituted 'ER' (HE) or 'DU' (THOU) according to the context. More recently, in the wake of feminist questioning of language, the use of 'Lord' has been addressed. The term is of masculine origin and perpetuates an equation whereby power and authority are vested in a God who should be beyond gender but is effectively male. Here the Buber-Rosenzweig solution becomes inappropriate and – though it is also unsatisfactory for many reasons – I have used 'the Eternal' when translating the four-letter name.

But what of the many other biblical designations: El, El Shaddai, El Elyon, El Berit, El Roi, El Olam, Adonai, Y H W H Tzevaot, K'dosh Yisrael, Pachad Yitzhak, Avir Ya'akov and the generic term Elohim? Most probably many of these were the names of local deities that Israel assimilated to their own concept of God. The story of Abraham's blessing by Melchizedek the King of Salem (Jerusalem) and priest of *El Elyon* shows how such a process might occur (Gen. 14:18–22).

One more word is needed about the term *Elohim*. This appears to be a general term for 'God' or 'gods' (and also 'powers', and possibly 'judges'). Even though it has a plural ending (*-im*), it always takes a singular verb when it is used to mean the God of the universe, who is known to Israel by the special name Y H W H. It is used in different ways in Scripture, often in conjunction with Y H W H, where the two may be used to indicate different aspects of the divine in the particular context. This distinction also became one of the central features in the development of the 'Documentary Hypothesis' about the origins of the Hebrew Bible, it being assumed that the names reflected different traditions about God from different strands of Israelite society that had been combined by a series of editors under particular social or political conditions. Current literary studies of the Bible have raised major questions about the legitimacy of such a distinction, but the hypothesis still seems to dominate studies of the Bible in academic circles. We will see below how the rabbis differentiated between the two names.

But given this variety of names and the difficulty of understanding their origins or significance, it is no wonder that opinions are divided about how Israel came to its conviction that there was only one God in the entire universe.

> You shall know today and take it to heart that the Eternal is God in the heavens above and on the earth beneath – there is no other. (Deut. 4:39)[1]

Did the idea evolve over time? Was it introduced by Moses out of his Egyptian upbringing and schooling, or did he learn it from his father-in-law, Jethro, the priest of Midian? Did it develop out of a kind of monolatry: Israel's God, the only God for Israel, who gradually came to be seen as the only God in the world? Or was it, as some suggest, a revolutionary idea that was born overnight and by its sheer simplicity and all-encompassing power conquered all opposition?

Certainly the Hebrew Bible in the form that has come down to us assumes this monotheism and seems unembarrassed to retain those texts and narratives that point to rival gods and idols that are forever tempting Israel to go astray. If we accept the biblical account of the emergence of Israel as a people – slaves in Egypt, wanderers in the wilderness for a generation, settlers on a new land, and refugees in exile – then they must have experienced God in many different guises: the multiple divine beings of Egypt; the invisible moving God of the wilderness; the fertility gods and goddesses worshipped on every high place and under every leafy tree in the land they entered; the all-powerful conquering gods of Babylon and their subtle theologies. So their God has to encompass and transcend all the different qualities to be found in each of these different environments and perform all their various functions.

These struggles can be seen, and are overtly described in the biblical narratives and prophetic complaints. In fact it is astonishing that 'monotheism' won out given the popularity of other gods. The most sophisticated king of all, certainly the great 'theologian', Solomon seems to have fallen foul of the seductiveness of a kind of symbiosis with the gods of the local nations. After the fall of Jerusalem the prophet Jeremiah, dragged unwillingly down to Egypt, has to withstand the taunts of those who complained that the destruction of the Temple and their exile was precisely because they had abandoned their 'authentic' god, not Y H W H but the 'queen of heaven' (Jer. 44:17)! After all if the measure of the legitimacy of your god is his or her ability to look after you, they had a genuine complaint – one that was to be repeated in different ways throughout Jewish history.

Nevertheless the assumption of the writers and editors of the Bible was that Israel had only one God, who was the God of the entire universe, even if the people went astray from time to time after other gods, which were no-gods. It is not always so self-evident how the biblical writers viewed the gods of other peoples – as legitimate and 'real' gods of that nation, as mere illusions, or as an attempt to worship the one true God that had somehow become distorted. (Certainly the Book of Jonah describes both the sailors who meet Jonah and the arch-enemy, the Ninevites, as coming to recognise the existence of only One supreme God, whom the sailors can identify with Y H W H, even if the Ninevites cannot.)

The challenges to this belief in the oneness of God came from many quarters. It was clearly an issue for the exiles in Babylon if we are to judge by the frequent assertions by the anonymous composer of the latter parts of the Book of Isaiah. God is frequently heard affirming that He is the first and the last, the only God from times past whose faithfulness would be manifest in the future. There is even a hint of some kind of dualism that the prophet has to combat when God proclaims:

> So that they may know from the rising of the sun and from the west that there is none besides Me, I am the Eternal and there is no other; who forms light and creates darkness, makes peace and creates evil. I, the Eternal, do all these. (Isa. 45:6–7)

But this 'oneness' of God sparks off other speculations. How can

God be 'out there' in the universe and at the same time somehow engaged with human beings in their small individual lives? Jeremiah has God ask the rhetorical question: 'Am I a God who is near and not a God who is afar off?' (Jer. 23:23) The reference point here has to be heaven to which God is 'near', as if answering the accusation that God sits in heaven and stays 'near' to His domain, and does not bother with the 'far' world of the earth.

Isaiah addressed the paradox of a God who is both utterly 'other' and remote, yet present in the world, with a formulation that has entered Jewish and Christian liturgies: 'Holy, holy, holy is *adonai tzevaot* (the Lord of Hosts), the whole earth is full of His glory' (Isa. 6:3). We have to understand that the word 'holy', *kadosh*, means something like 'other', 'apart', 'separate'. When repeated it means that God's 'otherness' is itself 'other'. When repeated three times it emphasises that God is utterly remote from any category we can comprehend or control. But at the same time God's 'glory', Hebrew *kavod*, from a word meaning 'weight', completely fills the world. God's 'presence' is everywhere. (In theological terms we would have to speak of God's simultaneous transcendence and immanence.)

With these passages and many others we find rehearsed in the Hebrew Bible many of the essential religious questions that will be explored throughout the subsequent centuries within Judaism, Christianity and Islam, each in their different ways inheritors of the biblical tradition.

By the time the biblical books became canonised and Judaism began its different evolutionary phases, the issue of the 'oneness' of God was quite resolved. The rabbis, the successors of the Pharisees who created 'Judaism' as we know it, had no doubts about the revolutionary nature of this belief in One God and that Abraham was the founding figure.

When Abraham was born king Nimrod tried to kill him so his father hid him for three years in a cave. When he left the cave he asked himself: Who created the heaven and earth and me? All day long he prayed to the sun, but in the evening the sun set and the moon rose. When he saw the moon and the stars round it he assumed that the moon created heaven and earth and that the stars were the moon's princes and courtiers. So all night he prayed to the moon. But in the morning the moon disappeared and the sun rose again, so he said: There must be a higher power over them, and to Him I will pray. (Genesis Rabba 61:16 and 95:3)

This 'One God' is no cold mathematical concept in the view of the rabbis. They were 'God-intoxicated' men who searched out in the Bible every possible clue to the qualities of God, and looked for God in every aspect of human existence.

The Divinity was felt by them, was present in their homes and schools, glorified their life, sanctified their work – no space or moment of existence, in the seen and unseen world, in the shadow of life and beyond the grave could be imagined without Him. Consequently, there is no aspect of primitive or advanced religious thought which has ever agitated the mind of man and has a bearing on Divinity and Godhead to which those sages remained indifferent, and to which they did not contribute their proper share in elucidating or developing them.[2]

Perhaps the best-known distinction the rabbis made is precisely between the two names of God that we have encountered: Y H W H and Elohim. By some time in the second century they had coined two terms which distinguished the names and the divine qualities they represented. Y H W H, they thought, expressed the *midat ha-rahamim,* God's attribute of mercy, while Elohim, showed God's *midat ha-din,* the attribute of strict justice. The world existed only because of the balance between these two powers within the Godhead. In a remarkable rabbinic homily, this tension is explained:

The matter is like a king who had some empty goblets. The king said: 'If I put hot water in them, they will burst; if I put cold water, they will crack.' So the king mixed cold and hot water together, and poured it in, and the goblets were uninjured. Even so, God said, if I create the world with the attribute of mercy, sin will multiply; if I create it with the attribute of justice, how can it endure? So I will create it with both so that it may endure. (Genesis Rabba 12:15)

In a variation on this theme, it is Abraham who makes the same point to God:

'Shall not the judge of all the earth do right?' (Gen. 18:25). Rabbi Levi said: Abraham said to God: 'If You wish to maintain the world, strict justice is impossible; and if You wish strict justice, then the world cannot be maintained. You cannot hold the cord at both ends at once. You wish the world and You wish justice. Take one or the other. Unless You are a little indulgent, the world cannot endure.' (Genesis Rabba, Lekh Lekha 39:6)

But the rabbinic imagination did not cease with the terminology of the Bible. They coined numerous 'names' whereby they addressed God or described divine qualities. Just to list a few: *Av Harahamim*, 'Father (source) of mercy'; *Avinu shebashamayim*, 'our father in heaven'; *ha-kadosh barukh hu*, 'the Holy One, blessed be He'; *ba'al ha-bayit*, 'the Master of the house'; *mi sheamar v'hayah ha-olam*, 'He who spoke and the world came into being'; *melekh malkhei ha-m'lakhim*, 'the king above the kings of kings', i.e. God as sovereign over all temporal powers; *tsur olamim*, 'the Rock of the Worlds', or simply 'Rock'. (Just to add a somewhat less solemn aside to this solemn listing, there was apparently a great debate among the drafters of Israel's Declaration of Independence, some of whom were religious but others secular, as to whether the name of God should be mentioned in it. In the end they agreed on a compromise and wrote about *tzur yisrael*, the 'Rock of Israel'. It worked because the religious assumed it referred to God, and David Ben Gurion, the first Prime Minister, assumed it referred to himself!). *Ribon ha-olamim* means, 'Master of the worlds', or *ribono shel olam*, 'Master of the world'. These last two are the terms used most frequently when addressing

God. *Rahmana* or *ha-rahaman* is the 'All-merciful'; *shekhinah*, the 'Presence', is a term developed in Kabbalistic, Jewish mystical thought which refers to the indwelling presence of God in the world, and was later adopted by the women's movement as indicating the feminine side of God.[3]

This latter name, and the commonly used concept of God as 'father', already hint at some of the problems that arise around the 'gender' or lack of gender of God. The image of God as father is somewhat problematic today. Freud has taught us to look with different eyes at the relationships between parents and children, and the women's movement has raised questions about the authority and power of fathers in our lives and the way describing God as 'father' impinges on the power of men over women. Rabbinic Judaism has no such ambivalence, and frequently depicts God as a stern but loving parent. Similarly rabbinic literature abounds with tales about 'the King', God, and his troubled relationship with a wayward son, Israel. The rabbis felt very strongly that our actions constantly distance us from God. Fortunately there are mechanisms of 'repentance', (the Hebrew term *teshuvah*, literally means 'return'), that allow for a regular reconciliation. If God is also 'judge', nevertheless God is accessible in surprising ways:

> When the children of Israel are summoned before the Holy One, blessed be He, the angels will say: 'Do not be afraid of the judgment. Do you not know Him? He is your fellow citizen, as it says: "He shall build My city and let My exiles go free" ' (Isa. 45:13); and they will also say: 'Do not be afraid of the judgment. Do you not know Him? He is your relative, for it is said: "The children of Israel, a people so close to Him" ' (Ps. 148:14); and they will also say: 'Do not be afraid of the judgment. Do you not know Him? He is your brother, for He said: "For the sake of My brothers and friends" (Ps. 122:8); He is even more; He is your father, for it says: "Is He not your father who has created you?" ' (Deut. 32:6) (Midrash Psalms 118:10)

The intimacy of the relationship between Israel and God is

expressed in a song that recurs several times on the Day of Atonement:

> For we are Your people and You are our God.
> We are Your children and You are our father.
> We are Your servants and You are our master.
> We are Your community and You are our portion.
> We are Your inheritance and You are our destiny.
> We are Your flock and You are our shepherd.
> We are Your vineyard and You are our keeper.
> We are Your work and You are our creator.
> We are Your beloved and You are our friend.
> We are Your own and You are our nearest.
> We are Your people and You are our king.
> We are the people known to You and You are the God made known by us.

The Imitation of God

One of the purposes of defining different attributes of God lies in our responsibility to imitate these good qualities.

> Our father our king: What is the task of the family of the king? It is to imitate the king. (Yalkut Shimoni on Leviticus)

> You are called merciful and gracious – so we should be merciful and give freely to all.

> You are called righteous – so we should be righteous.

> You are called loving – so we should be called loving. (Yalkut Shimoni on Deuteronomy)

> 'You shall walk after the Eternal your God' (Deut. 13:4). But how can a human being walk after God who is a devouring fire? (Deut. 4:24) It means walk after God's attributes – clothe the naked, visit the sick, comfort the mourner, bury the dead. (b. Sotah 14a)

In the Middle Ages, Jews were confronted with different philosophical and spiritual challenges to the concept of the 'unity' of God. Living in the Muslim world, where an even more rigorous monotheism could be found, the great philosopher Moses Maimonides made the belief in the unity of God one of thirteen principles of faith. But beyond God's unity, what could one say about the nature of God? The rabbis did not seem unduly worried about attributing all sorts of human qualities to God, though even they had some reservations about how far one should go.

> When Rabbi Hanina and Rabbi Jonathan were visiting certain towns in Judea, they entered a Synagogue and noticed that the reader was saying in his prayers, in addition to the standard words: 'God, great, mighty and awesome' the added ones 'glorious, powerful and majestic'. They stopped him on the basis that more was actually less, and it was only because Moses used these terms of God that we were allowed to use them. (Midrash Psalms 19:2)

(Another version suggests that it is like praising a man who had a lot of gold ornaments for his silver ones!)

But this caution about listing God's qualities was taken even further by Maimonides. He insisted that the only appropriate approach to describing the attributes of God was a *via negativa*. He concluded that even the attributes ascribed to God in the Bible and rabbinic teaching are only given because they indicate ways in which God acts in the world so that we can imitate such actions.

It must be evident even from this brief look at such a topic that entire mediaeval philosophical systems need to be taken into account, let alone the religious and cultural context, when attempting to get to the heart of it. The matter gets even more complicated when we introduce the Jewish mystical traditions which similarly wrestled with the problem of a God of whom one could say nothing, yet whom they wanted to experience and whose presence they felt in every aspect of life. They postulated a God about whom nothing could be said or known, the *En Sof* (without limit), so 'other' that this was not even the God spoken of in the Hebrew Bible. From that unknown God there 'emanated' a series of ten *sefirot*, stages from nothingness to the material universe that we know and inhabit.[4] There are numerous ways of understanding this process and the nature of the *sefirot*, from the most esoteric to the most popular. But the desire to understand how God exists in our life lies precisely in this tension between saying too much, which somehow diminishes God, or too little, so that God virtually disappears. The bibliography at the end of this chapter indicates some useful books for those who wish to follow these debates and theories further.

One God and One Humanity

But there is another consequence to the concept of the 'oneness' of God that has had a profound effect on Jewish thought, and indeed the thought of its 'daughter' religions Christianity and Islam. It is already explicitly stated in Genesis, namely the oneness of humanity, all descended from the first human creature, Adam, and all created 'in the image of God'.

> Only one man was first created in the world to teach that if anyone causes a single soul to perish, Scripture considers him as having caused a whole world to perish. And if anyone saves alive a single soul, Scripture considers him as though he had saved a whole world.
>
> One man alone was created for the sake of peace among human beings, so that no-one should say to his fellow: 'My father was greater than your father' . . .
>
> One man alone was created to proclaim the greatness of God, for people stamp many coins with one die and they are all alike; but God has stamped everyone with the die of the first man, yet none of them are alike. So everyone must say: 'For my sake the world was created.' (Mishnah Sanhedrin 4:5)

Nevertheless the rabbis took a pretty sanguine view of humanity.

In one midrash the angels debate about the appropriateness of creating human beings at all!

> Rabbi Simeon said: 'In the hour when the Holy One, blessed be He, was about to create the first human being, the ministering angels were divided into different groups. Some said, "Let him be created"; others said, "Let him not be created", for "Mercy and Truth have met (or fought) together; Righteousness and Peace have kissed (or taken arms against) each other" (Psalm 85:11). For Mercy said, "Let him be created, he will do loving deeds", but Truth said, "Let him not be created, for he will be utterly false"; Righteousness said, "Let him be created for he will do righteous deeds"; Peace said, "Let him not be created, for he will be full of discord." ' (Genesis Rabba 8:5)

> For two and a half years the Schools of Shammai and Hillel were divided. The former argued: 'It would have been better if human beings had not been created.' The latter argued: 'It was good that human beings were created.' They finally concluded: 'It would have been better if human beings had not been created, but now that they have been created, they should examine their behaviour!' (b. Eruvin 13b)

Theology in a Pop Song

It is not inappropriate to end this chapter on what is ultimately a highly complex philosophical and theological matter with a typical Jewish formulation. Some unknown poet in the Middle Ages put together a song, the first three verses of which speak of the transcendent God, unknown, unknowable, omniscient, who pre-existed creation, who has no equal or partner, etc. while the last two verses describe the immanent God, my redeemer, the rock to which I cling in times of trouble, my banner and the One to whom I entrust my body when I sleep. It is so popular that it is sung at the end of virtually every *Shabbat* morning service, and is so simple in its form that there are hundreds of tunes to it, fitting the mood of the most solemn or joyous occasion. (It will also fit almost any familiar melody from 'Waltzing Matilda' to 'Greensleeves'. A rock version made the charts in Israel.) The following version follows the rhythm, if not the rhymes, of the Hebrew original, and, with a bit of give and take, can fit most of the melodies as well.

Eternal God who ruled alone
before creation of all forms,
at whose desire all began
and as the Sovereign was proclaimed.

Who, after everything shall end
alone, in awe, will ever reign,
who was and is for evermore,
the glory that will never change.

Unique and One, no other is
to be compared, to stand beside,
neither before, nor following,
alone the source of power and might.

This is my God, who saves my life,
the rock I grasp in deep despair,
the flag I wave, the place I hide,
who shares my cup the day I call.

In my Maker's hand I lay my soul
both when I sleep and when I wake,
and with my soul my body too,
my God is close, I shall not fear.

Further Reading

Daniel H. Frank and Oliver Leaman (eds.), *History of Jewish Philosophy*, Routledge History of World Philosophies, Vol. 2 (London and New York, Routledge, 1997): an important collection of essays surveying the field of Jewish philosophy.

Neil Gillman, *Sacred Fragments: Recovering Theology for the Modern Jew* (Philadelphia, New York, Jerusalem, The Jewish Publication Society, 1990): a popular examination of contemporary theological issues from the perspective of a Conservative rabbi.

Louis Jacobs, *A Jewish Theology* (New York, Behrman House, 1973): a comprehensive introduction to the subject by a leading contemporary Jewish thinker and authority.

2

Two are the tablets of the covenant
The Jewish people and God

How odd
of God
to choose
the Jews
(William Norman Ewer).[1]

This little ditty sums up so much of the perception of the Jewish
people by outsiders, including the possibility that beneath the
urbane surface of the poem there may lie a kind of envy that has
expressed itself in far more vicious terms throughout Jewish
history. The Hebrew Bible speaks of a special relationship
between God and Israel. But though the Jewish people are the
direct continuation of biblical Israel, others feel that they have
inherited that role, either alongside the Jewish people or as a
replacement for them. If biblical Israel is chosen, it is to perform
a particular task in the world, to serve rather than to rule. As
much or as little as Jews have felt themselves to be 'chosen',
others have focused on the phrase 'chosen people' with quite
irrational feelings, often resulting in violent actions against us.
So it is important to explore how Jews have seen their relationship with God, particularly as expressed through the 'covenant',
the mark of that relationship.

There was a Jewish reply to Ewer to the effect – 'It's not so
odd, the Jews chose God!'[2] My colleague Hyam Maccoby turned
up the comment by one Cecil Browne:

27

But not so odd
as those who choose
a Jewish God
but spurn the Jews.

The Hebrew Bible bears out Ewer. God chose Abraham upon whom to build a new kind of model people living in a model society, exemplified by the qualities of 'righteousness and justice' (Gen. 18:19). But Abraham is an 'odd' choice to be the forerunner of a new humanity precisely because he is in some ways flawed, as, indeed, are all his successors. In fact it is a truism to say that almost no biblical character of any significance is shown without some weakness in his or her character also being displayed. Ultimately that is part of the strength of the Hebrew Bible and its value as a religious document. Such rigorous self-criticism leaves room for growth and change, for learning from mistakes and trying to improve. If such flawed and frail human beings can nevertheless serve God in some way, then we too should not despair. Moreover their weakness sets in a greater perspective the power and generosity of God.

The concept of a covenant, in hebrew *b'rit*, is inherited by the authors of the Hebrew Bible from their surrounding culture. Such covenants can be made in various ways. In one an overlord institutes a suzerainty treaty – his vassals agree to obey him though little is offered in return. Other such covenants are made between partners when they have equal obligations to one another. In a third the sovereign generously offers to do something for the partner, such as providing protection, without expecting anything in return. Elements of all of these can be found in the successive series of covenants that God makes with the world and with humanity. First, after the flood, God promises never to destroy the world again. Second, with Abraham a promise is made about Abraham's future: many children, a land of his own and protection from his enemies. The only tangible thing that God requires is the act of circumcision which is effectively the sign of the covenant (for more on this see chapter 8). Third, with Israel at Mt Sinai the most formal covenant is made, one which imposes obligations on both partners (Exod. 19, 24). The last covenant is with David and looks to the future.

The process of covenant-making at Sinai has a very special character. It takes place in three stages: God makes an initial offer which the people, led by Moses, accepts in principle. There follows a detailed negotiation when the 'laws', which constitute the terms of the contract, are heard by the people and agreed. Finally a ceremony takes place in which blood is sprinkled on the altar and on the people symbolising the two partners to the covenant. At each stage the people are given an opportunity to respond so that, at least in biblical terms, the covenant is voluntarily entered into by the Jewish people in full knowledge of what is intended, and at stake. For a covenant is more than merely a contract. For all that it is a legal document, it affirms a relationship. The Hebrew term *hesed* is used to describe the love and loyalty that exists between the partners in a covenant, a term and a theme we shall explore again in the final chapter.

God's opening offer sets the framework within which Israel is to see itself and operate in the world: 'You shall be for Me a kingdom of priests and a holy nation' (Exod. 19:6). The Jewish people has understood its existence as being governed by a covenant with God, and our history has been interpreted in the light of this relationship. Israel's hope was always the hope of redemption that God would one day bring for this people, this special treasure, God's own stiff-necked, stubborn, disobedient but beloved children.

The consciousness of God's care and protection of Israel is a major feature of biblical thought, both of the nation as a whole, and of those individuals, patriarchs, kings, prophets, who were somehow chosen to be its leaders and guides. Indeed the very paradox of Israel's weakness, smallness and general insignificance is the guarantee of God's necessary protection: 'The Eternal did not set the divine love upon you nor choose you because you were more in number than any people – for you were the fewest of all peoples, but because the Eternal loved you, and because God would keep the oath made with your ancestors' (Deut. 7:7).

In a variant on this theme, the unlikely younger brother Jacob is chosen above his elder brother Esau; David, the smallest and youngest of Jesse's sons, is to be anointed king; unwilling prophets, Moses the stammerer, Jeremiah (I am only an apprentice!), Amos (I am not a professional!), the 'suffering servant' of Second Isaiah (Isa. 52:13–53:12) – in turn the weakest, unlikeliest are called or chosen to be the bearers of God's word. Each in turn may suffer for their calling, but each is supported by God. To feel chosen in this sense is actually a mark of our inadequacy (or else a kind of inverted snobbery!) that reinforces what God can achieve despite the agents chosen for the task.

The drama of Israel's biblical history unfolds in the tension between their awareness of their dependence upon God, on one level at least of their consciousness, and their natural human assertion of their own strength – the celebration of their own success in times of prosperity and growth, the magical reliance on the tokens of their faith in times of trouble. Isaiah can warn a generation trembling before the allied armies of the Northern Kingdom and its neighbours that there is nothing to fear from these 'burnt-out stumps of firewood' (Isa. 7:4), because God will protect them. God will not allow Jerusalem, the place chosen for God's name and presence, to be desecrated. So Isaiah mocks the policy-makers, the military advisers and the fortifications and preparations for war (Isa. 22:8–14). And he is proved right in his time. But the prophet Jeremiah, a century later, must tell the same nation that now is the time when Jerusalem will fall, because a price must be paid for the people's excesses – and no invoking of the 'inviolability of Jerusalem' will make any difference (Jer. 7:3–15; 26:1–6). 'Let not the people tremble before the nations around them for they are but flesh and blood – let them stand instead in fear and dread, in awe and reverence before the Eternal their God.'

This latter sentence introduces us to a Hebrew term that is hard to translate. The verb *yarei* means 'to fear', but also 'to be in awe'. The 'fear of God', as we discover it in the biblical record, is compounded of dread and awe, of wonder and sometimes terror. It is that awe which draws people towards God as the most exhilirating, tempting and 'real' experience the human soul can attain, as the moth is drawn to the flame that will give it a moment of blazing glory, immortalise it and at the same moment destroy it. That was the fate of the sons of Aaron who brought a 'strange fire' to the altar, out of religious zeal in one interpretation, and were consumed by the divine fire that descended from heaven. They themselves became the sacrifices. Their passion for God literally burned them up (Lev. 10:1–3). But that same fear may send someone to the other end of the world, to the farthest reaches of his sanity, so as to avoid that encounter, as was the case with the prophet Jonah.

If there is a 'fear' to be experienced by the encounter with God, there is also another fear that has more to do with God's absence. It is a fear based not on reason or reality, not on enemies without or disease within. It is the fear of life itself, with its unreason and responsibilities; the fear that grips the throat as morning comes, and holds the sufferer shivering in bed, unable to face the day. The fear of change and newness, of disturbance and trouble, of the different, of the other – the fear of our own dissolution. A fear which demands reassurance and comforting, which will pay any price – the surrender of reason, will, justice and compassion – so as to drown for one moment the awareness of our own aloneness, of our nothingness, of our emptiness.

This latter fear the Jewish people has known and called by the name of 'exile', *galut.* And this fear has been its reality, its enemy, for a large part of our existence. It was a fear of which God had warned in one of the most chilling prophecies the Bible contains. It is found in what we might call the 'small print' at the bottom of the contract, the covenant with God. For, as with any contract, sanctions must be attached in case one of the partners reneges on the conditions. These can be found in the Hebrew Bible in Leviticus 26 and Deuteronomy 28, and are a grim description of what might come to pass. So disturbing are these words that when recited in synagogue as part of the cycle of readings from the Torah (see chapter 5), they are said in a lowered voice, as if the mere recital itself could set them in train. This is the price to be paid for disloyalty to God – exile from the land, and the state of being distant from God.

And as for them that are left of you, I will send a faintness

31

into their heart in the land of their enemies; and the sound
of a driven leaf shall chase them; and they shall flee, as one
flees from the sword; and they shall fall when none pursue.
And they shall stumble one upon another as it were before
the sword, when none pursues, and you shall have no
power to stand before your enemies. And you shall perish
among the nations, and the land of your enemies shall eat
you up. (Lev. 26:36–38)

And that was ever and again the reality of Jewish life – except
that time and time again the sword was only too real. At the
hands of Assyrians, Babylonians, Greeks and Romans; at the
hands of the Crusaders and the Almohade Muslims; of
Inquisitors, Cossacks and Nazis. And every time, in almost every
society, Jews encountered the same crazed mindless mobs,
venting their own pain, fear, frustration and bloodlust on the
nearest helpless victim, the perennial scapegoat.

How did Jews cope with these situations? It is important to
ask the question in the past tense, because for two hundred years
the old answers and responses have radically changed. For two
hundred years Jews have worn the secular clothing of the
Western world. Our God has also become distant, often replaced
with the smaller, equally invisible and pervasive, though un-
recognised, gods of our own society. Jews, like others, stand
unarmed and seek new answers. But first we can see the
responses of the past.

The first we might call the immediacy of tradition. The cycle
of the Jewish year, with its timeless repetition of the seasons of
Jewish life and experience, imposed a different sense of reality.
At Passover, whatever our material or spiritual state, we were
once again redeemed from slavery in an eternal Egypt. Midrash,
the rabbinic exegesis of the Bible, could always add a
contemporary note to relate the ancient story to new dilemmas.
Exodus 2:23 records that when Pharaoh died, the children of
Israel sighed because of their bondage and their cry came up to
God. The rabbis asked, why was it that when Pharaoh died, a
man who had so sorely oppressed Israel, only then did they
weep? One answer suggests that they applied the old adage –

better the devil you know . . . The next Pharaoh might be worse!
A second view was more pragmatic. The Pharaoh who imposed
slavery might be persuaded one day to repeal it. But his successor
would inherit an existing tradition and would be less likely to
change something of his predecessor. Another rabbi, perhaps
speaking out of direct experience of a totalitarian regime, had a
different answer. In Pharaoh's Egypt, like the police states of our
own century, one could not complain when things went wrong –
for that would amount to a criticism of the ruling power, a
betrayal of the revolution! So when Pharaoh died and a day of
public mourning was declared, the children of Israel seized the
opportunity to release all the pent-up bitterness and tears of their
situation, and wept so as to move the very gates of heaven – and
God heard their cry.

At *Pesach*, Passover – whether in comparative freedom or
waiting in fear for a knock at the door as the mob came screaming
the blood libel, that Jews had used the blood of Christian children
to bake their unleavened bread; or even in the concentration
camp where Jews composed a special prayer, apologising to God
that in the current situation they had not the possibility to eat
'unleavened bread', the special bread of the Passover period,
but must partake of the usual hard black bread that stood
between them and starvation – at Passover they were free again,
redeemed from Egypt, chosen by God, bowing to God alone.

At *Shavuot*, 'the Feast of Weeks', Pentecost, they received again
the Torah from God at Mt Sinai and entered into the covenant,
symbolised in some Sephardi traditions by reading a *ketubah*, a
marriage contract between God and Israel.

At *Sukkot*, Tabernacles, they once again experienced the
reality of the desert, the frailty of the shelter that is afforded to
human beings on earth, the total dependence upon the elements
and the providence of God.

On the ninth day of the Hebrew month of Ab, *Tisha B'Av*,
they lamented again the destruction of their Temple, and of
Jerusalem their holy city, and all the other destructions their
communities had known – so that this black day, this black fast,
served to release the bitterness and shame of their exile. But
every ninth of Ab is followed by *shabbat nachamu*, 'the Sabbath

of consolation', when the words of Isaiah 40 bring the promise of future restoration, the light of dawn at the end of the dark night: 'Comfort, comfort My people, says your God. Bid Jerusalem take heart and proclaim to her, that her time of service is accomplished, that her guilt is paid off; that she has received at the hand of the Eternal double for all her sins' (Isa. 40:1–2).

> Rabban Gamliel, Rabbi Elazar and Rabbi Joshua stood with Rabbi Akiva on the Temple Mount and saw a fox coming out of the Holy of Holies. The former three wept but Rabbi Akiva laughed. And thus he explained. 'The prophet Micah prophesied: "Zion shall become a ploughed field and Jerusalem shall become heaps" (Mic. 3:12). But the prophet Zechariah said: "Yet again shall Jerusalem be full of boys and girls playing in its streets" (Zech. 8:5). If the first prophecy was not fulfilled, I might fear that Zechariah's prophecy might not be fulfilled. But now that the former has happened, I know the latter will as well.' 'You have comforted us' said his companions. (b. Makkot 24b)

Everyone in Israel, all Jews, should consider themselves as if they personally had come out of Egypt – so runs the tradition of the Passover night. The soul of every Jew, born and unborn, stood at Mt Sinai at the revelation – so runs a rabbinic teaching. Today we are slaves, tomorrow we shall be free, reads the text of the Passover Haggadah, the home liturgy read on that night. 'Next year in Jerusalem!' it concludes.

The very curses of Leviticus and Deuteronomy, by virtue of being read in synagogue every year, became an inevitable, or at least potential, happening. And yet too, part of the cycle – to come but also to pass; to be suffered, but also to be survived.

Moreover, the enemies and troubles that arose at different times were also never entirely new. Rome was Edom, another name for Esau, the older brother who forever sought to slay his younger brother Jacob, and thus an archetypal symbol of any oppressive regime throughout history. What villain could be worse than Haman of the Book of Esther, who planned to exterminate the Jews? Only tragically, when the latest Haman, Hitler, came to power, many Jews had stopped believing in the power of that tradition, and had all but abolished the festival of Purim, which tells the story of Esther. They thought it was too barbaric, nationalistic and exotic, for the time of enlightenment and universal brotherhood they saw, or hoped they saw, about them. So they were blind to the truth for too long. Tradition was no longer strong enough to mould history to its pattern, and reality was not yet strong enough to waken them to truth.

So fear had its counterpart in hope – for the cycle of the year went round and round on its endless way. Yet that time of continuity and certainty is now past for all but a few. Two or three generations away from East Europe or North Africa, the assimilated grandchildren of Ashkenazi and Sephardi families stand both within and without those familiar walls, carrying all too often just a few pieces of the old pattern, sentimentalised memories of what once was. Most Jews are unable to return wholeheartedly to that past, because that would mean the sacrifice of comfort, or reason; and we live dissatisfied with the present, with its emptiness and its own threats. *The End of the Jewish People* and *The Vanishing Diaspora* are the titles of two books in recent decades that have evaluated the future of Jewish life outside the State of Israel. In this new post-war world, Passover is merely a family reunion and a meal. *Shavuot* is ignored. *Sukkot* is at best a kind of harvest festival. *Tisha B'Av* is a paradox for modern Israelis living in the physical Jerusalem, no longer a metaphorical one – restored yet not restored.

There is a current wave of 'Jewish renewal', which finds quite different expressions in different places; more radical in the United States, more 'folk'-orientated in Israel and certainly more conservative in Europe. There are also extraordinary achievements to be seen in small groups and emerging Jewish communities in the former Soviet Union. In trying to reinvest in Jewish traditions and rituals much is being achieved. But we are also in a radically different world and need to acknowledge how different things are from the past. It will take generations before we can fully understand the new kinds of Jewish self-expression and faith that are evolving today.

A second Jewish weapon of defence against fear was the last resort salvaged from the wreckage of hope, the only way to preserve sanity in a situation of helplessness: the self-mocking, self-effacing, bitter laugh, the gallows humour that changes nothing, except our attitude to that which cannot be changed. The origins of such a response, like so much else in Jewish life, can be found in the Hebrew Bible. The children of Israel stand before the vast Sea of Reeds. In front of them impassable waters; behind them the advancing army of Pharaoh. They cry to Moses: 'There weren't enough graves in Egypt that you brought us here to bury us?' (Exod. 14:11)

From the period of the Hadrianic persecution comes a story that could be repeated in virtually every subsequent period.

As the Emperor Hadrian was being carried through the streets of Rome, a Jew passed by. 'Long life to you, O Emperor!' the Jew greeted him. 'Who are you?' asked the Emperor. 'I am a Jew.' 'How dare you, a Jew, greet me!' Hadrian raged. 'Chop his head off!' Another Jew who chanced to pass by just then and saw what had happened decided not to greet the Emperor. 'Who are you?' demanded Hadrian. 'I am a Jew.' 'How dare you, a Jew, pass me by without greeting me!' raged Hadrian. 'Chop off his head!' The Emperor's counsellors were filled with astonishment. 'O Emperor, we cannot grasp the meaning of your actions. If you had the first Jew decapitated because he greeted you, why did you do the same thing to the second Jew because he did not greet you?' 'Are you trying to teach me how to handle those I hate?' retorted the Emperor. (Lamentations Rabba 3:60)

Behind such bitter humour lies tragic reality. On occasion the effect of persecution, chronic fear, could reduce Jewish responses to almost helpless passivity, and ironic, self-deprecatory wit could be the only response.

In his book *To Heaven with Scribes and Pharisees*, Rabbi Lionel Blue discusses Jewish humour and its entry into Jewish life.

Humour wells up in the Jewish people as the Temple goes down, together with the recognisable landmarks of Jewish life. Both Christianity and Judaism had to cope with worldly defeat. The former uses paradox and turns a worldly defeat into a victory of the spirit. The latter tries to live with defeat, as a normal condition of existence, and uses humour to do so. Almost surreptitiously, like a thief in the night, God's oddest and most healing gift stole into the hearts of His people, changing the dourness of their character. So the descendants of the stiff-necked Hebrews end up by doing His will on the New York and London stage or in a Hollywood film, changing bitterness into laughter and purging failure and depression.[3]

I could quote Lionel Blue endlessly in this context and would refer you to his many books. A further quote will introduce a third Jewish strategy for survival.

The greatness of Judaism does not lie in transcending suffering, but in reducing it to proportion. From experience, Judaism ought to put a cross at the centre of its faith. It does not, because this would mean a distortion of its task, which is to build God's kingdom in a chaotic world, and be His prisoners of hope.[4]

Judaism bases itself on what one may call the 'reality principle' – facing the world squarely as it is, and dealing with it on a day-to-day basis. This curious paradox, of living a day at a time, yet living at the same moment in the expectation of some ultimate divine intervention, the Messianic coming, is neatly summed up by the great mediaeval poet, Solomon Ibn Gabirol: 'Plan for this world as if you were to live forever; plan for the world to come as if you were to die tomorrow.'

Who Belongs in the Covenant?

If these are the conditions for belonging to a special covenant
with God, who is entitled to belong? That is one of the central
issues with which Jews are grappling today. In biblical Israel,
particularly when the people existed as an independent nation,
or nations, on a particular territory, outsiders could settle there,
marry into the people and at the same time accept the God of
Israel. The biblical category of *ger*, 'stranger', or to use the older
term, 'sojourner', referred to a 'resident alien' who had settled
and accepted the customs and laws of the people. The most
famous figure to follow this route is Ruth the Moabitess, after
whom an entire biblical book is named. At the moment when
she follows her mother-in-law back to Israel, she says: 'Your
people are my people, your God is my God' (Ruth 1:16). Putting
the 'people' first seems to have been the natural way – when you
joined a people you accepted their God as well.

Within the Hebrew Bible you were 'Israelite' if your father
was an Israelite, irrespective of who your mother was. The term
'Jew', literally 'Judahite', a member of the Kingdom of Judah,
only occurs in the late biblical book of Esther. Though the Bible
does not give statistics of how many 'non-Israelites' joined the
people, there are any number of references to them: 'a mixed
multitude' who joined the Israelites on their journey from Egypt;
a category of people known as 'those who fear the Eternal'
mentioned in the Psalms (118:4); and numerous individuals,
originally from different nations, according to their name or
designation, who crop up in the narratives as part of the people.
The fact that there are laws restricting Israelites from inter-
marrying with certain nations, and the attempt by Ezra the Scribe
to force people to divorce their non-Israelite wives after the
return from the Babyloninan exile (Ezra 10), all indicate the
degree of mixing with other populations at different times.

All this was to change as a consequence of exile. Instead of a
nation on its own territory, Israel became a 'faith community'.
Now someone was a Jew if their mother, no longer the father,
was a Jew; or if they entered the community by affirming their
belief in Israel's God. How this affirmation was to be done

developed over the centuries. From the earliest period two requirements have been essential – circumcision for a man, and entering a ritual bath, the *mikveh*, for both a man and a woman, as a kind of symbolic rebirth. In addition, since one was entering into a covenant, it was important to know some of the essential requirements of the laws within that covenant and agree to abide by them. How much, and how far one was to fulfil the *mitzvot*, 'commandments', seem to have varied considerably over the centuries, and remain a source of controversy today between the different parts of the Jewish world. (We will examine some of the causes of this in chapter 10.)

Throughout the almost two thousand years of the exile of the Jewish people from their homeland, individuals, and even on one occasion an entire people, have converted to Judaism. In the earliest period Judaism seems to have been a missionising religion, travelling over land and sea just to win a single convert (Matt. 23:15). (However the Gospel writer's view may be a little tendentious as he is referring to the Pharisees, the forerunners of the rabbis, of whom he was not fond, and he adds 'and when he becomes a proselyte, you make him twice as much a child of Gehenna, hell, as yourselves'!) Certainly many in Rome converted, and the Talmud attests to considerable curiousity about Judaism on the part of Roman 'matrons' as well as religious debates with emperors. There may even have been something of a race between Judaism and early Christianity to win over the larger number of converts – a race that ceased after Christianity became the State religion of the Roman Empire. From then on Jews existed as a minority, constantly under threat under Christianity, which seemed both to want them to convert or disappear, and at the same time still be around to witness to the truth of Christianity at the Second Coming. Under Islam they had a protected status as 'the people of the Book'. Nevertheless under both regimes anyone wishing to convert to Judaism, and indeed anyone helping them to do so, risked the death penalty for such apostasy.

With rare exceptions, over the centuries Jews became more and more cautious about welcoming anyone into the faith community. A would-be candidate was to be sent away three times and only if they persisted, and acknowledged that they were indeed unworthy to be accepted, then they might be taken further. Nevertheless despite the risks, people did choose to convert, amongst them a few Christian clergy during the Middle Ages who had studied the Hebrew Bible and were led from this to the Jewish faith. Such a move could only be seen as a threat by the Church and a number of them died at the stake as martyrs for their Jewish faith.

There was even the famous example of the Khazars, an independent kingdom in Eastern Europe between the seventh and tenth centuries, who converted as an entire nation to Judaism. Their origins are not clear, nor the extent of their kingdom. Individual Jews travelled to join them, though they remained largely independent of the rest of the Jewish world. The power of their empire was finally broken by Russian invasions. Little remains of their existence but numerous records speak of groups of Khazars continuing to exist in different Jewish communities after their kingdom fell.

In the modern period, Jewish attitudes to conversion did not change very much, with Orthodox authorities generally making it very difficult to convert and Reform ones being more welcoming. After the Shoah the Jewish world is divided between those who feel that we should close ranks and be suspicious of anyone who seeks to convert, and others who argue that given the vast numbers of Jews who have been lost we should be replenishing ourselves by at least welcoming converts, if not going so far as to seek them out with a missionising programme. But all such matters are complicated by the fragmented nature of Jewish life today, inner struggles for authority and general issues of Jewish status and identity that we shall examine in chapter 12.

Does the Covenant Extend to Others Outside Judaism?

If Jews are, on the whole, clear about the possibility of joining the Jewish faith, even if we may argue about how this is to be achieved, no such agreement exists about how to understand

Christianity and Islam in terms of their relationship to the original covenant with Israel. Clearly historical factors, most obviously the millennial persecution of Jews by Christians and the repeated attempts, up till today, either by force or encouragement to convert them to Christianity, place considerable psychological blocks before any attempt to evaluate or appreciate its religious significance. Questions about the nature of the Trinity, the apparent elevation of a human being to some kind of divine status, and the whole debate about whether the Messiah has come or not, were debated in the Middle Ages, often in confrontational situations with Christians, the 'disputations'. Hence they remain stumbling blocks even for Jews who would like to acknowledge in some way the legitimacy of Christianity from a Jewish perspective.

However, on a common-sense level the matter would seem to be resolved, at least for Jews in Western Europe or America. We live in a 'Christian' or 'post-Christian' society, largely secular, with neighbours with whom we share many attitudes and values, few of which are directly influenced by our particular religious affiliation. In fact it is that commonality of Western democratic socialisation that makes it difficult to differentiate Jews from their neighbours, as the rising intermarriage statistics suggest.

The Christian attitude to Judaism has undergone considerable changes in the wake of the document concerning the relations of the Catholic Church with other religions published by the Second Vatican Council (Vatican II) in October 1965, *Nostra Aetate*. Inspired by Pope John XXIII, it envisaged an entirely new and positive relationship between the Catholic Church and the Jewish people, culminating some thirty years later in the Vatican recognition of the State of Israel. Though ingrained Jewish suspicions inevitably remain, reinforced by the attitudes of other denominations within the Church, the climate of mutual respect and trust has grown considerably in Western Europe and America.

It is somewhat different in the State of Israel, where Christianity is more remote, and, perhaps in consequence, is perceived as a more threatening force. In part this is related to the political configurations that surround Middle Eastern religions in general, but it is also a reflex of the nature of Judaism in Israel today. It is not quite as polarised between 'ultra-Orthodox' or 'totally secular' as the popular view would suggest, but religion is certainly not an area that has been explored and developed with the range of options and nuances that Jews elsewhere experience. In some ways too, the Shoah continues to form Israeli attitudes, reinforced by a siege mentality created by generations of wars. Self-sufficiency is seen as an ideal and outside influences of any kind, let alone religious ones, as a kind of threat.

In Eastern Europe, particularly the former Soviet Union, a newly emerging Orthodox Church, with a few individual exceptions, has not yet even begun to come to terms with the openness to other faiths envisioned in Vatican II and carries with it still an ancient anti-Semitism that makes *rapprochement* extremely difficult.

Nevertheless for those Jews who follow the attempts by the Church since Vatican II to revise its relationships with the Jewish people, there is an openness to participation in interfaith dialogue and an attempt, despite centuries of mistrust, to forge a new relationship with, and indeed to seek to 'make theological space' for, Christianity. The exercise has been undertaken in the past. The mediaeval poet and philosopher Judah Halevi spoke of Judaism as the seed, and Christianity and Islam as the tree that have grown from it. However the fruit still contains the original seed.

> God has a secret and wise design concerning us, which should be compared to the wisdom hidden in the seed which falls into the ground, where it undergoes an external transformation into earth, water and dirt, without leaving a trace for him who looks down upon it. It is, however, the seed itself which transforms earth and water into its own substance, carries it from one stage to another, until it refines the elements and transfers them into something like itself, casting off husks, leaves, etc., and allowing the pure core to appear, capable of bearing the Divine influence. The original seed produced the tree bearing fruit

resembling that from which it had been produced. In the same way the law of Moses transforms each one who honestly follows it, though it may externally repel him. The nations merely serve to introduce and pave the way for the expected Messiah, who is the fruition, and they will all become His fruit. (Kuzari 4:23)[5]

In this century pioneer figures like Claude Montefiore, Leo Baeck and Franz Rosenzweig have explored this area. A contemporary Christian view would suggest that through Jesus, Christians also enter into the same relationship with God that Jews have through their birth into the covenant, but this is a long way from the kind of thinking commonly held by Jews. We are too close to the Shoah, and too much feeling remains that without the anti-Semitism of the Church providing the background, it could never have happened in the way and to the extent that it did. Vatican II notwithstanding, a suspicious Jewish world is watching to see how far Christianity has changed. Nevertheless there are many, and growing, opportunities for Jewish–Christian dialogue that have their own dynamic, and by their very nature they ack-nowledge the legitimacy and uniqueness of both traditions, even if the precise relationship between them remains problematical.

Far fewer problems arise with regard to Islam, whose strict monotheism was acknowledged by Maimonides as early as the twelfth century. The 'golden age of Spain' is a constant reminder of how a Jewish–Muslim symbiosis can work to the enrichment of both, intellectually, culturally and spiritually. Here it is the politics of the Middle East that casts a shadow over their relation-ship. Moreover Jews are no less prone than others to fall under the spell of Islamophobia, despite our history of being similarly scapegoated and victimised. The beginnings of Jewish–Muslim dialogue exist. On a religious basis the two faiths have far more in common with each other than either has with Christianity. Judaism sees no problem in recognising Islam as a 'daughter religion', but the actual relationship is always being held to ransom by politics.

With regard to other religions in general, Judaism has a far more open mind than its small size and apparent particularism would suggest. The rabbis conceived of certain general principles passed on by Noah to his three sons, and hence to all the nations of the world, these being known as the Seven Laws of the Sons of Noah, though the exact seven is subject to slight variations. They include the negative commands against idolatry, sexual misconduct, murder, blaspheming the name of God, robbery and cutting off the limb of a living animal. The one positive command is to establish courts of justice. Any society or individual that abides by these laws is certain of a place in the world to come. That is to say it is not necessary to go through Judaism to reach God.

I remember once being invited to the temple of an Indian sect for some kind of celebration and standing on a platform with representatives of other religious denominations. The stage was dominated by a huge representation of the particular deity, and from time to time people would come up and lay dainties at its feet. By all biblical standards this was 'idolatry' and my presence would seem to be highly problematic. But some of the rabbis taught that such forms of idol worship ceased to be a threat to Israel from the time of the destruction of the Jerusalem Temple. And anyway, contemporary idols are much more subtle and complex matters, though no less enslaving. (We shall return to this theme in the closing chapter.)

Prejudice and the unwillingness to enter into dialogue with 'the other' is a far greater threat to human survival, let alone to spiritual growth, than closing ourselves off. Perhaps we can understand the covenant requirement that we welcome the *ger*, the 'other', in a new way. For two millennia in the rabbinic interpretation it has served as a term for the 'righteous convert'. Perhaps today it can stand for anyone who is willing to meet us on our own terms and share the religious journey with us, just as we must do in return. Perhaps we can also resurrect the term from the Psalms, 'those who fear the Eternal', as a way of acknowledging the many others who celebrate in their different ways the One God.

The Two Tablets

The title of this chapter refers specifically to the two tablets of the covenant, the two tablets, written by God, containing the Ten Commandments, that Moses brought down from Mt Sinai. Those tablets Moses destroyed when he saw the children of Israel dancing round the golden calf, as if they had already broken off the relationship with God to which they had so solemnly agreed. Yet that was not the end of the story and a second set of commandments was obtained – but this time Moses had to carve them out himself. The divine–human collaboration was symbolised by this act. The prophets were to see in Israel's actions generations later a new threat to the covenant relationship with God. Despite their warnings, Jerusalem was destroyed and the people exiled, seemingly further proof that the covenant was destroyed. But those like Jeremiah who lived through the destruction could speak of a new or renewed covenant:

> Behold days are coming, an oracle of the Eternal, when I will make with the House of Israel and the House of Judah a new covenant. Not like the covenant which I made with their fathers on the day I took them by the hand to bring them out from the land of Egypt, for they set aside that covenant even though I was their husband, an oracle of the Eternal. But this is the covenant that I will make with the children of Israel after those days, an oracle of the Eternal, I will place My Torah within them and write it upon their hearts, and I will be their God and they shall be My people. No longer shall a man teach his neighbour, nor a man his brother, saying: 'Know the Eternal', for all shall know Me, from the least of them to the greatest, an oracle of the Eternal; for I shall forgive their sin and remember their failure no more. (Jer. 31:31–34)

With the emergence of Christianity came the assertion that the old covenant with Israel was irrevocably broken, and this new covenant was made with a new Israel, the Church. Yet Jews never acknowledged such an idea and remained faithful to the covenant that they saw as binding upon them throughout eternity. But that covenant required something on God's side as well – the protection and support without which Jewish life could not be sustained. There is thus a deep fissure in Jewish life since the Shoah, when it seemed, and to many it still seems, that God abandoned the Jewish people at their time of greatest need. Whether expressed in personal or theological terms there is a deep loss of confidence in that aspect of the covenant for a post-war generation. So what is the future of Israel's covenant with God? That is the subject of the last chapter of this book.

Further Reading

Walter Homolka, Walter Jacob and Esther Seidel (eds.), *Not By Birth Alone: Conversion to Judaism* (London and Washington, Cassell, 1997): a useful and up-to-date survey of current Jewish attitudes to conversion to Judaism, as well as a number of personal accounts by converts.

3

Three are the fathers of Israel
An overview of Jewish history

Abraham, Isaac and Jacob. We are so used to putting the three of them together, the founding patriarchs of Judaism, that we may not think about the implications of such a list. Why link three generations in this way? Why not two? Or four, since Joseph, Jacob's favourite son, was certainly significant both for his achievements and his role in Jewish history?

The solution may lie in the fact that three generations: father, grandfather and great-grandfather, may be the number of generations into the past that can be alive in our own time. So they are the living memories that can take us back into the past and tell us what happened in their own lifetime. Though there is no Hebrew term for 'history' as an abstract concept, the Bible uses the term *toledot*, 'generations', from the verb *yalad*, to 'give birth'. History, on that basis, is the living memory of those who are physically present to recall the past for us. But if that were all, then history would only be as old as the oldest survivor and would move down a generation with each death and new birth.

However there is also an 'oral memory' of key events and personalities which is passed on through stories, as well as being preserved by the trained memories of 'archivists'. For example, in the Hebrew Bible when Jeremiah is put on trial, the 'elders' are called in to give legal precedents quoting cases going back into the past (Jer. 26:17–23).

Memorising traditions alongside written records continued into the rabbinic period. In the Mishnah, the first codification of

Jewish law completed in the second century CE, we find the alarming statement: 'Rabbi Jacob says: "One who is walking along the road and studying and interrupts his studying and says, 'How lovely is that tree! How lovely is this field!' Scripture considers him as if he has forfeited his life" ' (Sayings of the Fathers 3:9). It seems at first glance a distinctly over-the-top endorsement of 'study above everything', or else a marked dislike for the appreciation of nature. But Jacob Petuchowski pointed out that the word translated as 'studying' is *shanah*, which means 'to repeat', hence the word *mishnah* itself, of which more in chapter 6. That is to say this passage refers to those teachers whose task it was to memorise large amounts of traditional teachings. They would then pass on what they had memorised intact to their students. So any chance remark they might make while doing this exercise of 'repeating' could well be misunderstood by their pupils as being part of the tradition itself and thus be incorporated and handed on, corrupting everything that came afterwards! Hence the drastic penalty.

The Hebrew Bible itself, by its very existence, testifies to the power of a third source of 'history', the written word. All of these ways of retaining, and hence controlling, the past are to be found in Judaism: the immediate history of family memories; the history conveyed orally by the collective memory of the people, particularly through ritual and liturgical life; the written records, frozen in time and form, but open to interpretation in the present.

To illustrate how these 'memories' operate, here are some rabbinic 'readings' of the past.

All three of the patriarchs in the biblical stories establish their relationship with God – Isaac and Jacob as successors to the covenant initially made with Abraham. So the name of God is often present when the three are named: God of Abraham, God of Isaac and God of Jacob. A Jewish teaching suggests that this formulation implies that each had to discover God in his own way. This view is reinforced by another formula commonly to be found in Jewish prayers: 'our God and God of our "fathers"'. Just as they in succession had to find God for themselves, so we too cannot simply inherit our relationship with God from our 'fathers' but must find it for ourselves. History alone is not enough. We have to create our own Jewish memories.

Thus the 'patriarchs' are venerated but also placed in a kind of perspective. They belong to the past but are also alive and present in our own generations as well. The rabbis taught: *ma'asey avot siman l'vanim*, 'the deeds of the fathers are a sign for the children' (b. Sotah 34a). A variation reads: 'The casual conversations of the patriarchs and their actions are a key to the redemption of the children' (Genesis Rabba 70:6). On this basis the patriarchs are 'types', their actions signalling the appropriate responses for their descendants in the situations of their own time.

Of course the tradition has to be selective about what activities of the patriarchs are to be imitated. The biblical Abraham nearly sacrificed his son; Isaac showed favouritism to one of his sons and broke up the family; Jacob deceived his father and cheated his brother. So it is rather the patriarchs as seen through the eyes of the rabbis that are to be our models, the written history of the Bible modified by its oral reworking.

In the rabbinic view Abraham was the model of the generous host (see how well he fed his three visitors in Genesis 18) and he and his wife Sarah were the first missionaries, bringing many to worship the One God. Does it not refer in Genesis 12:5 to the 'souls/lives' that they had made in Haran? Since only God can 'make' a life, this must refer to the souls they had converted to a life-enhancing relationship with the One God. (Abraham converted the men and Sarah the women!)

On this basis Jacob taught us how to deal with the threats posed by an enemy. When he returns home after twenty years in exile he is frightened at the prospect of confronting his brother Esau whom he had cheated out of his blessing. In the biblical account he sends ahead of himself gifts from his herds and flocks, divides up his camp and prays to God. The rabbis saw in his actions three necessary steps to take when confronted by such a threat. First prayer to God, then the attempt at appeasement through a gift, and only as a last resort the preparation for war (Midrash Tanhuma on Genesis 32:4). It must be noted here that in rabbinic thought, just as Jacob came to stand for the Jewish people, so also Esau came to represent any potential enemy, and one in particular. Thus Esau stands for 'Edom' the place where his descendants were located and then for 'Rome'. This enabled the rabbis, under Roman domination, to address issues currently facing the Jewish people through a kind of coded language, which is why Esau is treated in a very negative way. 'Interpretation' being a way of registering protest and advising on appropriate action.

Nevertheless the rabbis were not immune to the questions about how history is to be understood and read. It is well symbolised by their attempts to understand who wrote particular books of the Bible.

Who wrote the Scriptures? Moses wrote his own book and the section [in Numbers 22–24] about Balaam, as well as the Book of Job. Joshua wrote his own book and the last eight verses of the Book of Deuteronomy [which record the death of Moses]. Samuel wrote his own book and 'Judges' and 'Ruth'. David wrote the Book of Psalms, incorporating the work of the ten elders to whom individual Psalms are ascribed: Adam, Melchizedek, Abraham, Moses, Heman, Yeduthun, Asaph and the three sons of Korah. Jeremiah wrote his book and the Book of Kings and 'Lamentations'. King Hezekiah and his circle 'wrote' [edited] Isaiah, Proverbs, the Song of Songs and Ecclesiastes. The Men of the Great Assembly 'wrote' Ezekiel and the Twelve Minor Prophets, Daniel and the Scroll of Esther. Ezra wrote his own book and the genealogies of the Book of Chronicles up to his own time. (b. Baba Bathra 14b–15a)

In all of these cases the rabbis are attempting to see the biblical books in their historical context according to the chronology known to them. The tradition ascribes the composition of the books of Proverbs, Song of Songs and Ecclesiastes to King Solomon, so clearly here they are referring to the final editing, after Solomon's death. This is logical given the reference in the Book of Proverbs itself to a collection of Proverbs by Solomon that were published by 'the men of Hezekiah, king of Judah'

(Proverbs 25:1). Similarly, since the last eight verses of Deuteronomy speak of Moses' death, it is only logical that they would have been written posthumously by his servant and successor Joshua.

But with regard to this latter passage, there is another view:

> Eight verses of the Torah were written by Joshua, as it has been taught: 'And Moses the servant of the Eternal died there.' Is it possible that after he was dead Moses could have written these words, 'Moses died there'? Rather, up to there Moses wrote, but from there onwards Joshua wrote. This is the opinion of Rabbi Joshua, and some say Rabbi Nehemiah. But Rabbi Simeon said to him, 'Could the scroll of the Torah be short of even a single word?! Yet it is written: "Take this book of the Torah" (Deut. 31:26). Rather from here onwards [i.e. the last eight verses] the Holy One, blessed be He, dictated and Moses wrote it down with tears in his eyes.' (b. Baba Bathra 15a)

In these two opinions we see the divergence between an attempt at reading history 'as it really was' and the view that divine inspiration, or human imagination, transcends the limitations of mere chronology. For the most part the rabbinic tradition followed the line of Rabbi Simeon. In this way the patriarchs, for example, become 'types' that do not exist in some distant past. Rather they are present today – great-grandfather Abraham living just round the corner.

With modernity, however, the entire traditional construction of the past has been challenged through academic scholarship. The quest to discover 'what really happened in history', as opposed to what the tradition has selectively handed down, has become our dominant mode of thought for more than two centuries, and it has posed the greatest challenge to the validity and authority of the the tradition itself. We will see later its impact on the creation of modern Jewish religious groupings, but first it is necessary to give a brief overview of Jewish history – augmented by the time-line included as an appendix to this book and some suggestions for further reading.

The scholarly view of biblical history is familiar from modern encyclopaedias and commentaries. But these exist alongside serious debates as to how much 'real' history can be gleaned from the Bible itself. Like any writing created for a specific purpose it is selective in what it includes, its judgments on individuals or events are coloured. Apart from which it has been ideologically overworked by layers of editors, contains contradictory materials and for the most part exists in a historical vacuum with no outside corroboration for any of its main accounts. Archaeological findings offer only indirect information and are anyway notoriously subjective. If it were not for the Bible itself we would know nothing about Abraham, Isaac or Jacob, or for that matter King David or King Solomon. As to who wrote or edited these books, three centuries of historical-critical research leave us with a hopelessly fragmented theory of composition, and the occasional entrepreneurial bestseller claiming to prove who the real author was or where bits of the ark (Noah's and the one in the tabernacle) are to be found.

Were the Israelites actually descendants of an Abraham whose grandson, Jacob, went down to Egypt with his family to emerge four generations or four centuries later (the texts are contradictory) to conquer the land of Canaan? Or were they part of an indigenous population that rebelled and conquered their neighbours, as some scholars think today? Were they even in the holy land at all? One current theory, not taken seriously it must be admitted, locates all the biblical events in Arabia because of the coincidence of place names. Who was the Pharaoh of the exodus, if there was one, and where was the Sea of Reeds (not Red Sea of popular parlance) where they crossed on dry land? And anyway, how did they manage to do it? Six hundred thousand adult males makes for a couple of million families passing through a few miles of territory. The mathematics for the crossing itself suggest a figure of weeks or months. Pharaoh's army would have starved to death waiting to attack long before they were drowned. Was there ever a tabernacle in the wilderness, or is the whole account a political or pious forgery, a projection into the past of the Jerusalem Temple priesthood trying to establish their credentials and power?

Three are the fathers of Israel

The list of historical problems is endless and the scepticism understandable. Biblical criticism of the last centuries emerged in a society emancipating itself from the church hierarchies of its time and the scholasticism that dominated thought, preventing empirical evidence and new understandings from entering into a closed world. That having been said, the historical enquiry is fascinating in its own right, however inconclusive it may be. When augmented by the newer literary approaches to studying the Hebrew Bible, and a good dose of traditional Jewish exegesis to put the whole enterprise into some kind of perspective, something emerges. If they are not historical certainties, then at least they are an engagement with history which is also a quest for truth.

For what comes after the Bible there is no less confusion and complexity, though less religious investment on the part of tradition in the exact events.

The Diaspora, a Greek word meaning 'dispersion', 'scattering', refers collectively to all the places outside the land of Israel where Jews settled after the destruction of national life by the Romans in 70 CE. But in fact long before that historic catastrophe the dispersion of the Jews had been in progress. Of those exiled in Babylon after the destruction of the First Temple in 586 BCE, not all returned after the decree of Cyrus, and perhaps a majority put down roots and stayed there. Among those fleeing the Babylonians some had settled in Egypt, and a flourishing sanctuary in the Elephantine region of Egypt existed in the middle of the second century BCE. By the time of the Greek and later Roman overlordship of Judea large Jewish centres existed in Babylon-Persia, Syria, Antioch, Rome, Athens, Thessalonica, Bulgaria, Armenia, Cyprus, Carthage and Alexandria. In the first century CE there were Jews in Spain, and from the period of the Roman republic they were to be found in France and Germany. The Arab conquest in the seventh century brought not only Mesopotamian and Palestinian Jewry, but also all the communities throughout the Middle East and large parts of the Mediterranean world under the sway of Islam. The Jewish community in Spain experienced a Golden Age under Islam, then suffered successive persecutions under the Almohades, and subsequently at the hands of the Inquisition in Christian Spain whence they had fled, which culminated in the expulsion from Spain in 1492.

These exiles found homes within the Ottoman Empire, in locations ranging from Bosnia to Constantinople, from Salonica to Sofia; or else they regathered into new communities in North Africa, Amsterdam, London, Ferrara, Livorno, Vienna, Bucharest and other cities, still preserving their traditions and the Judaeo-Spanish language, Ladino. Thus two distinctive Sephardi civilisations developed, one oriental and the other occidental. (The term Sephardi derives from the name of an unknown land of exile *sepharad*, mentioned in Obadiah 20 and traditionally identified with Spain.)

As a contrast to the fate of the Sephardim, we may also consider the Ashkenazim, a term used to designate Jews who lived in Germany and East European countries, where the Judaeo-German vernacular (Yiddish) was spoken. (The name *ashkenaz* is to be found in Genesis 10:3 in the list of Noah's grandsons, and was traditionally associated with Germany.) Beginning with the First Crusade during the eleventh century, religious hysteria was whipped up against the Jews as convenient scapegoats when any trouble arose. After the Black Death in 1348–9, they were accused of poisoning the wells of Christians and in the aftermath armed mobs wiped out over three hundred and fifty Jewish communities, and tens of thousands of Jews, men, women and children, were murdered. One result was a massive flight of German Jews to the Polish provinces.

The details of the wanderings of these communities are beyond the scope of this account, but it will be clear that all aspects of Jewish life were affected by such migrations, leading to the appearance of local differences in custom and tradition. Some effects can be seen in matters of ritual and the prayerbook, for between the Ashkenazim and Sephardim there grew up differences in the liturgy and ceremonies, in the manner of pronouncing Hebrew and the character of the music of the synagogue. Variations in matters of Jewish law also arose, so that the great codifications had to be adjusted to include both traditions.

Three are the fathers of Israel

The repeated expulsions, wanderings and tragedies of Jewish communities over the centuries have led to what has been called the 'lachrymose' view of Jewish history. And there are enough records of destruction, long before the Nazi period, to justify this. Jews experienced eighteen major expulsions (and readmissions and re-expulsions) from European countries between 1290 and 1496. Contemporary accounts and liturgical poems record the repeated experience of mob attacks and massacres.

The Massacre at the Coronation of Richard I

In the year 4950 (September 1189–September 1190) evil was brought upon Israel from heaven. For there arose a King in the Isle of the sea known as Angleterre. And it happened on the day of their appointing him King, and when they put the royal crown upon his head in the city of London, in the palace which is within the city, and many folk were gathered there from France and from the isles of the sea, and there came likewise Jewish magistrates, and with them 'tenths' to bring to the King as a tribute, and bad men hastened to say that it was not allowed for Jews to look on the King's crown when the monks and priests crowned him, when they crowned the King at Orleans, and they thrust them forth and destroyed them, and the King knew not of this, and a rumour went to the city saying, 'The King has ordered the Jews to be converted,' and they went to fall upon them and slay them and their maidservants in their houses, and they slew about thirty men and some of the remainder slew themselves and their children ... (Ephraim ben Jacob of Bonn)

The same chronicler records the Massacre at York in 1190–91 and the Ritual Murder accusation at Blois, France, in 1171. In 1656 Bogdan Chmelnitzki, the Ukrainian Cossack leader, led an uprising against Polish rule in the Ukraine with the resulting massacre by the peasants of hundreds of Jewish communities. Over one hundred thousand were killed; many fled to Holland,

Germany, Bohemia and the Balkans. An anonymous poem records the horror of it:

> Dear people, let us weep and wail
> Over the dread events occurring in our days,
> In the year of the coming of the Messiah, the Cossacks pursue us
> With a dreadful cruelty, impossible to describe!
>
> The holy old community of Nemirov was dispersed;
> About this much will yet be written.
> With scythes the evil ones ran about, cutting us down like sheaves;
> Rather had we been taken prisoner by the Tartars.
>
> They chased and killed everyone alike,
> Many were drowned in the deep river;
> Those who swam were slain without mercy;
> No one was spared, young or old, poor or rich.
>
> Holy scrolls were mutilated and made into slippers,
> Holy Torah, how can it not anger you?
> Oh, woe, how they defiled your sweet words,
> That is why my eyes flow in a river of tears.
>
> Unburied the dead lie under the sun,
> One holy martyr covers another, the one underneath the better off.
> Oh, this unexpected terrible horror,
> Five hundred children drowned in wells.

If such massacres and expulsions were the most horrific of experiences, there were nevertheless other aspects of Jewish life in the Middle Ages that were also distressing. Since early times Jews had lived in separate quarters of towns, partly out of choice and to enable them to maintain Jewish institutions and religious practices. But often it was demanded of them, and the Jewish quarter allowed for a degree of self-protection in a hostile environment. However, when Jews requested to be readmitted to Venice, from which they had long been banned, at the beginning of the sixteenth century, they were allowed in on condition that they lived in the *geto nuovo* area, which could be closed in by walls, gates and drawbridges. From this beginning emerged 'ghettos' throughout Italy, accompanied by harsh laws restricting movement (the ghetto was closed at night and the Jews had to pay for the maintenance of the Christian gatekeepers), the wearing of a special badge and compulsory attendance at conversionary sermons. Since the boundaries of the ghetto were generally not allowed to be enlarged, they became increasingly more crowded and insanitary.

And yet there is also another side to the picture. Both Christianity and Islam had ambivalent relationships with Judaism. Their respective theologies required that Judaism be seen as inferior, and therefore subject to restrictions, in the case of Christianity, or, as in the case of Islam, high taxation because of their *dhimmi* status. Yet at the same time Jews were to be afforded protection. This effectively enabled Jews to play important roles in their respective societies, particularly as a merchant class, while individuals could acquire significant position and wealth. If they were considered inferior because of their religious status, they could often have equal opportunities in terms of the civil law and use the tensions between these sources of authority to their advantage. An early rabbinic formulation, *dina d'malkhuta dina*, 'the law of the land is the law', effectively allowed for a degree of autonomy within their society in all matters that did not specifically contradict Jewish religious requirements. Thus Jews were able to negotiate a collective relationship with the powers that be and regulate the inner life of their community according to Jewish law.

If each society within which Jews lived provided a different set of practical, political, cultural and spiritual challenges during the Middle Ages, the general situation began to deteriorate by the end of this period. Changes included: expulsions from England, France, Spain and parts of Germany; increased restrictions on rights of residence or movement; the gradual collapse of Poland accompanied by events like the Chmelnitzki pogroms mentioned above; changes in the Ottoman Empire also made it less favourable to the Jews.

Yet changes in the political nature of society, with the gradual emergence of the nation State, also gave Jews new kinds of status. After the American and French revolutions Jews were given equal citizenship rights, a process that had already begun in other parts of Europe. But the price that was paid was the loss of their collective status and its accompanying power to regulate their internal life. In Germany and Russia, at the beginning of the nineteenth century, communal institutions, like rabbinic courts, were abolished. Taxation became a matter for the individual citizen and was no longer regulated by the Jewish community as a whole. Thus the power to control the inner life of the community was gradually lost, leading to the situation that Jews experience today – full citizens of their particular society, but with a Judaism that has become 'privatised', a matter for individual conscience or interest, as opposed to a fully controlled way of life within a closed Jewish community. (The American Reform movement introduced the term 'Jews by choice' as a positive way of describing converts to Judaism. It was subsequently pointed out that in an open society, where nothing officially binds the Jew to the community, we are all 'Jews by choice'.)

Yet precisely this new openness produced new dangers, from without and within. If in the past anti-Jewish sentiment had been based on religious teachings or economic factors, the new 'anti-Semitism' – a word coined in the nineteenth century – based itself on pseudo-biological theories about race. But the old elements remained as well, and fuelled by economic and social insecurities at a time of rapid change, anti-Jewish hatred became a significant factor in turn-of-the-century Europe. Such was the setting for the notorious Dreyfus case in which a Jewish-French army captain on the General Staff was falsely accused of treason and sentenced to life imprisonment in 1894. The affair unleashed a wave of anti-Semitic reactions in France, but also led to a vigorous defence which culminated in his exoneration and reinstatement.

Reporting on the affair was a Viennese journalist Theodore

Three are the fathers of Israel

Herzl who was influenced to seek a solution to the 'Jewish problem'. His book *Der Judenstaat*, 'The Jewish State', was conceived as a blueprint for the creation of a Jewish homeland. Such nationalist ideas were current also in Eastern Europe, alongside Jewish socialist movements, but Herzl gave political form to them, convening the first Zionist Congress in Basle in 1897. Herzl burnt himself out in the pursuit of his goal, dying at the age of forty-four. A true visionary, he wrote in his diary after the Congress: 'In Basle I have founded the Jewish State. Were I to say this aloud today, the response would be universal laughter. Perhaps in five years, certainly in fifty, it will be there.'

After Herzl's death in 1904 the movement developed through practical colonisation in Palestine and continuing diplomatic negotiations. Between 1881 and 1948 the Jewish population grew from 24,000 to 630,000. One result of diplomacy was a letter from Lord Balfour on behalf of the British Government to Baron Lionel Rothschild, The Balfour Declaration of 1917, which stated:

> His Majesty's government view with favour the establishment in Palestine of a national home for the Jewish people, and will use their best endeavours to facilitate the achievement of this object, it being clearly understood that nothing shall be done which may prejudice the civil and religious rights of the existing non-Jewish communities in Palestine, or the rights and political status enjoyed by Jews in any other country.

Already in that letter one can see the seeds of the future conflict that was to arise between the Jewish immigrants and the native population.

It is possible that the Zionist movement would have led to no more than a number of large Jewish settlements in Palestine, including the revolutionary collective farm, the kibbutz. But the universal shock which followed the liberation of the concentration camps after the Second World War, the recognition of the systematic entrapment, transport and murder of six million Jews by the Nazi regime, showed just how vulnerable Jewish life could be. The creation of a Jewish State became a major political goal for Jews, supported by a wave of international sympathy for their plight, but also aided by the political realignments that took place at the beginning of the Cold War. On the 29th November 1947 the United Nations voted for a partitition of Palestine into two entities, exactly fifty years after Herzl's prophetic diary entry. On 14 May 1948 the British Mandate came to an end and David Ben Gurion declared the creation of the State of Israel. The immediate attacks of combined Arab armies rearranged drastically the initial partition plan, and subsequent wars, notably the Six Day War in 1967, changed borders and occupied areas alike. The intervening period has seen new alignments and gradual steps towards a comprehensive peace settlement with the neighbouring states and the Palestinian population that also seeks statehood. Thus the creation of the State of Israel has provided a refuge for Jews from all over the world, offered a new dimension to Jewish identity and life, but introduced new challenges to Judaism as it tries to come to terms with areas of public and political life that have not been addressed for two millennia.

These outer challenges of the modern world that led to the greatest tragedy in Jewish history, but also the greatest transformation in Jewish life in two millennia with the re-establishment of a national homeland, were matched by no less dramatic inner changes in Jewish religious life. Jews were presented with the opportunity of entering into this new world. Their commercial success brought them into the non-Jewish world, gave them a new status and the desire to justify it and maintain it. This meant enormous changes to their self-understanding. Yiddish, the Jewish language of Eastern Europe, was set aside and the vernacular language of their particular country adopted. When the Jews had lived as an autonomous 'state-within-a-state', their own authorities had power and sanctions, particularly the *cherem*, the 'ban' that could effectively excommunicate someone (as happened to Spinoza). In the new situation authority was now vested in the nation State itself and power over the individual members of the community was gone. In the well-known formulation of Clermont Tonnerre during the French Assembly debates on the Emancipation of the Jews: 'We must refuse

everything to the Jews as a nation, we must grant everything to
the Jews as individuals.'

It is difficult now to understand the ecstatic responses of Jews
to the possibilities opened up to them by their new situation.
Michael Williams illustrates the reaction of French Jewry in the
following way.

A hundred years after emancipation, the general tone of
the French Jewish community can be summarised in the
following quotations. Already in 1831, the Chief Rabbi of
Metz had called the decision of the French government to
give financial aid to rabbis in the east of France 'the greatest
act of justice that the Hebrew nation had obtained since
the destruction of the Second Temple' . . . 'The Revolution
of 1789' wrote a famous Jewish historian in the 1890s, 'was
our second law from Mount Sinai.' Another wrote 'the
Messianic age had arrived with the French Revolution, the
Messianic age had arrived with this new society of *liberté,
égalité, fraternité*'. The revolution was for one famous rabbi
'our exodus from Egypt, our modern *Pesach*'. For another,
'we must make the greatest efforts to arrive in the first rank
among all honest loyal workers in whatever careers are
opened to us. Let us offer the example of all civic and social
virtues, let us not cease to be irreproachable citizens, let us,
in a word, be the worthy children of France.' . . .

Théodore Reinach, in an extraordinary speech given at
a Jewish school in July 1898, at the time of the greatest
physical, psychological, moral and verbal violence directed
against the French Jewish community, said to the Jewish
children gathered before him: 'never confuse the real
France with the foam of hatred that rises unpunished but
temporarily to its surface. Continue to love her, this France,
with all your strength, with all your soul, as you love a
mother, even an unjust mother, even a mother *égarée*, a
mother wandering from the paths of maternity, because,
just because she is your mother and because you are her
children.'[1]

The Emancipation led to the creation of a variety of different religious responses and movements in the Diaspora. Reform Judaism in Germany was the first of these. The contrast between the forms of worship then present in the synagogue and those in the church led to the first stage of Reform – an attempt led by lay people to improve the decorum and aesthetics of the synagogue service. Steps included shortening the service, removing repetitions, introducing the sermon in the vernacular, choral singing with organ, adding prayers in the vernacular. The initiator of these was a successful businessman in the town of Seesen in central Germany. He founded a temple there in 1810 and later opened his home in Berlin to services in 1815. (As an aside it is worth noting that while the services he organised met with disapproval from the traditionalists there were no major problems. Instead it was the Prussian government that caused difficulties. King Frederick William III was concerned that a reformed Judaism might prove attractive to Christians and in 1821 issued a decree prohibiting Christian clergy and public officials from attending Jewish ceremonies as they might detract from the status of Christianity. In September 1823 the congregation was closed down.)

This initiative was followed in 1817 by a group of Jews in Hamburg who deliberately called their centre a 'temple'. This was a term in common use for a religious centre and helped differentiate it from the local synagogue. But it also carried deeper implications. The synagogue was meant to be a temporary institution until the real Temple in Jerusalem was restored. Calling this new centre a 'temple' said something about the final setting aside of these old aspirations. The Hamburg group produced the first Reform prayerbook in 1819, edited by two Jewishly educated laymen, and they used Talmudic arguments to justify their changes. They did not see themselves as innovators but rather as upholders of a continuous Jewish tradition. Support for these changes came from a number of rabbis. From Hungary Rabbi Aaron Chorin (1766–1844) wrote in its favour:

For a long time now I have noticed with regret the sad

situation of my coreligionists. A portion of them have surrendered to superstition, another to unbelief. While that harmful conglomeration of pious simulators, the Chasidim, spreads more and more and daily wins new supporters, another group eschews all religious obligations and declares as true only that to which the senses can witness . . .

During the past year a circular letter from a greatly honoured congregation in Germany informed me that about three hundred of the most highly respected heads of families had resolved to arrange their worship service in such a manner that it would comply with a sense of dignity, with the spirit of the age, and at the same time with the principles of Judaism, strictly interpreted in accordance with the Holy Scriptures and the Talmud. At the same time I was asked to state whether the teachings of the Talmud permit:

1. To cleanse our liturgy from later additions (Heaven only knows when and by whom they were added!) and to restore its pristine simplicity.

2. To say one's prayers in the understandable language of one's country, so that the heart of the worshipper may know what the lips speak.

3. To hold a service to the accompaniment of an organ, so that harmony and order, which are now lacking in our synagogues, might be reintroduced.

4. Or whether such changes are prohibited because of the rule, 'The customs of Israel have the force of Torah,' which, therefore, may not be altered.[2]

Despite expressing his anxieties about the responses his reply would evoke, Chorin said yes to all these changes.

Not surprisingly there was an immediate response from more traditionally inclined rabbis throughout Europe condemning these changes and asking the secular authorities in Hamburg to forbid this innovation. When this did not work, a book was published by leading traditionalist rabbis, which 'marked the beginning of an Orthodox party, opposed to any and all tampering with tradition'.[3]

Even though the Hamburg Reformers did not wish to break with tradition certain ideological elements were already present in their prayerbook. In 1807 the Paris Sanhedrin, a gathering of seventy-one Jewish notables, two-thirds of them rabbis, convened by Napoleon, had proclaimed that Jews would be loyal to the modern nation states in which they lived. This raised problems with regard to the many liturgical references to the return to Zion, the restoration of the Kingdom of Israel and messianic redemption. Also, from a contemporary point of view, certain other ideas like the physical resurrection of the body and the restoration of animal sacrifices raised problems. In an age that prided itself on reason, science and the rejection of superstition, the presence of mystical formulations, passages from the Zohar and reference to angels were also sources of embarrassment. What is particularly striking to anyone who knows Hebrew books is that the Hamburg prayerbook opened from left to right like any other European book, whereas traditional Jewish prayerbooks opened from right to left.

An example of their approach can be seen from the introduction to the Hamburg prayerbook:

> The desire for a return to Jerusalem was omitted because it is a wish from the heart of only very few. When Cyrus permitted the Israelites to return from the Babylonian exile only some 4,200 availed themselves of the opportunity. The rest stayed behind, demonstrating that one can be a good Jew without praying for a return to Jerusalem. The prayers for a return to Zion which we have retained can be taken in a spiritual sense; but we do not request that God transport us physically to Zion, because we are satisfied with the place where we live.[4]

While the Reformers were conscious of certain factors that influenced their decisions, other contemporary modes were also affecting them.

Whether they consciously realised it or not, these early reformers were influenced by factors other than the desire to simplify and modernise. One of those factors was German Protestantism. When Samuel Holdheim, the radical rabbi of the Berlin Reform Society, argued that the modern life of the Jew demanded the end of rabbinical autonomy, the separation of religious affairs from civil and political issues, the recognition of marriage as a civil act, he was reflecting the Protestant view of the supremacy of State over Church. The use of German vernacular was not only a modernist innovation, it was a Protestant innovation, as well. The women's gallery in the synagogue was abolished by these early reformers not merely because it was outmoded, but because the Protestant family pew was the vogue in Germany. Many Reform rabbis dressed in the fashion of the Protestant pastorate, with black gowns and white wing collars. It was hardly an accident therefore that the Jewish Reform movement was to reach its fullest development in countries that were predominantly Low Church: Germany and then the United States.[5]

While the liturgical reforms can be seen to fit within a particular social context, the intellectual background was provided by the emerging historical study of Judaism. For the Reformers such study enabled them to identify the processes of change within Judaism, which provided a justification for the innovations they also sought. The scholarly study of Judaism, the *Wissenschaft des Judentums*, emerged in the second decade of the nineteenth century among scholars who had been exposed to studies in German universities. They came from traditional Jewish homes and felt at first hand the clash between their own ahistoric Talmudic tradition and the historical and critical methods of contemporary scholarship. They began the meticulous work of documenting the texts and traditions of Judaism. But this historical approach had a double effect. On the one hand it reinforced a sense of loyalty to tradition, but on the other it undermined the authority of beliefs and practices whose origins could now be seen, which dealt a severe blow to Orthodox Judaism.

A series of rabbinical Synods were held in Germany between

the 1840s and 1860s at the instigation of Abraham Geiger (1810–74) leader of the Reformers, intended to address the changes to Jewish religious practice that were felt to be necessary. No ideological agreement was reached. Instead an inner conflict developed between those who wanted radical reforms and continuing development and those who wanted a more conservative approach. Issues like the shifting of the *Shabbat* to Sunday for the sake of the convenience of the worshipper, or whether to abolish circumcision, polarised the debate between the radicals and conservatives. At the Frankfurt synod of 1845 the irretrievable split finally occurred. The more conservative rabbis walked out, under the leadership of the man destined to become the leader of Conservative Judaism, Zechariah Frankel (1801–75).

It is important to mention the powerful opponent of these movements that sought change – Samson Raphael Hirsch, Chief Rabbi of the Orthodox community of Frankfurt. He realised that a simple literal reading of the tradition was no longer enough, so instead he sought a symbolic reading of it, an intellectualisation which identifies modern Orthodoxy as equally a creation of the post-Enlightenment, post-emancipation world. The motto which was adopted by his community and other like-minded 'modern Orthodox' ones was *Torah im derekh eretz,* a commitment to Torah in all its facets together with a full place within society.

By the end of the nineteenth century these three movements were still very alike in practice, the 'liberal' and 'conservative' wings of Reform, and neo-Orthodoxy. All three were led by rabbis with a university background and philosophical training. However slight the differences that may have been between them, they stimulated the creation of a variety of religious institutions of their own. The Reform Lehranstalt (Hochschule) für die Wissenschaft des Judentums, the Orthodox Rabbiner Seminar in Berlin and the (Conservative) Jüdische Theologicsches Seminar in Breslau became leading centres of Jewish scholarship. All three movements also produced prayerbooks.

To illustrate just how radical these could be, the prayerbook of the Berlin *Reformgemeinde* replaced the form and content of the traditional liturgy with what was effectively a prayer and meditation manual. The first edition appeared in 1845 and it was continually revised, going through ten editions by the early 1930s. This final version was reduced to a booklet of sixty-four pages – which was to cover services throughout the entire year. One of the preachers in this congregation, Immanuel Heinrich Ritter, explained the rationale for keeping the *Shema* (Hear O Israel) and the *Kadosh* (Holy, holy, holy . . .) in the original Hebrew:

> They are the pledge of allegiance and the watchword of Judaism, of which we are preserving the most ancient form – just as the Prussians and the Austrians are preserving their mottos *Suum Cuique* (To each his own) and *Unitis Viribus* (With combined strength) in Latin, even though they are speaking German today. By proclaiming those basic truths in both languages, we also want to point to their origin in the times and places of most ancient Asiatic culture, and to remind ourselves of the fact that the bases of Judaism have remained the same and that the present-day conviction of its adherents coincides with that of its first representatives [i.e. certain proof that it is a radical departure!].

In America the Reform movement became dominant as Jews moved out into the pioneer areas of the new country. The movement was pro-Bible, anti-rabbinic. It accepted the Higher Criticism of the Bible and the belief in 'Progressive Revelation'. The radical camp dominated American Reform, as expressed in the Pittsburgh Platform of 1885:

> We recognize in the Mosaic legislation a system of training the Jewish people for its mission during its national life in Palestine, but today we accept as binding only its moral laws, and maintain only such ceremonies as elevate and sanctify our lives, but reject all such as are not adapted to the views and habits of modern civilisation . . . We hold that all such Mosaic and rabbinical laws as regulate diet, priestly purity, and dress originated in ages and under the influence of ideas entirely foreign to our present mental and spiritual state . . . We recognize in the modern era of

universal culture of heart and intellect, the approaching of the realization of Israel's great messianic hope for the establishment of the kingdom of truth, justice and peace among all men. We consider ourselves no longer a nation, but a religious community, and therefore expect neither a return to Palestine, nor a sacrificial worship under the sons of Aaron, nor the restoration of any of the laws concerning the Jewish state . . . We reassert the doctrine of Judaism that the soul is immortal, founding this belief on the divine nature of the human spirit, which forever finds bliss in righteousness and misery in wickedness. We reject as ideas not rooted in Judaism, the beliefs both in bodily resurrection and in Gehenna and Eden . . . as abodes for everlasting punishment and reward.

As the movement developed, the Reformers realised that the role of traditional observance had been underestimated. So the Columbus Platform of 1937 reads: 'The Torah, both written and oral, enshrines Israel's evergrowing consciousness of God and of the moral law. It preserves the historical precedents, sanctions and norms of Jewish life, and seeks to mould it in patterns of goodness and holiness.' It affirmed Jewish peoplehood; the obligation on all of Jewry to help in the upbuilding of Palestine as a Jewish homeland – to be 'not only a haven of refuge for the oppressed but also a centre of Jewish culture and spiritual life'. They also stressed the need to preserve Sabbath, Festivals and Holy Days.

In the post-war era, all the Jewish movements, from the most radical to the most Orthodox, have moved towards a position of greater adherence to Jewish tradition. This is most marked in the growing numbers and self-confidence of ultra-Orthodox groups, helped by the power they hold in the State of Israel because of coalition politics that have made them indispensable till now for the formation of a government. The American Conservative movement has split over the issue of the ordination of women rabbis with a 'Traditional Conservative' wing breaking off. Even more radical movements like the 'Reconstructionists', an earlier breakaway from Conservative Judaism under the leadership of Mordechai Kaplan, and the American Reform movement will temper their radicalism (positive stands on the issue of homosexuality, outreach to intermarried couples) with a greater concern with the language and forms of traditional Judaism. Above all the concept of *amkha*, 'peoplehood', seems to dominate, as a response to the horrendous losses inflicted by the Nazis and a growing awareness of a shrinking Jewish community as more and more people intermarry with non-Jews and disappear from the Jewish community or maintain ever weaker links.

In Western Europe, each country has its own pattern of life, determined in some cases by large immigrations in recent years – North African Jews into France, Jews from the former Soviet Union into Germany. On the whole the post-war situation, particularly in countries occupied by the Nazis, has been one of quiet rebuilding, at least of the physical aspects of community life. Though officially Orthodox, neither the leaders nor members of congregations were really Orthodox, but they effectively prevented the development of any other kind of Jewish religious expression.

In Central and Eastern Europe, since the break-up of the Soviet Union, Jews are beginning once again to identify with Jewish culture and small social and cultural groups, kindergartens and even religious communities are springing up, though seventy years of communism have made them wary of the religious aspects of Judaism. The future of these communities is bound up with the politics of their society, and large numbers have already moved to Israel. By the middle of the 1990s the figure had already exceeded 700,000. Nevertheless a sizeable number, estimated as anywhere between one and three million (depending on how 'officially' Jewish are the people you wish to count) could establish in time a major force within world Jewry.

The incredible success story of the State of Israel, despite the enormous troubles that beset it, is another pointer to a challenging and changing Jewish future. The current population of around five and a half million includes immigrants from eighty countries. Over 80 per cent are Jewish, and with a relatively high birthrate compared to Jewish populations elsewhere, Israel is well on its way to being the largest Jewish community, exceeding the approximately five million Jews of the United States. Religiously the State is recognised as being polarised between secular and ultra-religious Jews, a product of the fact that the earliest settlers were socialist-minded and anti-religious. Small Reform and Conservative movements exist but have made little headway in terms of numbers, and their rabbis suffer restrictions of their right to perform marriages, burials and conversions, rights that they fully enjoy in every other Western society. But between these extremes are many variations of Jewish practice that individual Israelis perform, as well as spiritual searchings in many directions.

Part of the drama of Israel is simply that the Judaism conceived and developed in two thousand years of exile does not necessarily fit a Jewish society in its own homeland where different needs exist and different conditions prevail. The constant pressure of wars and political tensions, let alone the daily bread-and-butter challenges of earning a living and creating a new society, have pushed the classical religious questions somewhat into the background. Nevertheless study centres, traditional and radically new, do exist and the entire society is a kind of workshop for a future Judaism of as yet undetermined qualities and dimensions.

In all the changes and challenges described above, one revolution in Jewish experience has been omitted till now – the impact of the women's movement on contemporary Jewish life. That will be the subject of the next chapter.

Further Reading

Surveys of Jewish history

Haim Beinart, *Atlas of Medieval Jewish History* (New York and London, etc., Simon and Schuster, 1992): using the method popularised by Martin Gilbert (see next entry) of using maps to indicate main trends in Jewish history, this focuses on the Middle Ages and adds helpful textual notes.

Martin Gilbert, *Jewish History Atlas* (London, Weidenfeld & Nicolson, 1969, 3rd edn, 1985): an excellent overview of Jewish history presented in the form of maps.

David J. Goldberg and John D. Rayner, *The Jewish People: Their History and Their Religion* (London, Penguin, 1989): a well-organised and well-written survey of Jewish history.

Hyam Maccoby, *Judaism on Trial: Jewish–Christian Disputations in the Middle Ages*, The Littman Library of Jewish Civilization (Rutherford Madison Teaneck, Fairleigh Dickinson University Press, 1982): a fine account and record of the major mediaeval disputations which also shows the situation of the Jews under Christianity in the Middle Ages.

On the Nature of Jewish History

David Biale, *Power and Powerlessness in Jewish History* (New York, Schocken Books, 1986): a challenging re-evaluation of Jewish history.

Yosef Hayim Yerushalmi, *Zakhor: Jewish History and Jewish Memory* (Philadelphia, The Jewish Publication Society of America, 1982; Seattle and London, University of Washington Press, 1982): a fascinating examination of the tension between traditional memory and history reconstruction.

On Modern Jewish History

Michael A. Meyer, *Response to Modernity: A History of the Reform Movement in Judaism* (New York, Oxford, Oxford University Press, 1988): an excellent account of the rise and development of the Reform Jewish movement.

Jakob J. Petuchowski, *Prayerbook Reform in Europe: The Liturgy of European Liberal and Reform Judaism* (New York, The World Union for Progressive Judaism, 1968): a highly technical analysis of different Reform and Liberal liturgies by a master of the field.

W. Gunther Plaut, *The Rise of Reform Judaism: A Sourcebook of its European Origins* (New York, The World Union of Progressive Judaism, 1963): a valuable sourcebook for early Reform Judaism.

Howard M. Sachar, *The Course of Modern Jewish History* (London, Weidenfeld and Nicolson, 1958; rev. edn, Vintage Books, 1990): well-established survey of this period in Jewish life.

Four are the mothers of Israel
Changing roles of Jewish women

Even a few years ago this chapter would have been utterly different. Of all the themes covered in this book, none has undergone such a radical change in such a short time as the role and self-perception of women within Jewish society and life. The very designation 'four are the mothers of Israel' raises as many questions as it apparently answers. Women have been and are 'mothers of Israel', but they have also been, and are, more than mothers, and sometimes not 'mothers' in the biological sense but creators of human values and material advances in many other ways. What is different today, though there are clearly isolated individuals and situations in the past where the same rule applied, is that it is women who are defining for themselves the role they play within Judaism, as opposed to being the projected creations of male imagination and power.

Here I have to step back a moment and acknowledge my own difficulty in writing this particular chapter. We are in the middle of a revolution of consciousness, for both women and men, so it is very hard to find some kind of neutral ground on which to stand in describing it. If my sympathies are with what is going on I must nevertheless acknowledge that as a man I cannot, and possibly should not (one of the issues under debate) try to speak on behalf of women. Some women regard this as axiomatic; others may not see it as a problem at all as they consider themselves as either pre- or post-feminist.

Even in describing the issue one bumps into problems of

language which have wider ramifications. The phrase 'politically correct' has become something to joke about, and it can obviously go too far, but the way we discuss matters and the terminology we use, for subjects ranging from 'chairperson' to the ways we translate the names for God, do have consequences. The hippies of another generation could intone 'you are what you eat'. It is as legitimate to point out that 'you are what you say'; our language not only reflects our attitudes but creates them.

Above all there is the problem for anyone belonging to a 'power élite' entering the territory of, or claiming to speak on behalf of, those who are, or perceive themselves to be, past or present 'victims' of that élite. Without doubt Judaism as a patriarchal religion from its biblical period down to the present day has exerted control over the lives of women. If that is not the entire story, because there have been and are areas where women do exert power, this is largely because such 'freedom' has also been licensed by men.

Please excuse this long apologia. I wanted to get it out of the way to show that I am aware of some of the traps, even as I now prepare to step into them. (One of my women rabbi colleagues would by now be patting me on the head and saying, 'There, there, *bubbele!*')

The respective roles of men and women in Jewish thought take their starting point in the opening chapters of the biblical Book of Genesis, and much recent scholarship has been devoted to examining and re-examining these crucial texts. To sum up very briefly, there are two dominant images. In Genesis 2 woman is created out of 'the *adam*', so as to function as an *ezer k'negdo*. Literally it means 'a helper – opposite to him' or 'corresponding to him'. 'Helper' does not mean subservient in any way. God is described as a 'helper' of Israel (Ps. 121:2). Thus the combined phrase seems to suggest two equal entities defined by their correspondence to each other and a kind of symbiotic relationship. It is only after this pairing that the man, inevitably, names this new creation as *ishah*, 'woman', because she was taken from *ish*, 'man'. The word-play is intentional in the Hebrew, as in the English: the two of them are exactly equivalent. Moreover, the primordial *adam* only becomes recognisable as a human being, a 'man' when the 'woman' exists beside him.

But by the end of the following chapter of Genesis, another kind of relationship has been established. The story of the snake tempting Eve to eat the forbidden fruit will take us too far afield for our present purposes. Suffice it to say that the story can indeed be interpreted as a first act of disobedience against God, a 'fall from grace' and a terrible tragedy; but also as a successful strategy on the part of God to force the human pair out of their state of dependency in the Garden of Eden into self-consciousness and awareness, becoming as a result troubled, but responsible, adult human beings. Depending on which reading one makes, the respective roles of the woman and the man can be interpreted negatively or positively, but what is important is that the final image is of a soured relationship between them where the man passes the blame on to the woman in denial of his own responsibility, and the woman is presented as subservient to the man. But is that state intended to be a description of a new 'norm', or is it meant to show the degree to which things can deteriorate from the ideal relationship unless human beings do treat each other as mutually supportive and equal? Presumably the answer lies somewhere in the dynamism between these two diametrically opposed options, with human reality in any given case being expressed along some kind of continuum between them.

What now obscures the way in which this dynamic situation between men and women has been perceived in Jewish tradition is simply the fact that, apart from rare exceptions, the entire story, from the biblical period down to almost the present day, has been written and recorded by the 'boys'. The views and experiences of women have been given to us as filtered through male lenses, be they the writings of law-givers or homilists, poets or archivists, exegetes or editors. So what trust can one give to documents about the behaviour or roles of women in the past given this premise? The answer has to be that a certain amount can be trusted with qualifications and reservations; some more may be ascertained as a result of careful reading between the lines; perhaps more can be learned by the imaginative re-creation of that past using contemporary women's experience; and a lot of leftover material is simply indigestible or downright problematic.

If the Hebrew Bible is full of contradictory material, the patriarchal environment is a given. It is the autonomous, adult Israelite male who is addressed in the Ten Commandments (who has wives, children, slaves, animals and property) and who is also addressed directly at the covenant-making ceremony at Mount Sinai. Nevertheless the rights of women are asserted from time to time under the law – the most explicit and challenging being that of the daughters of Zelophehad who successfully plead to be allowed to inherit from their father in the absence of a male heir (Num. 27:1–11).

If women have a subordinate role in law, nevertheless they play significant parts in family life when it comes to decision-making. Moreover, at key moments of transition in the history of biblical Israel it is women who dominate the stage: the 'Hebrew midwives', the mother and sister of Moses, as well as the 'daughter of Pharaoh' in Exodus 1–2, but for whom there would have been no Israelites and no Moses; Hannah, the barren women, whose prayer for a son leads to the birth of Samuel who will usher in the period of the monarchy and anoint King David. Hannah created a history that would not otherwise have happened. The prophetess Huldah authenticated the scroll of the law found in the Temple and ushered in the major religious reforms under King Josiah (2 Kings 22:14–20). Without Ruth there would have been no messianic line down to and beyond King David. But for Queen Esther the Jewish people would have been destroyed. If these are merely the 'exceptions that prove the rule', they nevertheless have extraordinary significance.

In the rabbinic period things changed in two directions. Male authority and power were reinforced in the emerging Jewish society through the model of the rabbi-scholar. Nevertheless attempts were made by the rabbis to alleviate some of the disadvantages suffered by women under biblical law. Thus the freedom of a man to divorce his wife by merely dismissing her (Deut. 24:1) was hedged in with legal and financial considerations that protected the woman. However the rabbis felt, they could not (or did not wish to) reverse totally the biblical position and grant women the right to initiate divorce proceedings, so the situation remains unequal. Even though the Beth Din, the rabbinic court, took upon itself the right in certain circumstances to initiate a divorce on behalf of a woman, in practice this opportunity has rarely been taken. Various attempts have been made to introduce into the marriage document a conditional clause that would overcome this problem, but it has met enormous resistance within contemporary Orthodox rabbinic circles, partly because of the legal difficulties, but also because of issues of authority between the various Orthodox groupings.

One of the most tragic situations that arises out of this disparity is that of the *agunah*, the 'anchored wife'. This is a woman whose husband refuses to give her a bill of divorce, or else has disappeared, perhaps because he abandoned her, and cannot be traced, or who might have been killed, as happened in the Shoah, the Holocaust, but his body was never recovered. The woman is 'anchored' to him, unable to remarry.

Since Judaism is not monolithic there are inevitably contradictory views of women expressed within the tradition. In the words of Blu Greenberg: 'We find both equality and hierarchy, respect and condescension, deference and disability, compassion and callousness.[1]

There is a 'normative' view of the 'place' or 'role' of women in Judaism that has emerged over the centuries, though it is currently undergoing considerable re-examination in the present climate. Presumably it takes its origin from the obvious fact of the role of women in child-bearing and the conventional, if less biologically determined, role in child-rearing. The tradition, again following the normal cultural patterns of the wider society, defined the domestic sphere as the place for women to fulfil their religious obligations. Theirs were the tasks of maintaining the dietary laws, preparing for the *Shabbat* and Festivals, and taking responsibility for their own 'ritual purity', the laws preventing sexual contact during and immediately after menstruation. If women spent so much of their time looking after children – the need for a large family would almost guarantee this for a considerable part of her life – then, according to a rabbinic formulation, they could not be expected to perform all the *mitzvot*, commandments, that were given to the Jewish people. They were exempt from 'timebound' commandments, those that had to be performed at specific times of the day or year (Mishnah Kiddushin 1:7). This did not mean that they were forbidden to perform them but the effect, due to the accompanying cultural pressure, was virtually that.

Two areas in particular had a major impact in this respect – the exemption, which became exclusion, from religious study and from the regular, three times a day, public worship. In fact the two are interrelated because being unable to study, and thus learn Hebrew, women were often unable to follow or recite the statutory prayers. In the Middle Ages they were often dependent upon an educated woman who had studied enough Hebrew to lead them through the service.

Women at Prayer

Nevertheless, women were still under the obligation to pray, which was fulfilled in part by attending a service conducted by men. However from the seventeenth century we have a growing literature of specially composed supplicatory prayers for women, written in Yiddish, *tkhines*. Though usually composed by men, some were clearly written by women. Unlike the statutory prayers, which we will be examining in chapter 7, they express far more the personal situations and issues experienced by women, such as pregnancy or the wish for a child, recovery from illness and so on. Addressed to God, these prayers may rely on the merits or experiences of the matriarchs Sarah, Rebeccah, Rachel and Leah (in Yiddish: Sore, Rivke, Rokhl, Leye) for a positive response, or even ask them to intercede on their behalf.

> And I also ask our mother Rebecca to plead for our fathers and mothers, that they may not, heaven forbid, be separated from us. For you know well how one can long for father and mother. When Eliezer, the servant [of Abraham] took you away from your father and mother to your husband, Isaac [Gen. 24], you also wept copiously.

Therefore, you know how bad it is without a father and without a mother. May they have a year of life, a good year, and a year of livelihood, a year in which I and my husband and children will have sustenance and livelihood.[2]

It is difficult to read what was really going on behind the concept of 'timebound' commandments. Effectively it defined a particular role and domain for women, one which until modernity, and in many if not most traditional households still today, has been seen as fully appropriate and spiritually satisfying. It is sometimes justified by rabbis with the rationalisation that women have a greater natural spirituality than men and do not need the regular discipline of prayer, whereas men do! All such explanations, such as that women are more naturally nurturing, or men more naturally aggressive, may have some truth but have actually been used to maintain a particular status quo that works to the advantage of men. The effect of this combination of 'law and lore' has been, at least in the past, to keep women out of the synagogue where a lot of power resides in community life.

The women's movement of recent times, particularly in the United States, fought its earliest battles about precisely the place of women in public worship. In terms of the 'progressive' movements they could build on one and a half centuries of ideological equality, even if real equality had not been reached in practice. Women could certainly reach high positions as lay leaders, but then be unable to participate in the synagogue service where a man would normally have been honoured with an *aliyah*, being called up to the reading of the Torah. Compared to issues like the *agunah*, where real legal disability has a tragic impact on the lives of women, this may seem a relatively minor matter. But it is precisely the public recognition of equality and the accompanying authority that was considered to be important before tackling issues that were perceived as less easy to bring to people's attention.

Today there is a whole spectrum of different situations in synagogues and movements on these issues. In some, served by women rabbis or cantors, full equality is apparently the case, at least on the books. Nevertheless there are still emotional blocks on the part of some, men and women alike, against accepting women rabbis and they may suffer serious disabilities, particularly in matters of salary and contractual rights. Moreover, they tend to find themselves cast in the role of dealing primarily with educational or pastoral tasks within their congregations – 'women's work'.

In more 'conservative' congregations you may find typical inconsistencies – a woman may read the *Haftarah*, the prophetic passage, on *Shabbat*, but not read from the Torah scroll itself; she may wear a *tallit*, the prayer shawl, usually perceived as being a man's garment, but equally available to women, or be forbidden to do so; she may be permitted to carry the Torah scroll in procession or not, though nothing in Jewish law forbids this. (Here we see a good example of the common blend of ignorance of Jewish law – or a dangerous 'little learning' – combined with basic chauvinist attitudes. Among the arguments raised by those who object to women carrying the Torah scroll is the suggestion that the women may be menstruating and this will render the scroll 'impure'. There is actually no such problem in Jewish law in this regard.)

Resistance to such changes comes understandably from men, but women have proved to be equally negative, even within the 'progressive' movements. The changes imply a major change of role, responsibility and relative power in synagogue life that is not easy for all to accommodate and they clearly impact on patterns of home-life as well. Inevitably those who advocate change are accused of being 'political', whereas those who want to prevent change hardly recognise that they are being equally political. Nevertheless change is happening and a younger generation is much more open to egalitarian issues from the wider society, and indeed may simply take them for granted to the consternation of their parents.

In Orthodox circles a different set of problems appears since women are excluded from leading any part of a service where a *minyan*, quorum of ten adult males, is present. Though this was not the case in the early rabbinic period it became enshrined in Jewish custom and has virtually the power of law in traditional circles. Thus women can hear the Torah being read, but cannot be called up to recite the blessings as a man would. The basis of this, according to Jewish religious law, *halakhah*, is simply that since a woman is not under the obligation to do so, she cannot fulfil the task on behalf of others, namely the male quorum, who *are* obligated to do so. Nevertheless, legal niceties aside, precisely because of the impact of the women's movement on all parts of Jewish society, the pressure is on to open up this arena to women as well.

Some concessions can be seen in certain areas. For example, the 'progressive' movements have long recognised the unfairness of making a public fuss over a young boy reaching the age of thirteen and becoming *barmitzvah*, 'a son of the commandment', that is to say, responsible under Jewish law, and thus able to read from the Torah on behalf of the community, while ignoring what happens when a girl reaches the equivalent age (twelve). A *batmitzvah*, 'daughter of the commandment' ceremony is usually identical with that for the boy, and the girl then takes her equal place in the community afterwards. In Orthodox circles a *bat chayyil* ceremony has been devised, usually involving a number of girls together, but taking place on a Sunday rather than a *Shabbat*, though occasionally it may be held outside of the statutory part of the *Shabbat* service. The term itself is interesting as it derives from the passage in Proverbs (31:10–31) beginning *eshet chayyil*, 'a woman of valour' praising the domestic achievements of the ideal wife. (It is read to the wife by her husband as part of the traditional Friday evening *Shabbat* eve domestic liturgy, alongside the blessing of the children.) Clearly the ceremony indicates the role for which these young women are destined, and after the ceremony which may take place in the men's part of the synagogue, they are relegated to the women's section for life.

One consequence of the dissatisfactions with this situation has been the growth of the 'women's *minyan*', a prayer service run exclusively by and for women. There is no objection to this in Jewish law, and indeed it has happened in the past. It has to be strictly regulated. Only if ten men are present is a service a 'real' event, in terms of Jewish law, so even if ten women are present, they are effectively praying 'privately' together, hence certain prayers that normally require a quorum, cannot be recited – including the memorial prayer for the dead. Without a male quorum one can read from a Torah scroll, but not recite the blessings before and after. Despite these limitations, which do not apply in non-Orthodox circles, there has been a major growth of such women's prayer groups. Clearly there is a level where this has to do with a desire on the part of women for personal empowerment in the traditional forms of worship previously restricted to men; in part it is simply a wish to experience Jewish spirituality in its normative forms. There are doubtless other individual factors at play, things that are never questioned when men come together for services. But the mixture of personal and political, spiritual and psychological, piety and curiosity, are always present in a public liturgy which is a 'political' as much as a 'spiritual' event since it defines the nature, beliefs and values of a particular community.

As well as questions about the role of women in liturgical life, much recent work has been done on the language of the liturgy itself. In the post-war period many new translations of traditional and 'progressive' prayerbooks were produced simply because the language, often dating back to the early decades of this century, or in imitation of it, was too archaic to make much sense. But since the 1970s the issue of 'inclusive' language has also had to be addressed. Terms like 'man' which had long been assumed to 'embrace woman' as well, have been shown to connote men only. It became clear that so much of the language simply assumed that it was a man who was praying and it was felt that adjustments had to be made to make it more egalitarian – sometimes with corresponding changes in the Hebrew text as well.

There are also questions about where a woman might identify herself as even 'present' in the traditional prayers. The figures that are evoked are 'Abraham, Isaac and Jacob'. Where are women 'models' to be found? One of the most radical suggestions, and that which caused most debate in the 'progressive' movements that sought to implement such changes, was to include the 'matriarchs' alongside the 'patriarchs' in the first paragraph of the *Amidah*, the 'standing prayer', which is the central one of the liturgy. We will look at it in more detail in chapter 7, but suffice it to say that here the issue of the public acknowledgment of the equality of women was put to the test. Precisely because the prayer is so well known and so central, even though parts of it have been subject to variation in earlier centuries, it became the point of division between those who had already absorbed the change of consciousness brought about by the women's movement and those who had not. The arguments rage around many issues: a concern with 'tampering' with ancient traditions; the worry that by such changes one would be out of line with Jewish communities elsewhere – on the basis that wherever one went in the Jewish world at least one could feel at home in the synagogue service. Today there are a variety of prayerbooks that include the matriarchs, though the way of introducing them may vary. In some cases both the traditional and new versions are available and congregations or individuals can choose what to say.

A third issue is the problem of how to translate the name of God, something I mentioned in the Introduction. Moreover what does one do with the various terms used to describe God – in particular 'King' and 'Father'? While these derive from the biblical roots of Judaism and accurately reflect its patriarchal assumptions, they raise a variety of problems today. First, irrespective of gender issues, God as 'King' is problematic, since the 'kings' we know today are by and large powerless constitutional monarchs, and not the figure who holds the power of life and death over his subjects that is contained in this image from the ancient world. In fact the entire Jewish liturgy is based on an imagery that is hard to accommodate to a modern democratic society. But describing God as 'King' and 'Father' emphasises a masculine image that effectively reinforces all the male power structures in our society against which the women's movement and those who support it are struggling. Changing the liturgy to accommodate these issues is not going to change society, but once the problem is perceived it is impossible to leave the language and concepts as they are.

One interesting consequence has been to search within Jewish tradition for other possible images of God, including feminine ones, and introduce them also into our theological rethinking and renewal. The term *shekhinah*, from the Hebrew verb meaning 'to dwell', was used by the rabbis to indicate the tangible presence of God in the world, and was much developed by the Jewish mystics. The imagery associated with the *shekhinah* is that of a woman, and this led to the term being adopted by some women as a focal point of address in their prayer life. Naturally this leads to concerns being expressed about the possible challenge to the 'Oneness' of God, and the evoking of some kind of 'goddess'.[3] But it was also recognised by some that the *shekhinah*, as a subordinate female figure to God, reproduces the kind of sub-servient role that women are struggling to overcome. There are clearly no easy resolutions to these questions which are a matter of personal exploration and experimentation.

Since God should be 'above gender', one way out of the problem is to emphasise the different images of God in the tradition so as to indicate that all are only metaphors for some-thing that lies beyond them. Biblical tradition speaks of God both as 'father', and, albeit more seldom, as 'mother'. The following responsive reading in the form of a dialogue with and about God was composed for a new prayerbook for the Jewish Pilgrim Festivals that I co-edited for the Reform Synagogues of Great Britain:

> Can a woman forget the baby at her breast,
> show no love for the child of her womb?
> Even these may forget,
> but I will not forget you. (Isa. 49:15)

>> Our God in heaven,
>> remember Your covenant,
>> do not forget us. (Traditional prayerbook)

> Yet God, You are our father,
> we are the clay and You our potter,
> we are all the work of Your hand. (Isa. 64:7)

>> May the favour of our Living God be upon us
>> to establish us in the work we do,

and establish the work we do. (Ps. 90:17)

I have kept silent for too long,
kept still and restrained Myself.
Now I will cry out like a woman in labour. (Isa. 42:14)

> The soul is Yours
> and the body is Your creation;
> have pity on Your work. (Traditional prayerbook)

As a father is tender to his children
so the Creator is tender to those who worship,
knowing our nature,
remembering that we are dust. (Ps. 103:13)

> Do not send us away when we grow old;
> when our spirit fails do not forsake us. (Traditional
>   prayerbook)

As a mother comforts her child,
so will I comfort you. (Isa. 66:13)

> Fill the morning of our life with Your love
> to be glad and sing all our days.
> Give us happiness to match our sadness
> for times when we knew misfortune. (Ps. 90:14–15)

Never leave me, never desert me,
God of my safety.
Even if my father and mother desert me
the Eternal will care for me still. (Ps. 27:9–10).

> Hear our voice, show us mercy and compassion,
> accept our prayers willingly and with love.[4]

The prayerbooks of the major non-Orthodox Jewish religious
movements have gradually adapted to the new understandings
and expectations of women. With the greater availability of desktop publishing individual congregations have felt freer to experiment with printing their own different orders of service to express
their own local needs and values. But there has also been an
explosion of creative composition of rituals and prayers by

women to meet a variety of circumstances. In terms of language they include attempts to create new ways of addressing God that move beyond the patriarchal imagery and language of the past.

Some have experimented with traditional forms of liturgy, partly or radically adjusting them to meet the needs of women's groups. The Passover Haggadah, which contains the home liturgy for Passover evening, has often been used for experimentation, from socialist anti-religious versions to the *Haggadah for the Liberated Lamb*, a 'vegetarian manifesto'. *The Women's Haggadah*, edited by E. M. Broner, is conceived as a celebration of women's history and is the result of almost twenty years of experimenting with an alternative liturgy for the Passover evening by a group of women, including some of the leading feminist writers in America.[5]

The New Moon, *rosh chodesh*, has traditionally been a minor festival with particular associations for women. Jewish law indicates that it was customary for women not to work on this day, and the New Moon celebration has been adopted by many women's groups as a focal point for prayer and study.

Others have addressed, in particular, life-cycle events, including childbirth, naming ceremonies for girls, the onset of menstruation and menopause, mourning the loss of a foetus due to a miscarriage, the breakdown of a marriage or relationship, to mark the passing of the years. Most of this work has been done in the United States thanks to the sheer size of the community and the greater openness for experimentation.

Women at Study

The area of religious study has seen similar changes in recent decades after centuries in which the vast majority of Jewish women were excluded. Inevitably over the course of history individual women have emerged to make their mark in this area as well, but they are the exceptions that prove the rule. The glimpses we get of them are tantalisingly brief. Perhaps the best known is Beruriah, usually referred to as 'the wife of Rabbi Meir' rather than as a celebrated and significant scholar in her own right – a precise example of the way women tend to be viewed. The Talmud records a number of comments registered in her name, the most often quoted being her comments on the issue of sinners and sins.

> There were once some highwaymen in the neighbourhood of Rabbi Meir who caused him a lot of trouble. Rabbi Meir prayed that they should die. His wife Beruriah said to him: 'How do you conclude that such a prayer should be allowed?' In reply he quoted Psalm 104:35, 'Because it is written, "Let sins cease."' She replied: 'Is it written "sinners"? It is written "sins"! Further, look to the end of the verse: "and let the wicked men be no more." Since the sins will cease, there will be no more wicked men. Rather pray for them that they should repent, and there will be no more wicked.' He did pray for them and they repented. (b. Berakhot 10a)

The phrase 'look to the end of the verse', as a principle of deriving ideas from a text, became a standard practice.

The special quality of Beruriah is well captured in this account by an outstanding person, Henrietta Szold, whom we will meet again at the end of this chapter. Writing in the *Jewish Encyclopedia* in 1903 she explains:

> Her traits of character, gleaned from Talmudic passages, show her to have been a helpmate worthy of her great husband (Rabbi Meir), and to have possessed a personality corresponding to the emergencies of the troublous times following upon the failure of Bar Kokhba's insurrection. They betray intellectual qualities and attainments as well as womanly tenderness and staunch virtues. It is said that she studied three hundred Talmudic subjects daily (b. Pesachim 62b), and Rabbi Judah endorsed a decision of hers, on a question about clean and unclean, in which she went counter to the view of 'the wise' . . . (Tosefta Kelim B. M. i. 6)

There are other examples of her knowledge of Jewish

Scriptures and her almost coquettish playfulness, coexisting
with a capacity for righteous indignation . . .[6]

That 'coquettishness', mixed with a sharp thrust at male rabbinic
values, comes out delightfully in this little story:

> Rabbi Yose the Galilean was once walking on a road when
> he met Beruriah. He asked her: 'Which road should I take
> to go to the city of Lydda?' She answered: 'Foolish Galilean,
> did not the sages say: "Do not multiply talk with women!"
> (Sayings of the Fathers 1:5) You should have said: "Which
> way to Lydda!" ' (b. Eruvin 53b).

A famous story tells how she comforted her husband after the
death of their two sons. But it is precisely Beruriah who is the
subject of a nasty legend, recorded in Rashi's eleventh-century
commentary on the Talmud. The origins are unknown and it
goes against the character drawn in the Talmud both of Beruriah
and her husband:

> Once Beruriah scoffed at the rabbinical saying, 'Women
> are lightminded' (b. Kiddushin 80b), and her husband
> warned her that her own end might yet testify to the truth
> of the words. To put her virtue to the test, he charged one
> of his disciples to try to seduce her. After repeated efforts
> she yielded, and in shame committed suicide. Rabbi Meir,
> tortured by remorse, fled from his home. (Rashi on b.
> Avodah Zarah 18b)

We have here a sad example of the misogynist attitude that
surfaces from time to time in rabbinic writings. On the whole
Judaism does not succumb to the kind of polarisation commoner
in Christianity – the woman as virgin or whore. Nevertheless the
seductive power of women is a recurrent theme, starting with
the Book of Proverbs and surfacing in Talmudic stories of rabbis
succumbing to their sexual urges.

Some women redeemed from captivity were brought to

Nehardea. They took them to the house of Rabbi Amram the pious, and removed the ladder from the room in which they were to stay. While one of them was walking up and down in the room, a ray of light fell from the skylight on to the ground and revealed her. Rabbi Amram took the ladder which ten men could not lift up, and he lifted it by himself. When he had got half-way up the ladder, he forced himself to stop, and called out with a loud voice, 'Amram's house is on fire!' The rabbis came and complained, 'You frightened us with a false alarm.' He said, 'It is better that you should be falsely alarmed about the house of Amram in this world than that you should be ashamed of Amram in the world to come.' (b. Kiddushin 81a)

The traditional separation of the sexes, in education, in social life and in ritual life, characterised by the *mechitza*, the barrier that separates men and women in the synagogue (more usually represented by the women's gallery) is both a safeguard to piety (from the man's point of view) and an obvious source of titillation at the same time. Presumably at some level this sexual anxiety reflects the nature of all-male study circles and academies and the paradoxical seductiveness of asceticism in those with a more mystical bent.[7]

If the doors to the world of male study were closed to women, there are recorded cases of men teaching their daughters. Moreover individual names emerge of women who functioned as teachers at various times in the Middle Ages. But it is the modern period which gave the impetus and opportunity for women to improve their knowledge of Judaism, encouraged by the, at least ideological, support of the early Reform movement. But Jewish education for women was not restricted to the Reformers. After the First World War the Beth Jacob schools were established in Poland by Sarah Schnirer (1883–1938) – Orthodox establishments that combined traditional studies and industrial training. The growth of universal education, the entry of women into the professions and the world of work, the emergence of a Jewish middle class, all contributed to the growth of women's organisations concerned with welfare and education.

But the speed of change in the last few decades has been extraordinary. In 1978 a book was published which was to give the impetus to many women to reassess the role of Jewish women in the past. Written and edited by Sondra Henry and Emily Taitz it was called *Written Out Of History: Jewish Foremothers*. In the preface to the 1990 edition they explain:

> When we started our research in 1976, we looked for footnotes and minor bibliographic items to point the way to individual women. As we read Jewish history books we found that Jewish women were invisible, virtually written out of history ... Slowly, we found other figures of note. Beruriah, scholar of the Talmudic era (2nd Century CE) appeared first. She was followed by Deborah Ascarelli and Sara Coppia Sullam, Italian Jewish Renaissance poets (15th and 16th centuries); and Glückl of Hameln who wrote her memoirs in the 17th century ... We discovered Rebecca Tiktiner (died c. 1550), Benvenida Abrabanel (died 1560), and Eva Bacharach (1580–1651) who, despite prevailing restrictions, became serious scholars.

By the 1996 reprint they can note that:

> Instead of being 'written out,' Jewish women – in fact, all women – are being written back into history ... One of the reasons for this is women themselves. It is no longer unusual for Jewish women to occupy academic chairs in Jewish Studies departments of universities. The number of Jewish women students in both university graduate programs and community seminars has been growing fast and the interests of this changing population have helped shape Jewish Studies curricula ... Enrollment by women in rabbinic seminaries has also increased dramatically as Jewish women seek their spiritual as well as historical selves. This trend has made inroads even into the Orthodox community. Many Orthodox women's prayer groups are being welcomed into Synagogues and more are being formed ... In Israel more and more women are engaging

in the serious study of the Talmud, from which they were traditionally barred for centuries.[8]

One could add to the above categories that there are by now 'bibliographies of bibliographies' on aspects of Jewish women's studies.

Someone missing from the 1978 edition exactly illustrates the point about being 'written out'. After the fall of the Berlin Wall access was available to the records in Potsdam of the pre-war Jewish community. Among them were discovered the papers of Fräulein Rabbiner Regina Jonas. She had completed the course of rabbinic studies at the Liberal Hochschule für die Wissenschaft des Judentums in Berlin, but because of internal disagreements the seminary did not ordain her. Instead she received a private ordination, a common Jewish practice, from Rabbi Max Dienemann in 1935, which was later countersigned by Rabbi Dr Leo Baeck. She worked as a rabbi in Berlin during that time of the greatest tragedy facing the Jewish world. In 1942 she was deported to Theresienstadt Concentration Camp. In 1944 she was transported to Auschwitz where she was killed.[9] What has fascinated those who have researched her story is the total silence that surrounded her existence by those who survived from that period. Though when their memories were jogged some recollections surfaced. The first woman rabbi of modern times simply did not fit into a conventional perception of the Jewish world of that time, and so disappeared. But her story reminds us yet again of what the world lost, what developments might have taken place, but for the Nazi genocide.

If Regina Jonas was a rarity in 1935, the doors of Reform and Conservative seminaries have been open to women since the early 1970s. In the UK the Reform movement, which created the Leo Baeck College, debated the issue. (A number of individuals were asked already in the 1960s if they would accept a woman rabbi. As a representative of the 'youth' I was invited to write a reply and I am quite proud that I gave a definite 'yes' vote – though I must confess that at the time I had a pretty romantic idea of what it meant to be a rabbi.) The then Lecturer in Talmud at the Leo Baeck College, Dr Aryeh Dorfler was asked to rule on the subject and in an article in the magazine *Living Judaism* (Spring 1967) he wrote:

> Progressive Judaism has failed pathetically in the last hundred years, both in having neglected the intensive education of women in Judaism, in not having attracted them to the deeper study of Jewish sources, and in not having attracted them to the Ministry as a spearhead in the drive to invigorate Judaism within and without the Jewish home. Let us open the gates now, and after the destruction of our great, learned European Jewry, strengthen our ranks by recruiting gifted Jewish women to the Institutes of higher learning. This would indeed be in the spirit of those Sages who said, 'For the merits of the righteous women, the children of Israel were redeemed from Egypt.'

The admission of women to the rabbinate, together with all the other developments mentioned above, are clearly major stages in the development of Judaism in our time. Just how revolutionary this might be is indicated by Rabbi Barbara Borts:

> Some years ago ... two extraordinary articles were published. One, by Cynthia Ozick, claimed that Jewish women needed feminism for the purpose of sociological repair. We campaigned for equal rights – access to learning, to lay leadership roles, for our books to be published, for us to be trained as, and hired as, rabbis.
>
> No, retorted Judith Plaskow, this is insufficient, for how can we accept these roles if the underlying message is that we are interlopers, trespassers in the territory of the Jew, a man by definition, and his male God, one created in the other's image to return the compliment.[10]

Both of these issues, the sociological and the theological, are still to be addressed with full seriousness in large parts of the Jewish world. Nevertheless change is happening and Judaism is the healthier for it.

Earlier in this chapter I cited Henrietta Szold (1860–1945) on

Beruriah, and I would like to end with her. She was one of the leading figures in American Zionism and a pioneer worker for Youth Aliyah, the organisation that helps orphaned or disadvantaged children find a home in Israel. Her credentials as a Jewish communal leader could not be faulted, yet, as a woman, she suffered from the restrictions placed on a woman's role within the Orthodox synagogue of her time. When her mother died a friend offered to say *Kaddish*, the memorial prayer, on her behalf. She wrote to him the following reply which highlights both the difficulty of doing the right thing to help another, and the pain of someone taking a stand against convention.

It is impossible for me to find words in which to tell you how deeply I was touched by your offer to act as *Kaddish* for my dear mother. I cannot even thank you – it is something that goes beyond thanks. It is beautiful, what you have offered to do – I shall never forget it.

You will wonder, then, that I cannot accept your offer ... I know well, and appreciate what you say about, Jewish custom; and Jewish custom is very dear and sacred to me. And yet I cannot ask you to say *Kaddish* after my mother. The *Kaddish* means to me that the survivor publicly and markedly manifests his wish and intention to assume the relation to the Jewish community which his parent had, and that so the chain of tradition remains unbroken from generation to generation, each adding its own link. You can do that for the generations of your family. I must do that for the generations of my family.

I believe that the elimination of women from such duties was never intended by our law and custom – women were freed from positive duties when they could not perform them, but not when they could. It was never intended that, if they could perform them, their performance should not be considered as valuable and valid as when one of the male sex performed them. And of the *Kaddish* I feel sure this is particularly true.

My mother had eight daughters and no son; and yet never did I hear a word of regret pass the lips of either my mother or my father that one of us was not a son. When my father died, my mother would not permit others to take her daughter's place in saying *Kaddish*, and so I am sure I am acting in her spirit when I am moved to decline your offer.

The date of her letter is 16th September 1916. How far have we really moved in nearly eighty years?

Further Reading

Judith Z. Abrams, *The Women of the Talmud* (New Jersey and London, Jason Aronson, 1995): a popular examination of different issues relating to women in the pages of the Talmud.

Rachel Adler, *Engendering Judaism: An Inclusive Theology and Ethics* (Philadelphia and Jerusalem, The Jewish Publication Society, 1998): a major theological attempt to envision a truly egalitarian Judaism.

Susan Benin (ed.), *Celebrating the New Moon* (New Jersey and London, Jason Aronson, 1996): a scholarly account and anthology of women's New Moon celebrations.

Sondra Henry and Emily Taitz (eds.), *Written Out of History: Our Jewish Foremothers* (New York, Biblio Press, 1996): a pathfinding exploration of the roles played by Jewish women in Jewish life.

Susannah Heschel, *On Being a Jewish Feminist* (New York, Schocken Books, 1983): an excellent early collection of essays on different aspects of Jewish feminist ideas.

Elizabeth Koltun (ed.), *The Jewish Woman: New Perspectives* (New York, Schocken Books, 1976): an important early collection of articles, including one by Deborah Weissman on Sarah Schnirer, the founder of the Beth Jacob schools.

Judith Plaskow, *Standing Again at Sinai* (San Francisco, Harper and Row, 1990): a major attempt at creating a Jewish feminist theology.

Four are the mothers of Israel

Sybil Sheridan (ed.), *Hear Our Voice: Women Rabbis Tell Their Stories* (London, SCM Press, 1994): women rabbinic graduates of the Leo Baeck College explore the issues they confront in their careers and religious lives.

Ellen M. Umansky and Dianne Ashton, *Four Centuries of Jewish Women's Spirituality: A Sourcebook* (Boston, Beacon Press, 1992): a fine anthology of examples of different explorations of women's spirituality.

5

Five are the books of the Torah
How Jews read the Bible

I once had a rather unkind thought, though in part based on experience. If you asked someone whether they had read the Bible and they said no and were embarrassed – they were probably Christian. If the answer was no and they were proud of it – they were probably Jewish.

This is an awful generalisation and may simply be a reflection of the particular Jewish community of a particular age that I know in Britain. It is a product of poor Jewish education, often an offputting childhood experience of synagogue life – boredom and a disconcerting feeling that Judaism was about doing certain ritual things quite detached from any values. The 'Bible' if we ever came across it was probably not even a Jewish version. My family had a Gideon Bible on a shelf at home for reference, 'borrowed' from a hotel room some time in the past. Anyway, in its black-bound King James English version it was clearly a Christian document, and therefore taboo. The Jewish 'Bible' that we did know was the *chumash*, and to be more precise the Hertz *chumash*, usually a heavy, dark-blue volume with the Hebrew text and translation and an English commentary beneath. The word *chumash* is Hebrew for 'five' and is the traditional term for the 'Five Books of Moses'. Because it is Jewish practice to read the complete set of these five books, the Torah, on a weekly basis in synagogue, any number of traditional versions of the *chumash* with numerous Hebrew commentaries dotted around the page, are available. They will often be single volumes containing just one of the five books, with the order of the *Shabbat* service at the back so that they doubled as textbook and prayer-book.

Whatever else they contained there would be the Targum, the Aramaic translation (versions of which date from the second to the fifth century CE), and the commentary of Rashi, the greatest mediaeval commentator (1040–1105). Older copies might carry the name of some Eastern European centre of Jewish life of the last century where they had been printed, like Warsaw or Lublin. The pages would be yellowing and crumbling, while bits of cardboard would fall out of the binding. If the binding came off some mysterious Hebrew text was revealed under the stitching. Such volumes turn up from time to time in people's attics and they remember that *saba*, grandfather, used to use it.

However my generation that grew up in Britain after the war was assimilated and mostly ignorant of Hebrew of a sufficient level to read and understand the biblical text let alone a Hebrew commentary, printed, as if to vex one further, in a special type-face with unusual letters known as 'Rashi script'. This is another typically misleading term, since it is not the kind of writing used by Rashi. Instead, when early editions of the Hebrew Bible were printed, Rashi's commentary was included and a particular typeface was chosen, presumably to distinguish it from the biblical text itself. The same 'Rashi script' was subsequently used for all the classical commentators, who surround the biblical text in the larger editions of the 'Rabbinic' Bible. They seem to fence it in but actually open it up to infinite understandings. ('Rashi script' remains a hazard for those beginning today to delve into the world of mediaeval Jewish commentators. New editions of the *miqraot gedolot*, the Rabbinic Bible, use the normal square Hebrew script for Rashi and the others, though it feels distinctly 'inauthentic'!)

The Hertz *chumash* is a hefty volume, especially for a child, but it was also a godsend, being something with a bit of content to leaf through during the seemingly endless Saturday morning services in my Orthodox *shul* (synagogue). It was also big enough to conceal a comic or other less spiritually uplifting literature. The 'Hertz' was worthy of our loyalty, even if the translation, that of the Jewish Publication Society of America (1917), was a bit archaic in places. (But then so was the translation of the old Singer's prayerbook that we used on Saturday mornings. Whatever else I knew about God, the prayers told me that 'Thou quickenest the dead', a mysterious act that suggested some kind of macabre race. Much of our Judaism felt somewhat archaic because of these translations.)

Chief Rabbi Joseph Herman Hertz (1872–1946) was loyal to tradition in his own special way, combative when confronting the heresies of modern historical criticism, but not above quoting Christian scholars and divines when they said something flattering about this ancient Jewish document. Thus in his preface to the first edition of 1936, presumably in anticipation of criticisms he expected, he wrote:

> Jewish and non-Jewish commentators – ancient, medieval, and modern – have been freely drawn upon. 'Accept the true from whatever source it come' is sound rabbinic doctrine – even if it be from the pages of a devout Christian expositor or of an iconoclastic Bible scholar, Jewish or non-Jewish. This does not affect the Jewish Traditional character of the work. My conviction that the criticism of the Pentateuch associated with the name of Wellhausen is a perversion of history and a desecration of religion, is unshakeable . . .[1]

The Hertz *chumash* was literally the Bible of the Barmitzvah boy trying to learn the Hebrew text by heart for recital in synagogue on the date nearest his thirteenth birthday. But I also remember my father arguing points of interpretation from Hertz with his neighbours in adjacent seats, which was presumably his own way of getting through the service between the parts of it that he loved to sing. If our ancestors knew their *chumash with Rashi*, we knew our *chumash with Hertz*.

Copies can still be found in most synagogues, lined up on the bookshelves at the back, though other volumes have sought to take its place. Out of the Reform movement in America comes the 'Plaut Chumash', which is Hertz brought up to date according to more recent biblical scholarship and an eclectic liberal outlook. It includes 'Gleanings' at the end of each section made up of traditional and modern comments, from Jewish and even more non-Jewish sources than Hertz, aimed at providing additional insights or spiritual instruction. It has found its place in 'progressive' communities in the USA and Britain alongside Hertz.

In his introduction Gunther Plaut, a distinguished German-born, American Reform rabbi and scholar, summarises the Orthodox view on revelation then explains a 'progressive' view:

> We believe that it is possible to say: The Torah is ancient Israel's distinctive record of its search for God. It attempts to record the meeting of the human and the Divine, the great moments of encounter. Therefore, the text is often touched by the ineffable Presence. The Torah tradition testifies to a people of extraordinary spiritual sensitivity. God is not the author of the text, the people are; but God's voice may be heard through theirs if we listen with open minds.
>
> Is this true for every verse and story? Not in our view. But it is often hard to know whether the voice that speaks has the ring of permanence or resounds to the apprehensions and misapprehensions of a particular age. Our own insights are not so secure that we can judge past ages with any ease of superiority. In the face of the unique tradition before us, modesty and caution are a necessary rule.
>
> This does not mean, however, that we abdicate all judgment, treat legend as fact, or gloss over those texts which represent God in anthropomorphic terms. This commentary is neither an apology for, nor an endorsement of, every passage. It will present the modern readers with tools for understanding and leave the option to them.[2]

Nothing could be further from the approach to Torah of what has come to be the successor of Hertz in Orthodox Jewish circles, a series under the general title 'ArtScroll'. These are beautifully produced hardback and paperback volumes (a paperback Hertz is as inconceivable as a Victorian matron in a miniskirt!). They reflect a new American Orthodox vitality and assertiveness. The authors know their pious constituency and are determined to keep them on the straight and narrow path, as the introduction to the Book of Esther, the first in the series, puts it:

> It must be made clear that this is not a so-called 'scientific' or 'apologetic' commentary on the Megillah [*megillat ester*, the Scroll of Esther]. That area has, unfortunately, been too well-covered resulting in violence to the Jewish faith as well as to correct interpretation. It is in no way the intention of this book to demonstrate the legitimacy or historicity of Esther or Mordechai to non-believers or doubters. Belief in the authenticity of every book of the Torah is basic to the Jewish faith, and we proceed from there. It comes as no surprise to me – nor should it to any Orthodox Jew – that the palace in Shushan, as unearthed by archealogists [sic], bears out the description of the palace in the Megillah in every detail . . . [So why mention it? Methinks the lady doth protest too much . . .][3]

They are also very clear about who belongs in such a volume: 'No non-Jewish sources have even been consulted, much less quoted. I consider it offensive that the Torah should need authentication from the secular or so-called "scientific" sources.'[2]

Just to indicate that contemporary Jewish Orthodoxy has many faces, there is a series of Bible commentaries, *Da'at Miqra*, 'Knowledge of Scripture', alas only in Hebrew, produced in Israel by the Mossad HaRav Kook, a publishing house of impeccable Orthodox credentials. In contrast to the ArtScroll, the various writers, though basing themselves on traditional Jewish exegesis are quite prepared to look at 'secular or so-called "scientific" sources', though they are understandably careful in how they use them. The inside cover contains a disclaimer:

> This commentary is based on the one hand on the classical traditional exegesis, beginning with the commentary of our

sages, of blessed memory, and concluding with those commentators of the traditional-scientific tendency, and on the other side brings into consideration, and is helped by, the results of modern scholarly research in the areas of exegesis, philology, history, geography, archaeology, etc., *insofar as these researches do not contradict Jewish tradition.* [my italics]

Clearly these two remarkable products of contemporary Jewish Orthodoxy are ideologically worlds apart, and it is important to show how diverse such views can be.

To return to the ArtScroll series, the remarks quoted above are presumably meant to be an attack on Chief Rabbi Hertz's kind of symbiosis, even though he did represent, with great dignity and success the 'orthodoxy' of a previous generation. The attack here is probably also on a celebrated and popular series of single-volume commentaries on the entire Hebrew Bible published by the Soncino Press in the 1940s that have gone through numerous reprints. They have served for the rest of the Hebrew Bible as Hertz did for the *chumash*. Here too, although the scholars were mostly Orthodox and drew on impeccably Jewish sources, they too were not unwilling to call upon non-Jewish scholars when their comments seemed appropriate. But this seems not to be the case anymore. The latest revised Soncino editions, clearly under the influence of the ArtScroll series, and presumably in competition to reach the same market, have also 'purified' the old commentaries of 'extraneous' matter.

Though Jews may argue intellectually about the appropriateness of the use of the term 'fundamentalism' to Judaism – after all it had its origins in describing a Christian group in America – the cap does seem to fit. Or, as my colleague Fr Gordian Marshall prefers to describe the phenomenon, it is 'selective literalism'. For such commentaries, every event of the Hebrew Bible is literally and historically true, as are all the comments, including the legendary material, of subsequent generations of 'authentic' rabbinic scholars. This 'authenticity' naturally includes Rashi and scholars with a more mystical or chassidic tendency – less popular, presumably because more dangerous in the hands of the uninitiated, are those like Abraham Ibn Ezra (thirteenth century) whose intellectual training in his native Muslim Spain led him to ask different kinds of philosophical, grammatical, philological and even historical questions to the text.

The ArtScroll series has its critics within the Orthodox world. Rabbi Dr Alan Unterman notes how our present sense of history stands in contrast to the timeless present experienced by earlier Jewish generations. Because of this the quotations from the *Aggadah*, the narrative comments of rabbinic tradition, are actually being used in a radically new way:

> Our dilemma is that we belong to a modern culture in which history, not merely as an academic subject but as a basic assumption of politics, news, and most intellectual pastimes, is fundamental. This leads to the secularisation of *aggadah* as a kind of 'Jewish' history – in a way as disreputable as 'Jewish Science'. Orthodox writers in the English language, particularly in projects like the American ArtScroll Series, have secularised *midrash* and *aggadah* as revisionist history.[4]

It is probably clear from the above discussion where my sympathies lie in this matter. Hertz is in many ways out of date, but he represents a fine blending of Jewish 'learning' and respect for modern scholarship so typical of the Orthodox Jewish clergyman of the pre- and immediately post-war period in Britain. However my disagreement with the ArtScroll approach does not diminish my respect for the enormous breadth of traditional learning, care, and rigorous control, that have gone into the production of these volumes. If book sales and statistics mean anything the ArtScroll understanding of Jewish Scripture is the popular wave of the future, with the 'right-wing' religious politics that goes with it.

By starting at this 'end' of the story of Jewish Bible exegesis I have rather put the cart before the horse. So it is necessary to tease out some of the classical strands, but first a few more background points and reminiscences.

Five are the books of the Torah

Attached to the biblical reading on the *Shabbat* morning is a short extract from the prophets, the Haftarah, which also has to be learnt and chanted (with a different kind of melody) by the Barmitzvah boy. The origins of adding a prophetic reading are obscure. One theory is that it was introduced when the Romans banned the public reading of the Torah in synagogue. By introducing instead a prophetic reading that alluded to the Torah portion of the week in some way, the Torah was invisibly evoked and present. When the ban was no longer in force, the practice continued. (The theory cannot be entirely true because at least one series of prophetic readings over the summer are deliberately chosen to precede and follow *Tisha B'Av*, the ninth day of the month of Av which commemorates the destruction of both Temples. In the weeks beforehand the readings contain warnings of the prophet that unless Israel changes its ways, Jerusalem will indeed fall; the readings afterwards, leading up to the Jewish New Year, are words of consolation and comfort, setting us in a more optimistic frame of mind as we approach the great annual judgment.)

But apart from these seemingly random selections the rest of the Bible, its contents and order, were unfamiliar apart from the few books that belonged to special festivals and fasts. So we all knew 'the Scroll of Esther', mentioned above, because that was the book read at the festival of Purim when we got to boo and make a lot of noise with rattles and anything else we could get our hands on at the mention of the wicked Haman who sought to exterminate the Jews. Of course we also added cheers for Esther and Mordechai, which was not prescribed by Jewish law. Recent generations have also taken to cheering the hapless Vashti, the previous wife of King Ahasuerus, who by refusing to appear at her husband's whim at his six-month banquet, got herself demoted and possibly executed. Her act of defiance of male power has earned her the praise of feminists, as opposed to the seemingly overcompliant Esther. But it can also be argued that Vashti's defiance was only a pyrrhic victory, while Esther simply played her cards better and won the game in the long term.

Neither the Song of Songs, read at Passover, the Book of Ruth read at Pentecost, nor Ecclesiastes, read at Tabernacles, got the same prominence in my memory of childhood. Collectively, together with Lamentations, read on *Tisha B'Av*, they constituted the *megillos* (according to the Ashkenazi pronunciation of my youth) or *megillot* (in today's Israeli-orientated Sephardi form), the five scrolls.

I suppose we knew some Psalms since they cropped up in the liturgy, but apart from providing a good singalong (Psalm 29 sung lustily while the scroll was paraded on its way back to the ark where it was stored; parts of the 'Hallel' Psalms (113–118) sung on festivals), they were just lost in the liturgy amid the myriad words read, recited, mumbled, chanted or sung during the endless *Shabbat* morning service. If today I know a lot more about the Hebrew Bible it is the result of my professional career, and had I been an average *shul*-goer I doubt I would have learned much more about it.

It was not always thus, and indeed there are Jewish circles today where one grows up with a far greater familiarity with the Hebrew Bible, though again confined to the areas mentioned above. But here we enter into another kind of Jewish paradox that will be further explored in the next chapter on the 'Six parts of the Mishnah'. For many 'outsiders' the Jewish people are simply the 'folk of the Bible' who are still around today. Some are convinced that we still sacrifice animals in the Temple, presumably pluck out 'an eye for an eye and a tooth for a tooth' when given the slightest opportunity and were actually born in Jerusalem even if we speak with a good English accent.

The fact of the matter is that the Hebrew Bible, for over two thousand years, has *not* been the central document that determines Jewish *actions* even if it is a constant source of Jewish *reflection.* Instead the very nature of rabbinic Judaism depended upon a view that alongside the 'written Torah', given by God to Moses on Mt Sinai, was an oral commentary to it, the 'oral Torah' or 'oral law', which enabled us to apply the teachings and legal precepts of the Hebrew Bible to new or changing circumstances. (We shall look at the central documents, the Mishnah, Talmud and later Codes and Responsa in the next chapter.) The paradox goes deeper than that, since one of the injunctions of

Deuteronomy is that we should neither add to nor subtract from these words or commands of God (Deut. 4:2; 13:1). Yet the entire Jewish enterprise for two thousand years has been precisely to 'add to and subtract from' these words in the sense of interpreting and re-interpreting them for our own time, place and circumstances. Effectively by 'shutting down' the biblical record, by freezing these 'Five Books' and then the rest of the Hebrew Bible as unchangeable 'Scripture', the door has to be open to interpretation, and it is evident that the Judaism of the past two thousand years is that which was built up painstakingly by successive generations of rabbis, sometimes in quite clear contradiction to the biblical text itself.

This should be neither surprising nor shocking, for such is the nature of all revealed Scriptures. They are fixed in time and space by the moment at which they are given, or at least committed to written form. However their very 'givenness' is the challenge they offer to present practices that are inevitably different. Even when our beliefs at a certain time are scandalously at odds with the perceived ancient values of our Scripture, themselves mediated through the interpretations of previous generations, a way can always be found to 'understand' the Scripture afresh, whether those who do this are conscious or not of the radical nature of their activity. (After all the new meaning, alongside so many others, must, by definition, have *always* been present in the text, since it was an omniscient God who gave it.) The fact of a given text being perceived as revelation, or 'Scripture', means that it cannot be sidestepped or avoided but must be confronted at all times and forced to conform with what are recognised to be the best of contemporary values.

The problem with modernity is that we have stepped outside that process and evoked 'history' to examine the very origins of the Hebrew Bible, which undermines the 'divine authority' of everything that flows from it.

The beginnings of this process of 'reinterpretation' of the Bible begins within the Bible itself. When the prophet Amos talks about rich people misusing the law against the poor 'in the gate' (where legal matters were settled) (Amos 5:12), he is referring to the specific language of a law in Exodus 23:6. When the Psalmist says that God 'made known His ways to Moses' (Ps. 103:7), he is citing a verse from Exodus 33 (v. 13) and then goes on to meditate on the merciful qualities of God that are revealed in the following chapter (compare Ps. 103:8–11 with Exod. 34:6–7), a passage we will examine in greater detail in the last chapter. The list of such 'interpretations' is endless, though there is much debate among scholars about who is quoting whom.

The important thing is that from the very earliest stages of the post-biblical period the Scriptures were examined for clues as to the meaning of contemporary events, as well as for expanding particular laws that operated within God's covenant with Israel. It is no accident that the Gospel writers and Paul have constant reference to the 'Old Testament' either to explain some aspect of the life of Jesus as conforming with previous prophecies, or to justify some theological innovation. This was a perfectly natural phenomenon in the Jewish world to which all these writers belonged. Less well known outside of Judaism, but of extra-ordinary importance, is the huge body of what was to become rabbinic interpretation of the 'Torah' that spans a period from the second century BCE (Before the Common Era) right up to the tenth century, to be followed by as great a body of work of interpretation under the dominant societies of Christianity and Islam up to the modern period. Only a brief outline and a few examples of this activity can be given here and indeed much scholarly work has still to be done on this complex field.

The key term we need to know is 'Midrash'. From a Hebrew root '*d-r-sh*' meaning to 'search' or 'seek out', it means to explore in depth the different levels of meaning contained within a word, and in particular how that meaning can be affected by the context in which it is found. While the rabbis were sometimes interested in clarifying the plain meaning of the text, for which the term *pshat* was coined, more often they used the new explanations they found as a springboard for some kind of teaching. If every word was the revealed word of God, then nothing could be redundant or without deep significance for the life of the Jewish people. Thus there arose a body of Midrash, later edited into various collections, which is usually classified under two different categories: *Midrash Halakhah*, expansions of legal texts; *Midrash*

Aggadah, literally 'narrative Midrash', a term covering the widest range of anecdotal, historical, homiletic, moralising materials, with a well-defined literary structure, often seeking to fill apparent gaps in the biblical narrative.

For the legal exegesis, the rabbis developed various principles whereby, for example, texts in different places could be compared so as to derive a new law. Sometimes the procedure would indeed work in such a way: a principle would be derived from a biblical verse and applied to a new situation. But it could also work the other way – a law had come into being, presumably from the cultural environment in which the rabbis found themselves, and the Bible was scoured for a text that could be used to justify the practice.

For example the complex Jewish dietary laws, which include distinguishing between meat and milk foods and keeping them apart, are based on a half-verse which is repeated in identical form three times (Exod. 23:19; 34:26 and Deut. 14:21), 'You shall not seethe a kid in the milk of its mother.' The verse itself is open to interpretation: does it literally mean you shall not cook a kid in the milk being supplied by its mother, or that you shall not kill and cook an animal that is not yet weaned, while it is still taking its mother's milk, which would be an act of cruelty against the mother? Or is it simply a reaction against some ancient pagan custom current in the biblical period whose meaning has simply been lost? The fact that it recurs three times allows the rabbis to speculate on a whole variety of details that can be derived from such a repetition – that it refers to domestic and wild animals, that it applies within the land of Israel and outside, or while the Temple stands and after the Temple has been destroyed. What about cooking it in the milk of another species? The debates run on for pages in what is one of the earliest of the midrashic collections, Mekilta de-Rabbi Ishmael Tractate Kaspa 5.[5] A further discussion in the Talmud (b. Hullin 115b) derives three basic prohibitions: cooking meat and milk together, eating them together or deriving any benefit from such a mixture. Elsewhere 'milk' is elaborated to include any dairy product. Then the debate concerns how long after eating one of them the other may be consumed. In short the highly complex system of dietary laws beginning with the Bible and its midrashic interpretation then takes on a life of its own – something we will look at further in the next chapter.

Midrash Aggadah is of a different order. We first meet Abraham in the Bible when he is seventy-five years old. What was his life like before he encountered God? How did he come to the belief in one God? What legends are associated with his birth? Here there are remarkable parallels between the Gospel stories of Jesus and midrashic tales about the events preceding the birth of both Abraham and Moses. They belong to a familiar folkloric genre explored by Joseph Campbell in *The Hero With a Thousand Faces*. The birth of a 'hero' is often put at risk by a ruler, warned that a child will be born who will somehow subvert his or her power, so measures are taken to kill the child who is rescued by divine or miraculous intervention. Thus King Nimrod tried to kill Abraham in the midrashic version.

When Abraham goes to sacrifice his son Isaac (Genesis 22), the text merely tells us that 'three days later' he arrived at the place. What were Abraham's thoughts during this journey – the rabbis have Satan tempting him not to obey God, reflecting on what must have been Abraham's own inner psychological processes. Who were the two unnamed young men who accompanied Abraham on his journey? One Midrash assumes they were Ishmael his first son and Eliezer, mentioned by Abraham as someone likely to inherit what he had if he died childless. So the rabbis elaborated on a discussion between them on how they would carve up Abraham's money once Isaac was dead!

One of my favourite midrashic tales is a warning against hubris. The rabbis were quite happy to live with the anachronism that significant figures like Abraham or David would know all about the later development of Jewish life. David complains to God that in the Jewish prayers there is frequent reference to 'Abraham, Isaac and Jacob' but not to 'David'. Surely he was important enough to merit inclusion with the patriarchs? God points out that the three patriarchs were all tested and came through. Was David prepared to risk such a thing? Of course, came the answer. God gives him a clue as to the nature of the test to help him, namely that it will concern a woman. David is ready! After this conversation, David wanders on to the roof of his palace and glancing down sees a woman bathing – and thus begins the episode with Bathsheba that will begin the downfall of David and destroy his family life.

The examples are literally endless and anyone who wishes to enjoy them can do so in a number of collections.[6] However I do have to point out that the world of Midrash is a law unto itself and that those who want to enter it have to acclimatise themselves to its own kind of discourse, rules and subtleties. I cannot resist quoting the exasperation of E. H. Plumptre, the Dean of Wells, who wrote a commentary on the Book of Ecclesiastes for the *Cambridge Bible for Schools and Colleges* in 1890. In his section on 'Jewish Interpreters of Ecclesiastes' he writes:

It is, perhaps, natural in dealing with a book which presents so many difficulties both in particular passages and in its general drift, to turn to the interpreters who belonged to the same race and spoke the same language as the writer. How did they understand this or that expression? What did they gather from the book as its chief substantial lesson? And of these we look naturally, in the first instance, with most interest and expectation to the book which gives us the expression, not of an individual opinion, but of the collective wisdom of Israel. We have heard, it may be, high things of the beauty of the Haggadistic mode of interpretation that prevailed in the schools out of which the Mishna, the Gemara, the Targum, and the Midrashim sprang. We open the Midrash, or Commentary, on Koheleth [Ecclesiastes] in the hope that we shall see our way through passages that have before been dark, that some light will be thrown on the meaning of words and phrases that have perplexed us. What we actually find is answers to the parable of the blind leading the blind and both falling into the ditch (Matt. 15:14); rules of interpretation by which anything can be made to mean anything else; legends of inconceivable extravagance passing the utmost limits of credibility; an absolute incapacity for getting at the true meaning of a single paragraph or sentence – this makes up the store of accumulated wisdom to which we had fondly looked forward. Instead of a 'treasure' of 'things new and old', the pearls and gems, the silver and the gold, of the wisdom of the past, we find ourselves in an old clothes' shop full of shreds and patches, of rags and tatters. We seem, as we read, to be listening to 'old wives' fables' and old men's dreams. A suspicion floats across our mind that the interpretations are *delirantium somnia* in the most literal sense of the word. We involuntarily ask, Can these men have been in their right minds? Are we not listening to a debate of insane Commentators? Is not the Midrash as a *Critici Sacri* compiled and edited within the walls of Colney Hatch? Of other expositions it is true that they 'to some faint meaning make pretence'. Of this alone, or almost alone, it may be said that it 'never deviates into sense'.[7]

Well you have been warned! The odd thing is that Plumptre then goes on to give examples of the things that have so upset him, and for the life of me, presumably because I have been trained to enjoy the *Sortes Midrishianae*, as he calls it, they all seem very reasonable ways of meditating on a strange text that seems to beg for precisely this kind of development.

Ecclesiastes 1:7 'All the rivers run into the sea, yet the sea is not full.' Of this verse we have a wide variety of interpretations: (a) All wisdom is in the heart of man and the heart is not full. (b) The whole law [presumably 'Torah'] goes into the heart and the heart is not satisfied. (c) All people will join themselves to Israel and yet the number of Israel will still grow. (d) All the dead pass into Hades and Hades is not full. (d) All Israelites go on their yearly pilgrimage to Jerusalem and yet the Temple is never crowded. (f) All riches flow into the kingdom of Edom (= Rome), but in the days of the Messiah they shall be brought back.

Incidentally, on the rabbinic point that although the Temple was full during the pilgrim festivals no one complained about feeling crowded, there is a debate about what was the nature of the miracle – that there was room for everyone or that no one complained!

But Plumptre should not have the last word on what is one of the great Jewish gifts to humanity, however unlikely it may seem from his observations. For all its complexity and the subtlety of its composition – and not all of it is of equal value – the Midrash is an extraordinary achievement of . . . Perhaps of literature, but also of exegesis, of fantasy, of spiritual adventure. Certainly it is an astonishing display of human imagination. But more than even this, by opening up the Hebrew Bible in its own unique way it also rescued the Bible from possible oblivion – relegated to the dust-heap of ancient scriptures to whet the curiosity of archivists and antiquarians. The rabbis opened the Bible up to their and subsequent generations, they made it relevant to daily needs and dramatic situations, and took it to places it would never have dreamed of going. If their work was not systematic or logical or consequent, so much the better as a reflection of the un-bounded creativity of the God who gave it to them. Even more than that, the rabbis by their different approaches also saved themselves from a legalism that might have strangled them as well – for *Halakhah*, Jewish law, has its own eminent logic that leads to ever narrower perceptions and tighter regulations. It is in the creative tension between *Halakhah* and *Aggadah* that Judaism was able to develop both its breadth and the chance for its own repeated self-transcendence.

Abraham Joshua Heschel writes beautifully on the play between these two aspects of midrash.

Halakhah represents the strength to shape one's life according to a fixed pattern; it is a form-giving force. *Aggadah* is the expression of man's ceaseless striving, which often defies all limitations. *Halakhah* is the rationalisation and schematisation of living; it defines, specifies, sets measure and limit, placing life into an exact system. *Aggadah* deals with man's ineffable relations with God, to other men, and to the world. *Halakhah* deals with details, with each commandment separately; *aggadah* with the whole of life, with the totality of religious life. *Halakhah* deals with the law, *aggadah* with the meaning of the law. *Halakhah* deals with subjects that can be expressed literally; *aggadah* introduces us to a realm which lies beyond the range of expression. *Halakhah* teaches us how to perform common acts; *aggadah* tells us how to participate in the eternal drama. *Halakhah* gives us knowledge; *aggadah* exaltation. *Halakhah* prescribes, *aggadah* suggests; *halakhah* decrees, *aggadah* inspires; *halakhah* is definite, *aggadah* is allusive.

To maintain that the essence of Judaism consists exclusively of *halakhah* is as erroneous as to maintain that the essence of Judaism consists exclusively of *aggadah*.

The interrelationship of *halakhah* and *aggadah* is the very heart of Judaism. *Halakhah* without *aggadah* is dead, *aggadah* without *halakhah* is wild.[8]

The same tension was expressed to me once by an Orthodox Rabbi: 'A *baal halakhah* (a "master" of *halakhah* alone) is a naked giant; a *baal aggadah* (a "master" of *aggadah* alone) is a dwarf in full panoply.'

We have no space to explore here in detail the subsequent development of Jewish Bible commentary. It is important to stress however that throughout the Middle Ages up to the present day there was a virtually unbroken tradition of examining and re-examining the biblical text in the light of contemporary knowledge. Up until the Emancipation it took place within a fairly well-defined Jewish world, one which shared an overarching legal system and a variety of other ritual, cultural and spiritual factors. These gave a coherence to the whole. When Jews encountered major intellectual or spiritual challenges from the world outside they retained a sense of continuity in time with past traditions, and horizontally in space with other Jewish communities. Even people operating in such different cultural environments as Rashi (Rabbi Shlomo Yitzhaki, 1040–1105) in Christian France, and Abraham Ibn Ezra (1093–1167) living in Muslim Spain, shared a number of assumptions – including the background of rabbinic tradition, the Hebrew language itself and, of course, the belief that the Bible in its entirety was the revealed word of God.

Both of these key figures were, in their own way, and according to the norms of their time, rigorously critical and broadly educated scholars. Rashi in particular seeks to clarify the plain meaning of the text, an emphasis present in the Christian scholarly environment of his time. At the same time he is the master of rabbinic tradition, writing a commentary on the entire Talmud that is indispensable till today. His commentary on the Hebrew Bible, accompanying the biblical text in one of the earliest printed Hebrew Bibles, was in turn influential on later generations of Christian scholars, particularly those responsible for the King James translation of the Bible. Abraham Ibn Ezra was a typical product of the rich Islamic culture of his time. He was a philosopher, philologist, grammarian, mathematician, astronomer and physician and brought all these disciplines to his study of the Hebrew Bible. He was even prepared, very cautiously, to ask awkward questions about the authorship of the Pentateuch, even when this went against the received tradition.[9]

With the onset of modernity all this was to change, and it was a Jewish scholar, though one who was excommunicated from the Jewish community for his writings, who became the pathfinder. Baruch (also known as Benedict de) Spinoza (1632–77), writing in his *Tractatus Theologico-Politicus*, virtually defined the approach that was to become the modern historical criticism of the Bible.

The history of Scripture should consist of three aspects: 1. an analysis of the Hebrew language; 2. the compilation and classification of the expressions of each of the books of the Bible; 3. research as to the origins of the biblical writings as far as they can still be ascertained, i.e. concerning the life, the conduct and the pursuits of the author of each book, who he was, what was the occasion and the epoch of his writing, whom did he write for, and in what language. Further it should inquire into the fate of each book; how it was first received, into whose hands it fell, how many different versions there were of it, by whose advice it was received into the Canon, and lastly, how all the books now universally accepted as sacred, were united into a single whole.[10]

What was shocking here is the attempt to go behind the received texts and the received Jewish tradition, to stand on some allegedly objective ground outside of them and evaluate them from this historical perspective. The last few centuries of 'secular' biblical scholarship have indeed been dominated by this approach, with both Jewish and Christian 'conservatives' fighting a rearguard action against the trend, either by addressing and debating the suggestions made by the modernists or by apparently dismissing and willfully ignoring them. Which brings us back to the approaches we saw at the beginning of this chapter.

Of course that is not the end of the story. Recent Bible scholarship has begun to move away from the historical-critical approach to examine the Bible more as a literary document. Jewish scholars, in America and Israel, with precursors like Martin Buber and Franz Rosenzweig in pre-war Germany, have begun to take the lead in this kind of approach. In some ways this new interest in examining the text in the smallest detail, close-reading, takes us back to the methods of the rabbis. The peculiarities of phrase or language or repetition that they used as a springboard for their imaginative teaching, are used by their modern colleagues to understand the levels of meaning of the text. If the rabbis were looking at each word and letter to find in it traces of God, today's scholars, no less dedicated, are looking for the presumed intention of the author or, if that cannot be determined, the myriad ways the audience might receive what was written. For both it is the quest for meaning that dominates and it may be this that has attracted Jews back into the arena.

Today the Hebrew Bible is open to many different approaches for those who wish to study it. Nevertheless its role in Jewish life today remains marginal. As a source of Jewish religious practice its place has long been taken by the Talmud (see the next chapter). It is taught in Israeli schools, both religious and secular, as the national literature of the State, so must inevitably share the fate of classroom overfamiliarity and indifference. It is even less well-known in Diaspora communities, even in translation, since opportunities for such study after childhood Sunday school classes are even fewer. Hence my cynicism at the opening of this chapter. But I must also point out that, particularly in America, where concerns about the falling off of Jewish life have led to many experiments in Jewish education, there are new approaches to the Hebrew Bible that may make it more available and attractive. The Internet now offers sites where you can learn to chant the biblical text appropriate to your Bar- or Batmitzvah portion, or discover on-line commentaries on the weekly Torah portion. With desktop publishing various groups are sending out similar weekly digests or creative readings of the Torah to subscribers. Perhaps a cyber Bible may succeed in the future where the solemn blue- or black-bound volumes of the past have failed. For now the Hebrew Bible remains a treasure available to all, studied intensely by a few, but a closed book to many.

Further Reading

For More on Jewish Bible Study

Jonathan Magonet, *A Rabbi's Bible* (London, SCM Press, 1991).

Jonathan Magonet, *A Rabbi Reads the Psalms* (London, SCM Press, 1994).

For those who wish to sample the flavour of rabbinic and mediaeval Jewish Bible exegesis, presented in a lively style and with an eye to modern literary modes of study, try the remarkable series of volumes by the late Professor Nehama Leibowitz, translated and adapted from the Hebrew by A. Newman: *Studies in . . . Bereshit (Genesis)* (1972); *Shemot (The Book of Exodus)* (1976); *Vayikra (Leviticus)* (1980); *Bamidbar (Numbers)* (1980); *Devarim (Deuteronomy)* (1980) (Jerusalem, The World Zionist Organisation, Department for Torah Education and Culture in the Diaspora.)

Some Current Jewish Bible Commentaries

N. Sarna (general ed.), *The Jewish Publication Society Torah Commentary* (Philadelphia, New York, Jerusalem, 1989): N. Sarna, *Genesis* (1989); N. Sarna, *Exodus*; B. A. Levine, *Leviticus*; J. Milgrom, *Numbers*; J. H. Tigay, *Deuteronomy* (1997): the most recent scholarly, Jewish, English-language commentaries on the Pentateuch – technical but excellent.

The Megillah: The Book of Esther: A New Translation with a Commentary Anthologized from Talmudic, Midrashic and Rabbinic Sources, translated and compiled by Rabbi Meir Zlotowitz (New York, ArtScroll Studio Press, 1976): the first of a series of Bible commentaries reflecting contemporary ultra-Orthodox views on the Bible.

J. H. Hertz (ed.), *The Pentateuch and Haftorahs* (London, Soncino Press, 2nd edn, 1962): a classic, even if outdated in its scholarship.

W. Gunther Plaut (ed.), *The Torah: A Modern Commentary* (New York, Union of American Hebrew Congregations, 1981): good modern introductions to the individual volumes of the Pentateuch; some detailed clarifications of the text and interesting if idiosyncratic meditative comments at the end of each section.

Collections of Midrash in English

Hayim Nahman Bialik and Yehoshua Hana Ravnitzky (eds.), *The Book of Legends: Sefer Ha-Aggadah: Legends from the Talmud and Midrash*, translated by William G. Braude (New York, Schocken Books, 1992): the classic collection edited by the leading modern Hebrew poet, Bialik. The excellent English translation was a labour of love by Rabbi Braude who completed the proofreading just before he died.

Louis Ginzberg, *The Legends of the Jews* (New York, Simon and Schuster, 1961): this is the one-volume abridged version. Those who wish to learn more of the background should go

Five are the books of the Torah

for the full five-volume set with its excellent notes.

A Rabbinic Anthology, selected and with an Introduction by C. G. Montefiore and H. Loewe (Cleveland and New York, Meridian Books, The World Publishing Company; Philadelphia, The Jewish Publication Society of America, 1963): an Orthodox rabbi and a Liberal scholar enjoy a civilised conversation as they edit this remarkable collection of *Aggadah*.

Six are the 'Orders' of the Mishnah
On Rabbinic Judaism and Rabbis

Moses received the Torah at Sinai
and handed it on to Joshua
and Joshua to the elders
and the elders to the prophets
and the prophets handed it on to the Men of the Great
  Assembly.
They used to say:
Be careful in judgment,
raise up many disciples
and make a fence around the Torah.
Simon the Just was one of the last of the Great Assembly.
He used to say: On three things the world stands:
On Torah,
on the Temple service
and on loving deeds.
Antigonos of Socho received the tradition from Simon the
  Just . . .
Yosé ben Yoezer of Seredah, and Yosé ben Yochanan of
  Jerusalem received from them . . .
Yehoshua ben Perachyah and Nittai the Arbelite received
  from them . . .
Yehudah ben Tabbai and Simeon ben Shatach received
  from them . . .
Shemayah and Abtalyon received from them . . .
Hillel and Shammai received from them . . .

Six are the 'Orders' of the Mishnah

(Sayings of the Fathers 1:1–12)

This is how the Rabbinic tradition recorded its origins as the inheritors of the Torah: Moses to Joshua to the elders to the prophets. This is familiar biblical territory, though we might be surprised at the prominence given to the 'elders', who usually blend into the scenery in the biblical stories. The chain of tradition is passed through this line. Notably it does not pass through priests or kings. The Pharisees, the predecessors of the rabbis were in conflict with the Sadducees, presumed to be the priestly and royal leadership of the time. The Torah in question was the 'oral Torah', in contrast to the 'written Torah', the Five Books of Moses. At Sinai, according to rabbinic teaching, alongside the latter, God gave Moses a method of understanding it, an oral tradition, not to be recorded, but to be handed down by word of mouth.

That there was commentary and explanation to accompany the public reading of the Torah is clear from the Bible itself. When the exiles returned from Babylon, the people assembled and Ezra the Priest had the 'scroll of the Torah of Moses' brought before the assembly, women and men alike and all who could understand to hear it. 'And they read in the book of the Torah of God with interpretation and giving the meaning and they made them understand the Torah' (Neh. 8:8). It was the same Ezra, known also as 'the Scribe', who 'set his mind to explain the Torah of the Eternal and put it into practice, and to teach Israel statutes and judgments' (Ezra 7:10). Here we meet the *soferim*, 'scribes' – a word derived directly from *sefer*, 'a book' – whose task it was to instruct the people in their tradition.

Somewhere in this practice over the centuries evolved what was to become the 'oral Torah', itself an ever-growing body of material. Presumably that is why there is a repetition of the phrase 'handing on' in the above listing when we come to the 'Men of the Great Assembly'. A new stage, outside the biblical record, has been reached. What precisely this body was is not certain, but it is clearly a significant transitional stage in the creating of what was to become 'Pharisaic' and later 'rabbinic' Judaism. From this stage on the tradition is handed down through 'sages', scholars, listed in pairs, whose favourite teachings are also reverently passed on. Indeed we see here the beginning of a tradition of teacher–pupil learning which will elevate the role of the teacher to the same significance as one's biological parent.

> Just as we are commanded to honour and revere our father, so are we obligated to honour and revere our teacher, even more than our father. For our father brings us into the life of this world, but our teacher, who teaches us wisdom, brings us into the life of the world to come. (Maimonides, Mishneh Torah, *hilkhot talmud torah* (Torah Study) 5:1)

That respect was shown, among other ways, by ensuring that one passed things on *b'shem omro*, 'in the name of the one who said it', and thus it was transmitted down through the generations.

In the twelfth century, the great Jewish philosopher and legal authority Moses Maimonides classified in his Mishneh Torah the relationship between teacher and student.

> There is no honour higher than that which is due to teachers, no reverence more profound than that which should be bestowed upon them. Our sages said: the reverence for your teacher should be like your reverence for heaven (Sayings of the Fathers 4:12).
>
> Just as the students are required to honour their teachers, so should teachers honour their students and welcome them, as our sages said: 'Let the honour of your student be as dear to you as your own' (Sayings of the Fathers 4:15). We should take care of our students and love them, for they are the children who give delight in this world and in the world to come.
>
> Students increase the wisdom of teachers and broaden their minds. Our sages said: I have learned much from my teachers, more from my colleagues, but I have learned most from my students (Ta'anit 7:1). (Maimonides, op. cit. 5:1, 12–13)

We should pause here for a moment and recognise something of great significance. It may be that we are too familiar with the idea of universal education, and would anyway trace it back to ancient Greece, to appreciate the significance of the Jewish practice of expounding the Torah. But whatever else it might become, Judaism was not to be a mystery religion, whose secrets were the property of some priestly caste alone that was effectively a power élite. All were to be instructed in the Torah and its understanding, and, significantly, this applied to men and women alike, despite the patriarchal nature of the society in which this value emerged.

Just to give the flavour of the rabbis' views on study, let me quote a few of their observations on the subject. The first reflects the very real tragedies they experienced in their desire to place Torah above all else, but also the sense of the divine purpose behind all that occurred to them.

> When Moses descended from Mount Sinai, and saw the abominations of Israel [dancing round the Golden Calf], he gazed at the tablets of the Ten Commandments and saw that the words had flown away, so he broke them at the foot of the hill. At once he fell dumb. He could not say a word. At that moment a decree was passed concerning Israel, that they were to study these same words in the midst of sorrow and in the midst of slavery, in migration, and in confusion, in pressing poverty and in hunger. But for the sorrow they have suffered, the Holy One, blessed be He, is destined to reward them during the days of the Messiah many times over. (Seder Eliyahu Rabba 19)

The following passage illustrates both the rabbinic way of taking a biblical verse and attempting either to locate its context or invent a suitable one for it. It also shows great humour as well as familiarity with the problem, common to students of all times and ages, of getting up in the morning.

> The lazy man says: 'There is a lion in the way, a lion in the streets!' (Prov. 26:13). Solomon [the 'author' of the Book of Proverbs] tells us about the lazy man. When they say to

him: 'Your teacher is in the city, go and study Torah from him,' he replies: 'I am afraid of the lion that is in the way!' And when they say: 'See, your teacher is right here in town, get up and go to him,' he says to them: 'I'm afraid in case there is a lion in the streets!' They tell him: 'Look, he's living right by your house.' He says to them: 'But there's a lion outside!' They say to him: 'He's in your house!' He replies: 'But what if I go and find the door is locked!' Finally when he does not know what to reply he says to them: 'Whether the door is open or locked, I want to sleep a little bit more!' (Deuteronomy Rabba 8:6)

It has to be pointed out that any such chain of tradition as the one listed at the beginning of this chapter carries with it some kind of polemic purpose. It is designed to show how that history of origins is to be understood and to reinforce the authenticity of what has come down and the authority of those who have received it. So this one too reflects internal conflicts within the Jewish world, as is so often the case in Jewish history. The predecessors of the rabbis, the Pharisees (Hebrew: *perushim*, 'those separated', or 'separatists') stood in conflict with the descendants of the aristocratic priestly families, the Sadducees, whose power base was the Temple. The Pharisees transferred much of ritual life from the Temple to the synagogue, placed great stress on study and personal religious observance and gradually played a greater and greater role in the civil and political life of Jewish society. By the first century CE they appear to have represented the beliefs and practices of most of the Jewish people.

Incidentally it must be pointed out here that, although the Pharisees are frequently attacked in the Gospels, it would seem that Jesus belonged to their number, as is evident from the many teachings held in common. The rabbis criticised the same hypocrisies that Jesus did. What was clearly an internal Jewish argument became distorted when seen from outside and used for polemic purposes as the early Church sought to assert its separate identity. The followers of Jesus represented just one of the many Jewish groups that were in debate and struggle at that time, including the Zealots, who sought political independence from Rome. But with the disastrous failure of the revolts against Rome and the destruction of the Temple, the Pharisees emerged as the leaders of the Jewish people Thus the year 70 marks a crucial turning point in Jewish history. According to a famous Talmudic story, Yochanan ben Zakkai had himself smuggled out of the besieged Jerusalem and established an academy at Yavneh where he gathered scholars and set about rebuilding Jewish life. He is the last to be named as 'receiving the tradition from his predecessors', namely from Hillel and Shammai (Sayings of the Fathers 2:9). His students are now called 'rabbi', the title that marks them as scholar, teacher, judge and spiritual leader of the people.

The 'Mishnah' of the title of this chapter refers to the compilation of existing legal traditions, the 'oral' law, edited about 200 CE, the work being attributed to Rabbi Yehudah Ha-Nasi. The term itself means 'repetition' of the oral tradition, the method whereby the teaching was studied and handed on to others. It has six divisions, the 'orders' of our title, each of which has seven to twelve 'tractates', in turn subdivided into chapters. The orders deal with subjects as varied as the festival calendar; agricultural matters; damages; 'women' – dealing with marriage, divorce; and ritual purity.

There is much debate among scholars about the relationship between the Mishnah and the Midrash that we examined in the previous chapter. Which came first? Did the interpretation of the Bible (Midrash) lead eventually to the need to compile the emerging laws; or did the laws themselves develop semi-independently? Probably both processes took place at the same time.

Over the next two to five centuries the rabbis undertook a major examination of the contents of the Mishnah leading to two enormous compilations of comment and discussion: the Palestinian Talmud (edited in about the fourth century) and the Babylonian Talmud (edited by the seventh century). The Mishnah, together with its expanded commentary, the *gemara* (lit. 'completion'), together constitute the Talmud, a term derived from the verb *l-m-d* to study or teach.

The Palestinian Talmud shows evidence of incompleteness, probably because of the deterioration of Jewish life in Palestine. The Babylonian Talmud, considerably larger, became the 'second Scripture' of Judaism, to the study of which Jewish men dedicated themselves for a lifetime. The *yeshiva*, 'academy', became the focal point of Jewish intellectual life. The greatest aspiration for a Jewish family was to have a son who could dedicate himself to the life of the Talmud scholar, or to marry their daughter to one.

The Babylonian Talmud is an extraordinary, highly complex work, edited with great literary finesse. In it the rabbis debate the relationship between the laws of the Mishnah and other compilations and the Hebrew Bible. But they also explore in exacting detail and with rigorous logic the application of these laws to everyday life and experience, incorporating and debating the different traditions, opinions and circumstances that surround any given subject. Both the majority and minority opinions are cited when a conclusion is reached. By preserving the dissenting voices the possibility is left open for renewing the debate should circumstances change. The arguments sometimes resemble an elaborate chess game in which different potential sequences of events are discussed with their alternatives, so that to follow the argument several such moves have to be held in one's head at the same time. Topics are explored to the limits of their theoretical possibilities, even when these lead to practical absurdities. Studying the Talmud is a training in mental agility and the development of a kind of organic logic as much as it is a record of legal debate. If at times it reads like the unedited minutes of an endless committee meeting, the Hansard of rabbinic discussions, some kind of structure can always be discerned. The range of topics covered reflects the desire to address the whole of life while trying to establish the will of God for the conduct of the Jewish people. The historian Heinrich Graetz describes it as follows: 'The Talmud must not be regarded as an ordinary book, composed of twelve volumes; it possesses absolutely no intrinsic similarity with any other literary production, but forms, without any figure of speech, a world of its own which must be judged by its own peculiar laws.'[1]

Rather than talk about it let us look at one tiny extract which shows how far-ranging such a discussion can be. This passage is one I am particularly fond of as it was one of the first pieces I learnt when I began my rabbinic studies. The passage occurs in the middle of a long discussion about the contents of the Grace after Meals which by that time had evolved into an elaborate series of four blessings. The question is raised, where do we learn in the Torah that we should say a blessing after we have eaten? The square brackets in what follows indicate the unwritten thought processes that go on between the written words of the text, without which it would hardly be comprehensible!

Our rabbis taught: Whence do we learn from the Torah that we should recite a blessing after eating food? [The answer is in a biblical verse itself] as it says: 'You shall eat and be satisfied and bless [the Eternal your God for the good land which He has given you]' (Deut. 8:10). This refers to [the first paragraph of the grace which thanks God who] 'feeds everyone'. [The continuation of the biblical verse] 'the Eternal your God' refers to [the second blessing about] God's providence. 'For the land – this refers to the [third] blessing about the land'. [The word] 'good' [in the verse] refers [specifically to the phrase in this third blessing about] rebuilding Jerusalem [in our day], [and the proof for this is that there is a biblical verse] which speaks of 'this *good* mountain [namely Jerusalem] and this Lebanon' (Deut. 3:25). 'Which He has given us' refers to [the fourth and last verse which states] 'who is good and does good'.

This only tells me that I should recite a grace after I have eaten, how do I know that I should say a blessing before [I have eaten]? You could say that it is an argument from minor to major: If when you are satisfied you want to say a blessing, if you are hungry [and food is set before you] how much the more [would you want to recite a blessing!].

[There is here an intervention from Rabbi (Yehudah Ha-Nasi) who gives a different reading of the same verses quoted above. He points out that the fourth blessing of the grace does not need a biblical proof text to justify it as it was actually introduced by a special decree at the Academy at Yavneh. During the revolt against Rome, the Romans forbade the burial of Jews who had been killed at Bethar. When this order was finally revoked and the bodies were buried the additional blessing was added, namely that God 'is good and does good'.]

[Since the previous opinion had been based merely on the logic of the argument from minor to major, the rabbis are still looking for an authentic biblical verse to justify reciting a blessing before eating. So the text then continues:]

This only tells me that I should recite a grace after I have eaten, how do I know that I should say a blessing before? That is why the biblical verse explicitly states 'which He has given you' – from the moment when He has given it to you [you should feel obligated to recite a blessing, that is, even before you eat].

Rabbi Yitzhak says, we do not need this [proof], for does not the verse say: '[You shall serve the Eternal your God] and He will bless your bread and your water' (Exod. 23:25). [For what follows you have to remember that the Hebrew text of the Bible consists only of consonants and in order to read a word you have to add the vowels yourself, though the tradition has determined what they should be. Since different vowels can make the word have different meanings, the rabbis were quite happy to change the vowels to make the word yield new meanings whenever they wanted to – as will be the case here.] So do not read 'and He will bless', but [read the verb instead as an imperative] 'bless [your bread]!'. And when is it called 'bread'? Before one eats it!

Rabbi Natan says, we do not need this [proof], for does it not say [in the Book of Samuel when Saul goes looking for his father's missing donkeys and meets a group of young women on their way to the well who tell him how to find Samuel the prophet] 'When you come to the city there you will find him before he goes up to the high place to eat, for the people do not eat until he has come because he blesses the sacrifice and afterwards those who are invited eat' (1 Sam. 9:12).

[This would appear to be the clincher, since here we have a situation where it is explicitly stated that before people eat someone recites a blessing. But the Talmud does not stop here, as if the rabbis, exhausted by this complicated argument, stay around for a little banter. (This is something of a projection on to the text since there is no certainty that the rabbis named above ever met except in the mind of the editor or editors of this passage!)]

[Literally,] 'And all this, why?' [Why did these young ladies give such a long and convoluted answer about where Saul could find the prophet Samuel? Alas in the first answer to this question we see a glimpse of the kind of chauvinism the rabbis sometimes display. An anonymous rabbi says]: 'Well you know how women like to talk!' But [Rabbi] Samuel said: 'They wanted to look upon the beauty of Saul, for does it not say: "From his shoulders and upwards he was taller than all the people"' (1 Sam. 9:2). But Rabbi Yochanan said [quoting a proverb] 'No two kingdoms should overlap by as much as a hairsbreadth.' [Samuel was the current ruler and Saul was to be his successor, the first king, and if he had arrived too soon there could have been a clash between them, so the women, unbeknown to themselves, were acting on God's behalf in delaying Saul.] (b. Berakhot 48b)

Certain things emerge from the above passage. First that it is well organised and structured so that there is a logical sequence to the solutions offered to the problem – ending with the biblical verse that actually provides the answer. By this means the logical suggestion of the anonymous speaker (if after you have eaten you want to bless, how much more so beforehand when you receive it), the pressing of the verse 'which He has given you' to mean 'from the moment He has given it to you', and Rabbi Yitzhak's changing of the meaning of 'He will bless your bread' to the imperative 'bless your bread!', all get their space in the argument. It also shows the sorts of argument that might win out on other occasions, arguments from minor to major, manipulation of the text and indeed the introduction of historical information in the case of the decree instituted at Yavneh. Even the concluding part has its value, even if the first example is rather uncomfortable, since Rabbi Yochanan manages to introduce into what might otherwise appear to be a casual conversation evidence of the workings of divine providence.

If the Talmud (and it is generally the Babylonian Talmud that is quoted in Jewish sources in the following centuries) kept the argument open, things began to change after the great codification of law by Moses Maimonides. Living in Spain under the influence of Islamic philosophy and law, he attempted to draw together the many complex arguments of the Talmud into a systematically arranged code, written in a clear and simple Hebrew, which would make the decisions readily available to everyone. Whether intending to or not, he set in motion the move away from the deliberate openness of the Talmud back to the formal structure of the Mishnah.

Just to see what happened to our discussion above, here is Maimonides' summary, together with other related materials in his typical succinct style:

It is a positive command from the Bible to recite a blessing after eating food, as it says: 'You shall eat, be satisfied and bless the Eternal your God' (Deut. 8:10). But he is not obligated according to the Torah unless he is actually sated, since it states specifically: 'You shall eat, be satisfied [sated] and bless . . .' Based on rabbinic enactment, this means 'if he has eaten anything the size of an olive he should recite a blessing'. [Olives in the Talmudic period seem to have been quite large, about the size of a partridge egg!]

Moreover, according to rabbinic enactment one should recite a blessing on all food beforehand and afterwards enjoy it . . . So too one should recite a blessing before enjoying a sweet fragrance. Indeed, all enjoyment without reciting a blessing is a sacrilege. Similarly, by rabbinic enactment, one should recite a blessing after all that one has eaten or drunk, that is if he drinks a quarter [of a *log*] or eats the equivalent of an olive. But if one merely tastes one need not recite a blessing either before or after if it is less than a quarter of a *log*. (Mishneh Torah *hilkhot b'rakhot* (Laws of Blessings) 1:1–2)

Maimonides called his work the *Mishneh Torah*, a term borrowed from Deuteronomy 17:18, a phrase which was understood to mean 'a second law', and which gave rise to the name 'Deuteronomy' itself (though in its context the phrase actually refers to 'a second [that is "copy"] of the Torah' to be written by the king). The use of such a term earned him considerable criticism for his apparent arrogance in putting his own work on a par with the Torah of Moses itself! He had predecessors in attempting to codify Jewish law, but the clarity and elegance of style, comprehensiveness of approach, together with the authority of the man himself gave his *Mishneh Torah* considerable impact. Moreover his successors in this activity, Rabbi Jacob ben Asher (1269–1340), author of the *Arba'ah Turim* and Joseph Karo (1488–1575), author of the *Shulhan Arukh*, built on his work.

If today the *Mishneh Torah* is cited by Orthodox teachers as an authoritative and authentic example of traditional Judaism, they forget that at the time it caused enormous controversy, so much so that the Jewish world became divided into two camps pro- and anti-Maimonides over the next few centuries, with the different parties refusing to marry with each other! One reason for the controversy was his suggestion that his code would make the study of the Talmud less necessary! However the real debate surrounded precisely the fact that he had systematised the 'law', without citing his sources or the reason for his particular decisions in cases where the Talmud was inconclusive. As a result there grew up a number of supercommentaries trying to explicate the reason for his decisions in particular cases. But despite the controversy, the door was open to a new kind of authority in Jewish life, less amenable to debate and more based on this and subsequent codes. Perhaps the greatest Jewish thinker of all time, it was said of him: 'From Moses to Moses, there was none like Moses.' His other extraordinary contribution to Jewish thought, no less controversial, was his philosophical work *The Guide to the Perplexed*, in which he attempted to reconcile the tradition of Torah with contemporary philosophical views and challenges. If he seems at times too much the intellectual it is worth conjuring with an image I once heard used to describe him – 'he was a cold fire'.

Maimonides' code was fully comprehensive, including laws concerning the Temple and regulations for the priests, even though the Temple had been destroyed a thousand years before. In part this was necessary since he believed in the coming of the Messiah and the restoration of the Temple. However in contrast, in the *Guide to the Perplexed*, written for a different audience, he expressed the controversial view that the sacrifical system was only a concession to the practices of the day, and that God's aim was to allow the Israelites to use the types of worship that they were used to so as ultimately to wean them off them entirely. That is also why sacrifices were restricted to the Temple alone whereas prayer and other personal religious practices could happen anywhere. (*Guide* III, 23) This clearly implies that the need for the Temple had also been transcended, despite wishing for its restoration, one of the many apparent contradictions between Maimonides' legal and philosophical writings.

Another reason why Maimonides retained laws of no obvious relevance for his time was that a legal system has to be comprehensive, since the laws or principles that work in one area may have relevance for another. But his successors in the field of codifying Jewish law confined themselves to laws that had practical consequences for their contemporaries. The last great code, the *Shulhan Arukh* ('the prepared table'), was composed by Joseph Karo, an authority on Jewish law and a mystic who was part of the circle of Jewish mystics living in Safed in the sixteenth century. Karo had already written a major commentary on the work of his predecessor Jacob ben Asher, which he considered his major work, while the *Shulhan Arukh* was a shortened synopsis intended for 'young students who could meditate on it, learn it by heart and learn the *halakhah* from their youth'. Coming out of the Sephardi world he had ignored the variations on Jewish law to be found in Ashkenazi circles, and appropriate supplementary variations were added to remedy this defect by Moses Isserles, which he called the *Mappah*, the 'tablecloth' on Karo's 'prepared table'. In typical fashion this code too acquired its super-commentaries from eminent scholars and then, probably due to the fact of its being printed, it became the authoritative textbook of Jewish law.

If codes and supercommentaries tend to get frozen within the pages of a book, life nevertheless moves on and new issues constantly arise. Out of the need to address them there arose another kind of Jewish literature: *she'elot uteshuvot*, literally, 'questions and answers', which go by the more dignified term 'Responsa'. The practice goes back to the Talmudic period, and flourished through the Middle Ages, of addressing halakhic questions to rabbis who were deemed to be authorities in Jewish law. Whereas in this earlier period rabbis would range far and wide over Talmudic and other sources to give their replies, after the publication of Joseph Karo's *Shulhan Arukh* this became increasingly the source on which people relied.

The Responsa literature is a mine of information on the state of Jewish life and the kind of questions that arose within the communities. Subjects might range from whether it was appropriate for married Jewish women to follow the fashion of wearing wigs to questions about appropriate areas of study, from matters of civil law to issues of Jewish status. Today Orthodox rabbis working in the same tradition address questions about surrogate motherhood, euthanasia in the case of someone on a life-support machine or genetic engineering.

One extraordinary example of a Responsum that had a major impact on the life of certain Jewish people resulted from the chance visit in the middle of the last century by a distinguished rabbi to the Viennese Institute for the Deaf and Dumb. The 'deaf-mute' had been considered from Talmudic times as a category of person who was exempt from the *mitzvot*, 'commandments', alongside the 'imbecile'. When it was recognised that with such training they could communicate like anyone else, their status was completely changed to that of a normal person.

The world of the Responsa, of Orthodox communities who look to particular rabbis for guidance continues to exist, particularly in the United States and Israel. It is a world with considerable spiritual power for those who feel at home within it, though it has its own complex and subtle divisions, loyalties and challenges. From the 'left' it feels itself assaulted by modernity itself, and some parts of it feel they must fight a rearguard action against modern expressions of Judaism. But it is also under pressure from 'ultra-Orthodox' groups whose single-mindedness and, it must be said, intolerance, makes their 'modern-Orthodox' or 'central-Orthodox' coreligionists feel threatened as well. Such pressures make even minor innovations within the traditional system very difficult and open to denunciation by those 'to the right'. It is a world that I cannot claim to know in any real way and have only observed from outside, helped by a number of Orthodox colleagues who belong, sometimes uncomfortably within it. (Though discomfort within Judaism seems to be an essential experience from time to time. Anything that is really alive must experience the difficulties of change, conflict and loss.)

But Orthodox Jewry, for all its relative power (in Israel) and 'presence' in Jewish life, is not the only expression of Judaism, and in terms of numbers is actually the smallest religious grouping. The vast changes in Jewish life since the Emancipation have radically affected the degree to which Jews feel themselves to live within the confines of Jewish law. When areas of Jewish law passed into the hands of civil authorities the classical role, and indeed authority, of the rabbi as judge virtually disappeared or became an area of specialisation. In the nineteenth century Jews experiencing the new open society wanted their rabbis to have a broader culture, a university education and a firm grasp of Jewish history and philosophy. Some countries even demanded such university qualifications in order that rabbis be recognized by the State, and here we can see the degree to which societal pressures encouraged both the emancipation and ultimately assimilation of the Jews. When the existing *yeshivot*, the traditional academies for Talmud study, were unwilling to accept such conditions the modern rabbinic seminary was born, bringing contemporary academic approaches to traditional Jewish materials, the *Wissenschaft des Judentums*, 'scientific study of Judaism', approach. A somewhat unkind response to this new development from more traditional circles was the comment: 'When rabbis became "Rabbi Doctors", then Judaism became sick!'

Within a sixty-year period during the nineteenth century the major seminaries were created that were to transform the image, education and role of the modern rabbi in response to the new situation of Jews in Western society: 1827 Padua, later Rome; 1829 Metz, later Paris; 1854 Breslau; 1885 Jews' College, London; 1872 Vienna; 1872 the Liberal Lehranstalt (Hochschule) für die Wissenschaft des Judentums, Berlin; 1873 the Orthodox Rabbiner Seminar, Berlin; 1875 the Reform Hebrew Union College, Cincinnati; 1877, Budapest; 1886 the Conservative Jewish Theological Seminary, New York.

The 'new' rabbi adapted from the Christian clergy of the time not only the black gown, even the clerical collar, but also a changing role as preacher, scholar and *Seelsorger*, 'pastor'. But each Jewish society adapted in its own way. In America, particularly in the Reform movement, the rabbi, preaching 'prophetic Judaism' became a social activist. In Germany, the intellectual sermon, arduously prepared, became the trademark for some. (It was said that the more the sermon was above the heads of the congregation, the more they appreciated their rabbi for his learning.) In all cases the rabbi remained a teacher, and as often as not a kind of 'social engineer', holding together the often very disparate groups that made up the average congregation, addressing on their behalf contemporary issues and trying to sort out the inevitable conflicts that arose within. It must also be pointed out that the rabbi, being as human as the next person, could also contribute to the divisions, but was also placed in a peculiarly ambiguous position – the confidante of many, but also likely to be embroiled in the personal disputes or ideological battles that affected the same people. As Lionel Blue has often pointed out, the synagogue is the place where religion and the world meet each other; the hope is that the world will become more religious as a result, but as often as not, the religion simply becomes more worldly.

It is my privileged position to head a rabbinic seminary, one of the few created since the end of the Second World War. The express purpose was to become the successor of the Berlin Hochschule that served to train rabbis for the German Liberal movement. The fact of being created at a time of considerable turmoil in the Jewish world has enabled us both to embrace the classical studies of Jewish tradition, from a modern (and maybe post-modern) perspective, but also to try to find out what are the skills and qualities needed to deal with today's Jewish community and the wider society in which we live. The role of the rabbi is undergoing major changes as is the way it is perceived. The following may help explain something of what is happening.

In January each year we review the application forms of those who wish to be considered as candidates for the rabbinic programme at Leo Baeck College. They are invited to tell us what they see as the role and qualities of a rabbi. While the answers vary from applicant to applicant, they share many common views about the enormous range of tasks they feel rabbis should perform.

- Learning and teaching – enabling others to share in the experience of Jewish study.
- Confident leadership and profound humility. Strong enough not to be looking for affirmation or praise through the role.
- Leader, teacher and counsellor – as leader, a model of living Jewishly.
- Qualities: compassion, integrity, calmness, strength of character and mind. A sense of humour. Love of God and of Judaism.
- Represents Judaism to the Jewish community and non-Jewish world.
- To lead the congregational services; pastoral work; social work.
- The link between people and Jewish tradition.
- A spiritual leader. A diplomat in dealing with the congregation. Multifaceted skills in areas of counselling, inspirational leadership . . .
- Active in both community and personal development. Instill pride in being Jewish.

- Available at all times of need and crisis.
- The central pivot around which the community revolves. The one who sets the tone in spiritual and material matters.

This complex range of tasks and qualities mirrors pretty well the different expectations people have about the rabbi. It points to the possibilities and potential within the role, but also the great burdens the rabbi has to bear.

The candidates still see the rabbi through the eyes of the average congregational member, which has its positive and negative aspects. At one end is the old joke that the rabbi is invisible six days of the week and incomprehensible on the seventh! At the other may be a deep respect for a particular rabbi who has had an important influence on them. For the rabbi is indeed at times a counsellor and friend, supporting individuals and families throughout all the stages of life, sharing their joys and comforting them in times of sadness or trouble. The rabbi is also expected to be a teacher of old and young alike, though not all rabbis are particularly good at working with such different age groups.

He, or she, is to be the spiritual leader of the community – though here too there is an inner tension. For rabbis are the salaried employees of the congregation. They have to learn how to tread the delicate tightrope between setting their own leadership goals and winning the support for them of a changing voluntary leadership who may have quite different priorities, but who ultimately pay the salary.

The rabbi may be the only 'professional' working in a synagogue so that many of the tasks that would normally fall upon the administration end up in his or her lap. How do you free yourself of those kinds of burdens so that you can do the things you feel to be more important? And how do you keep up some kind of order in your life when the phone can ring at any moment with the news of a death or emergency that has to take priority over the sermon you are trying to finish in time?

If there are others working for the synagogue, such as administrators or educators, the rabbi may have to develop managerial skills so as to work with this professional team and ensure that the many skills available to the congregation are employed in the best way.

Some of these roles would seem strange to a rabbi of even a few generations ago who had a far greater authority as judge and arbiter in the practical minutiae of community life or who would have been expected to devote far more time to traditional study. In our more democratic age, the distance from the rabbi has shrunk and if the rabbi has authority today in his or her community it is less because of the title and far more because it has been earned through personal qualities.

Already it must be clear that there are too many expectations raised by the very title 'rabbi'. No one can fulfil them all well (and at the same time!) which leads to major problems for rabbis. When the expectations are so unrealistic how do you accept your limitations? Where do you get the self-confidence to admit that you cannot do everything, that you have strengths and weaknesses like anyone else and learn to arrange your work so as to develop the former and make sure that others do the things you do not do well? How do you lead your congregation to accept that the rabbi is human in this respect so that a more realistic shared task is developed? What kind of support or supervisory system do you need personally, considering the burdens you carry? How do you manage your time and set limits under such enormous pressures? Perhaps the hardest word for a rabbi to say is 'No!'

Most rabbis are acutely conscious of what they consider to be their personal inadequacies. The problem is not so much the kind of roles they feel they should fulfil, most of which reflect the idealism, spiritual commitment and willingness to serve the Jewish people that they have brought to the task. Rather it is in the lack of boundaries to the many roles, the blurring between their public and private life, and the assumption that a rabbi must be always on call, a workaholic, committed twenty-four hours to the service of his or her community. All too often it is not the rabbi alone who is under scrutiny but also the rabbi's spouse and children who may suffer considerably from being in the public eye. They may then find that for the rabbi the congregation and its needs tend to come first before family.

The rabbinate is one of the few professions where it is not only what one knows or does that matters, but who and what one is. It is the person as a whole that is on offer to the Jewish world and the wider community.

I fear that I have painted a rather bleak picture but that is not my intention. It is simply that in a modern society with all its challenges and tensions, and given the tragic drama of Jewish life this century with the scars it has left, the rabbi is one of the few 'generalists' around who is often the first to have to deal with the problems of others. So the rabbi is somewhere between the 'General Practitioner', the first port of call, and an 'Ambassador-at-large', representing Judaism to the world at large. How do you maintain your own inner spiritual, intellectual and emotional resources in such a demanding profession?

I was once challenged at a public discussion on this subject by someone who felt that it was wrong to speak of the rabbinate as a 'profession'. Surely it was a 'vocation', a calling to serve God. The person was right to make this point – though I pointed out that no rabbi would survive very long if he or she did not have a whole range of professional skills – acquired in five years' of studies, but continually developed and refined in the years of service to the community. The truth is that the modern rabbi has to live up to both sets of criteria, bringing a spiritual dimension to a highly complex professional task, and bringing many professional skills to the development of the spiritual life of a complex Jewish community.

How do rabbis stand up under the pressure? In a word, badly. Many of them suffer the syndromes associated with high-stress occupations – including health, psychological and marital break-downs. Like others in the public spotlight rabbis may seem specially attractive to members of the opposite sex and disastrous mistakes in this direction are also not unknown. Mostly, however, it is a case of low-grade exhaustion that leads from time to time to serious 'burn out'. The oft-repeated story from America has it that at a conference of rabbis an announcement came over the hotel loudspeaker system: 'Would all those rabbis who are happy in their current job please assemble for a meeting in the phone booth in the lobby!'

It may be that non-Orthodox rabbis have it worse than their Orthodox colleagues whose tasks, at least from outside, seem more clearly defined and limited – but that may simply be a fantasy. Some groups are simply freer to talk about their problems than others.

Nevertheless two factors may change something of the pressures, or at least moderate them. The first is the recognition that there is a problem in the lack of boundaries and unrealistic expectations. This has led to the examination of possible support systems needed by rabbis – whether by greater collegiality and the sharing of burdens or the use of some kind of professional supervision for the work itself, on the social worker or counsellor model.

The other factor is the growing number of women rabbis who have begun to move away from an early attempt to ape the worst workaholic characteristics of their male peers. Women rabbis with families still find themselves more committed to running households and raising children than their male counterpart. This is one of the findings of some studies done in America by women rabbis themselves. This means, quite pragmatically, that less time is available for the congregation, so different strategies have to be explored and a clearer role defined, giving greater tasks to lay or other professionals in the running of the synagogue. The values of personal space and family time are now more on the agenda of male rabbis as well, though the old work ethic has a habit of sneaking up on them.

All of which is not even to touch on the sheer weight of the responsibility carried, the feelings of inadequacy when compared with the great figures of the past and a feeling of ignorance of a tradition that can never be studied and understood enough. Two sayings indicate the nature of this personal challenge. The first comes from Rabbi Dr Leo Baeck, the leading figure of German Jewry during its darkest hours, who survived Theresienstadt concentration camp: 'A message is not the preaching of a preacher but the man himself.' Few rabbis would disagree with the sentiment, but in their private moments, most must shudder at its implications. The other comes from Zussya of Hanipol, a strange ecstatic figure among the early Chasidim. When he thought about his end and what it would be like to stand before the judgment he said to himself: 'If they ask me, "Zussya, Zussya, why couldn't you be like Moses?" Then I can say, "How could I be like Moses?" I'm only Zussya! But if they ask me, "Zussya, Zussya, why couldn't you be like Zussya?" Then what am I going to answer?'

If all the above seems too depressing, the following piece by Rabbi Alexandra Wright helps redress the balance:

The dynamic of the rabbi's relationship with the congregation is vital and unique. What other individual becomes privy to so much intimate and personal knowledge about a group of people? What other individual can watch children in a community grow, enter their teenage years and move into adulthood? What other individual can sit weeping with the family of a dying person, be with them to help them through a funeral and *shivah* [mourning period] and see the imperceptible hand of time effect its healing process? How many times must the rabbi confront the stark and painful knowledge that all is not right with the world – that marriages teeter and fall, that children suffer because of cruelty or more simply a lack of understanding of their needs; that there is much cynicism and loneliness, sickness and prolonged grief?

Again and again one must turn from ingesting this crucial knowledge and feeling it as a microcosm of one's own experiences, to articulate the transcendent goodness and justice of God. I find myself living on a kind of cusp, my belief in God and the intrinsic order of the Universe constantly challenged and perforated by what I become witness to; and yet at the same time living as part of a community, as the privileged witness of their gratitude, love and beneficence. There is restoration and my healing comes about in the middle of the rough and tumble of community life and the relationships that are made there.[2]

It seems appropriate to end this chapter with a blessing that was probably originally inserted into the *Kaddish*, the memorial prayer, to mark the passing of a great teacher. Whatever its origins it is a plea that rabbis receive the practical and the spiritual support that they need.

> For Israel and for the rabbis, for their pupils, and the pupils of their pupils, who devote themselves to the study of Torah, in this place and in every other place; let there be for them and for you great peace and favour, love and mercy, long life, ample sustenance and redemption from their Father who is in heaven.

Further Reading

On the Talmud

Hyam Maccoby, *The Day God Laughed: Sayings, Fables, and Entertainments of the Jewish Sages* (London, Robson Books, 1978): a delightful compilation showing the human side of the masters of Jewish tradition.

Adin Steinsaltz, *The Talmud: The Steinsaltz Edition: A Reference Guide* (New York, Random House, 1989). This is the introductory volume to an extraordinary achievement to 'translate' the entire Talmud initially into modern Hebrew and subsequently into European languages by Rabbi Adin Steinsaltz. This volume is very much the Talmud 'from within' with detailed explanations of the terminology and methodology of Talmud study.

Günther Stemberger, *Introduction to the Talmud and Midrash*, translated and edited by Markus Bockmuehl (Edinburgh, T. & T. Clark, 2nd edn, 1996): a superb scholarly introduction to the entire field of rabbinic literature.

Six are the 'Orders' of the Mishnah

On Rabbinic Law and Thought

Louis Jacobs, *Jewish Law* (New York, Behrman House, 1968): samples of Jewish legal texts across the centuries with excellent commentary and explanation.

Barry W. Holtz (ed.), *Back to the Sources: Reading Classic Jewish Texts* (New York, Summit Books, 1984): a useful survey of the major areas of Jewish thought – Bible, Talmud, Midrash, philosophy, Kabbalah, Chasidism and prayer – by authorities in the field.

Seven are the days of the week
On Shabbat and Jewish liturgy

The great exponent of cultural Zionism Ahad HaAm (Asher Ginzberg, 1856–1927) wrote that 'More than Israel kept the Sabbath, the Sabbath kept Israel.' Certainly some of the biblical prophets castigated Israel for doing their business on the Sabbath day, and it was the constant theme of the sermons of my own childhood. Yet without doubt the Sabbath, *Shabbat*, is a central pillar of Jewish existence.

This separating out of an island in time, a special day, belongs to a whole range of 'separations' and 'distinctions' within Judaism. The very act of creation begins with just such a series of divisions and distinctions: between light and darkness, day and night, the waters above the firmament and the waters below. With each further differentiation, tasks are assigned and boundaries drawn. Time too is given its distinctive identity – there are six days for doing work and a seventh day of rest.

It has been said that whereas Christians build cathedrals in space, Jews build them in time. The *Shabbat* with all its complex structure is precisely that. Incidentally I prefer to use the Hebrew term *Shabbat* because it carries a different set of overtones to the English 'Sabbath' – though it is interesting to note that 'Sabbath' is effectively a loan word in the English language, presumably because there was no equivalent word or concept into which it could be translated.

The development of the *Shabbat* and its unique quality is well described by Solomon Goldman:

The [Jewish] Sabbath, as we know it, is a far more elaborate pattern than its biblical prototype. For it is the produce of a complex of sublime faith, poetic fantasy, extreme promptings of the imagination, legal acumen, theological speculations, excessive piety, crushing poverty, bitterness of humiliation, exile and persecution, good common sense, and the sheer love for life. The rabbinic, as the biblical, Sabbath aimed at the same several objectives, all of which were to culminate in one, perhaps unattainable, ideal. First, it was to constitute a day of physical relaxation, of complete rest, when all manner of work such as, for example, carrying a load, treading wine-presses, ploughing, harvesting, and buying and selling are prohibited. Second it was to teach man to be kind to the beast and more particularly to his fellow-man, be they slaves or aliens. Third, it was to be a joyous day spent at home with one's family and not in loitering abroad. Fourth, it was to be a day of intellectual stimulation, free from idle talk. Fifth, it was to be a day of spiritual delight or ecstasy. Sixth, it was to link the Jewish people to God, to His function as Creator, and to their emergence as a free people. In other words, it was to be a holy day; that is a day by means of which the Jew was to have every week a foretaste of the ideal world order, which it was his responsibility to help bring into existence.[1]

The *Shabbat*, at least in its 'secular' guise as 'the weekend', is so much a part of our existence that we take it for granted and fail to see what a revolutionary event it was. Though the world of the Ancient Near East saw the seventh days that ran through a lunar month as being special, often days of ill omen, they were still tied to the lunar calendar as such. But the Biblical *Shabbat*, by formally dividing time into the six days of work and the seventh of rest, actually imposed a totally artificial measurement of time upon the world. Because the lunar month is not exactly 28 days, *Shabbat* time breaks the power of the moon in determining time. In effect it imposes God's 'time' upon the world, and is another biblical way of asserting that God is creator and sovereign of the universe, the ruler of nature, and not subject to it. It is a quite revolutionary assertion in a world where the forces of nature were worshipped. Moreover its insistence on human freedom and the legitimacy of rest as an expression of that, caused bewilderment among other peoples with whom Jews came in contact long after it was an integrated part of Jewish life.

The *Shabbat* begins and ends with 'separations'. The blessings we recite on Friday evening over the wine and the day itself are known as the *kiddush*, 'sanctification'. However the translation 'sanctification' does not convey a number of the nuances of the Hebrew root *kadosh* with its original sense of separation, being set apart. At the end of God's work of creation, 'God blessed the seventh day and *vay'kadesh*, "made it special", because on it God ceased from all his work which God had created and made' (Gen. 2:3). By reciting a blessing specifically about the special nature of the *Shabbat* when we usher it in, we 'hallow' it, 'set it apart', proclaim its 'holiness', 'otherness', and thus in the same act 'make it holy'.

> Blessed are You, Eternal our God, Sovereign of the universe, whose commands make us holy, and who delights in us. Willingly and with love You give us Your holy *Shabbat* to inherit, for it recalls the act of creation. This is the first day of holy gatherings, a reminder of the exodus from Egypt. Because You chose us to be holy among all peoples, willingly and with love You gave us Your holy *Shabbat* to inherit. Blessed are You, Eternal, who makes the *Shabbat* holy.

The blessing notes that the *Shabbat* recalls two things, the creation of the world and the exodus from Egypt – a reflection of the two motives for the *Shabbat* given in the two versions of the Ten Commandments (Exod. 20 and Deut. 5).

By this proclamation of the holiness, otherness of the *Shabbat*, we actually create this special, different time and living space in the world. Depending on your own relationship to it, it may be perceived as an enormous freeing from the mundane drudgery of the world, a day of light, freedom and joy. But for others it is an awkward time, seemingly hemmed in by restrictions and inconveniences that one is better off without. A third position is to be selective in one's choice of what to observe. (Which reminds us of a famous riposte by Jesus on being accused of doing what was not lawful on the *Shabbat*: 'The Sabbath was made for man, not man for the Sabbath' (Mark 2:27). The same saying can be found in the Midrash in the name of Simeon ben Menasya (*Mekhilta Ki Tissa Shabbat* 1[2] which suggests that both were quoting a text that had long been around, and that debates about how *Shabbat* should be observed were as old as the concept itself.)

It requires a considerable act of will and imagination to make the kind of investment that brings the *Shabbat* to life, one that flies in the face of our conventional trivialisation of leisure. For the other side of *kiddush* as separation *from*, is *kiddush* as a setting apart *for*. The Jewish marriage ceremony, known as *kiddushin*, contains the statement by the groom (and a version by the bride in non-Orthodox ceremonies today), 'Behold you are *mekudeshet*, set apart, for me . . .' By reciting the *kiddush* we set the day apart for God, we 'align' ourselves with the One who is wholly 'other', and indeed can experience the dimensions of *Shabbat* described by Solomon Goldman above.

The *Shabbat* is 'special' only in relationship to the rest of the working week, and the world of work is in no way to be despised or put down, for it is every bit a part of God's creation. What the *Shabbat* does is to highlight two perspectives on that world that we need constantly to understand and 'remember' if we are to exist and function within it. First that the world is God's creation which sets the boundaries upon our ambitions, personal and collective, and our freedom to exploit the world. Much biblical material, legal, poetic and prophetic, concerns itself with our responsibility to the earth, including the need for its own seven-yearly *Shabbat*. In this sense the Bible already anticipates by three millennia our belated ecological concerns. But second, by reference to the exodus from Egypt, a boundary is set upon our right to exploit and 'enslave' one another. These two ideas are captured by the psychoanalyst Erich Fromm:

The goal of man is to live again in peace and harmony with his fellow men, with animals, with the soil. But this new harmony is different from that in paradise. It can now be obtained only if man develops fully in order to become truly human, by knowing the truth and doing justly, by developing his power of reason to a point which frees him from the bondage of man and of irrational passions . . . On the Sabbath, in the state of rest, man anticipates the state of human freedom that will be fulfilled eventually when the Messiah will come. The relationship of man and nature and of man and man is one of harmony, peace and non-interference. Where work is a symbol of conflict and disharmony, rest is an expression of dignity, peace and freedom . . . That is why the Sabbath commandment is at one time motivated by God's rest and at the other by the liberation from Egypt. Both mean the same and interpret each other; rest is freedom.[3]

The hypothetical or intellectual awareness of 'rest' or 'freedom' are not enough – it is the experience of them, week after week on the *Shabbat*, that, in theory at least, allows for the infiltration of such values into the world. But such experience of rest and freedom must be consciously created, preparations must be made, a pattern of the day set, because pattern, habit and familiarity provide the framework within which uniqueness and spontaneity can find their place. The *Shabbat* too needs its 'work'. The Exodus version of the Ten Commandments asks us to 'remember' the *Shabbat*, which led to the idea that throughout the week one collects special choice foods and saves them up for the *Shabbat* itself – thus the interaction between the two is constantly present. The 'separation' is not between absolutes, but is part of a continuum of expectation, bounded by ceremonials that open and close the special day.

If the rest of the week also has its spiritual significance this is brought out by the prayer-life of the Jewish community. In the limited space available we can only look here at the outline of one of the three daily services so as to give some indication of its inner dynamic. For more information about Jewish liturgy and prayer see the books cited at the end.

Over the Threshold

We are about to enter the central prayer of the Jewish liturgy. It has a number of names. First and foremost it is *ha-tefillah*, *the* prayer. The one to be recited three times a day, with subtle variations for the *Shabbat*, festivals and different seasons of the year. It is also called the *Amidah*, literally 'the standing [prayer]', because it is recited while standing before God. Indeed it is noteworthy that Jews generally stand or sit when they pray, and reserve the act of kneeling or prostration on the ground for one period of the year alone, the High Holy Days of the New Year and Day of Atonement, and even then we do it very seldom.

Its third name is one of those delightful absurdities or inconsistencies that reminds us that liturgies are human compositions. It is known as the *shemoneh esray*, the Hebrew for the number 'eighteen' (benedictions) though it actually contains *nineteen* separate blessings. Indeed it must have had only eighteen at one time, but one was divided or another added – and scholars still debate the matter. It is the Jewish equivalent to a baker's dozen.

What matters for our purpose is less the number of individual blessings than the way in which they are organised and structured. They consist of three introductory ones and three closing ones which remain relatively unchanged throughout the cycle of the year – though minor additions reflect the rainy season of nature and the penitential season of the Jewish New Year. It is the central thirteen benedictions that are subject to change, being entirely replaced on *Shabbat* with a single blessing, and with one or more variations for the different festivals. Whereas the thirteen daily blessings are a selection of petitions made by the Jewish people individually and collectively to God, that of the *Shabbat* is geared to the particular qualities of rest of that day. It is as if the *Shabbat* is not only a day of rest for us, but also a 'day off' for God, when our constant demands for attention and support have to cease. And if that seems a whimsical idea, it came very alive to me once when explained by my teacher Rav Sperber. Think of the self-control it must have taken, he said, for Jews in times of great distress and suffering, nevertheless to refrain on the *Shabbat* from pouring out their sorrows and prayers for help to God. Seen in that light, of the heroism of self-restraint, the change in the quality of that blessing on *Shabbat* takes on an unexpected poignancy.

I visited him once in Jerusalem and he spoke about the hard times in the East End of London before the war. He took a *Shobbos* (Ashkenazi pronunciation of *Shabbat*) afternoon stroll out to Whitechapel. He passed a Jew who asked him when *Shobbos* went out. Sperber told him and asked, since you work on *Shobbos*, why do you want to know? 'I have to work because Saturday is the day people get paid, and if I don't work today, my family has nothing to eat next week. But I don't smoke because it's *Shobbos*.' 'You keep *Shobbos*, I told him, and we wept together,' said Rav Sperber. And we wept again around the table.

The first of the thirteen petitions in the *Amidah* is in some ways a key to Jewish self-understanding.

> You grace human beings with knowledge and teach mortals discernment. Grace us with the knowledge, discernment and understanding that come from You. Blessed are You, Eternal, who graces us with knowledge.

The first request of the community of Israel is for knowledge. It is possible that this statement that knowledge has been given to humanity by God as an act of 'grace' is a rabbinic assertion that the knowledge gained by Adam (the word used in the blessing for 'human beings') on eating from the tree in the Garden of Eden (Gen. 2:17) should not be seen negatively, and certainly not as a 'fall' from divine grace. This knowledge, however we came by it, is ultimately a given, a fact of life, granted us by God, with which we are equipped to survive in the world. The word 'knowledge' here is the same as that used of the tree in the Garden – 'of the *knowledge* of good and evil'. However this phrase in biblical terminology seems to signify 'all things' and not just a moral distinction between good and bad. The same word is used of 'sexual knowledge' between Adam and Eve when she first conceives. It is therefore a knowledge that is intuitive and grows through intimacy and relationships with others. The word 'discernment' comes from a word meaning 'between' and suggests learning how to discriminate. It implies refining our ability to distinguish and clarify in the intellectual and moral sphere. The third term, 'understanding', seems to mean intellectual ability, though it also contains the sense of appropriate and wise conduct that leads to success, material and spiritual, in the world.

In the blessings that follow, this understanding leads us to recognise our distance from God and the need continually to 'repent/return' and ask forgiveness and pardon from God. These lead in turn to requests for the welfare of the individual and the community and a series of petitions for the restoration of the Jewish people to its land, with all the messianic overtones.

Let us return to the introductory and closing blessings which help establish the context common to all the different daily, *Shabbat* and festival services.

> Blessed are You, Eternal our God and God of our ancestors, God of Abraham, God of Isaac and God of Jacob, the great, the mighty and the awesome God, God beyond, generous in love and kindness, and possessing all; who remembers the faithful love of our ancestors and therefore in love brings rescue to the generations, for such is His being. The sovereign who helps and saves and shields. Blessed are You, Eternal, the shield of Abraham.

(We have seen in chapter 4 how this paragraph has been amended in some recent liturgies to include the matriarchs alongside the patriarchs.)

> You, O Eternal, are the endless power that renews life beyond death; You are the greatness that saves. You care for the living with love. You renew life beyond death with unending mercy. You support the falling, and heal the sick. You free prisoners, and keep faith with those who sleep in

the dust. Who can perform such mighty deeds, and who can compare with You, a Sovereign who brings death and life, and renews salvation. You are faithful to renew life beyond death. Blessed are You, Eternal, who renews life beyond death [Literally: who brings the dead to life].

You are holy and Your name is holy and the holy ones praise You day by day. Blessed are You, Eternal, the holy God.

The first blessing is almost an anthology of terms used for God in the Hebrew Bible. God, who is also the God of our ancestors, is 'the great, the mighty and the awesome God' (Deut. 10:17). 'God beyond', is an attempt to retranslate the more familiar 'most high God' (*El Elyon*) without the mythological implication that God is sitting somewhere up in the sky. The name itself, as we noted in chapter 1, was introduced by Melchizedek, the king of Salem (Jerusalem) when he blessed Abraham (Gen. 14:20) and from his phrase 'Who has delivered (*migen*) your (Abraham's) enemies into your hand' comes the closing phrase of the blessing, 'shield (*magen*) of Abraham'.

The entire blessing seems to be a way of drawing together these names, and thus qualities and attributes, of God known to Israelite and Jewish tradition – thus asserting that they all represent aspects of the same God, and evoking the memory of those qualities for this moment of encounter.

The second blessing concentrates more specifically on God as the master of life and death, and particularly with reference to the resurrection of the dead. If the first blessing concentrated on the historical relationship between Israel and God, the second one asserts the daily sustenance and nurture we receive, throughout and even beyond life. But the emphasis on the resurrection of the dead is also a reflection of an old inner Jewish religious controversy about physical resurrection that eventually became part of the conflict between the Sadducees, inheritors of the old Priestly traditions, and the Pharisees, creators of what was to become normative rabbinic Judaism. This is another reminder that liturgies always have a social and political purpose as well as their overt spiritual content.

Seven are the days of the week

The third blessing is closely related to the sixth chapter in the Book of Isaiah in which the prophet has a vision of God's throne in the Temple and sees the *serafim*, fiery angelic beings, standing beside God and singing God's praises with the words, 'Holy, holy, holy is *adonai tzevaot* (the Lord of hosts), the whole earth is full of His glory' (Isa. 6:3). This particular blessing is amplified considerably in different daily and festival services so as to include the Isaiah passage and other related ones; thus it forces us to move beyond our own human dimensions and needs into a recognition of that transcendent reality beyond our grasp as we seek to encounter God. The God we can approach as did our ancestors, who is present to respond to our human needs, is also utterly outside our limited perception and control, a God who rules the cosmic forces of nature and myriads of unknowable worlds and creatures. So we must live with this twofold reality. In recognition of this, there is a tradition that as we recite the words 'holy, holy, holy', we go up on tiptoe, as if trying to reach those same divine heights where the angels are singing God's praises.

Let us hold in our minds for a moment the nature of these three blessings, known respectively as *avot* (ancestors), *gevurot* (powers – of God) and *kedushot* (holiness), and turn to the concluding three.

Eternal our God, accept Your people Israel and their prayers. Restore the service to Your holy house and in love and favour receive the fire-offerings of Israel and their prayer; and may the service of Israel Your people be always acceptable to You. Let our eyes see Your return to Zion in mercy. Blessed are You Eternal, restoring Your divine presence to Zion.

We declare with gratitude that You are our God and the God of our ancestors forever. You are our rock, the rock of our life and the shield that saves us. In every generation we thank You and recount Your praise for our lives held in Your hand, for our souls that are in Your care, and for the signs of Your presence that are with us every day. At every moment, at evening, morning and noon, we experience

151

Your wonders and Your goodness. You are goodness itself, for Your mercy has no end. You are mercy itself, for Your love has no limit. Forever have we put our hope in You.

And for all these things may Your name, our Sovereign, be blessed, exalted and honoured forever and ever. May every living being thank You; may they praise and bless Your great name in truth for You are the God who saves and helps us. Blessed are You Eternal, known as goodness, whom it is right to praise.

Set true peace upon Your people Israel forever. For You are the Sovereign, the possessor of all peace, and in Your eyes it is good to bless Your people Israel at every time and in every hour with Your peace. Blessed are You Eternal, blessing Your people Israel with peace.

Again a clear pattern emerges from this sequence. The first blessing, *retzeh*, 'be pleased', is a way of saying: 'Please accept all the petitions that we have just laid before You.' More specifically it echoes the pleading of a people in exile from their homeland asking God to return and restore the sacrificial worship in the Temple.

In gratitude for past favours, and obviously in hopeful anticipation of new ones to come, the second of these closing blessings, *modim* (we 'thank', or 'rehearse' in the sense of making a public statement), is a public acknowledgment of God's kindness through thanksgiving and praise. It is a powerful assertion of the miraculous nature of life itself and of the bread-and-butter realities of everyday existence.

The third blessing is a kind of farewell greeting, slightly longer in the morning version than the evening version quoted here. In asking for 'peace' it is effectively a liturgical equivalent to the standard Hebrew and indeed Arabic greeting, 'peace be upon you', *shalom aleikhem*. It is called *shalom rav* (great peace) in the shorter version or *sim shalom* (grant peace) in the longer one.

What is the image or assumption upon which all these six opening and closing blessings are built? It appears to be the entrance of a group of petitioners into the court of a king. As they enter they present their credentials – 'we are the children of

Abraham, Isaac and Jacob with whom You have had a special relationship.' The king is then praised for his many qualities, particularly the fact that he holds the power of life and death over the petitioners. But, lest they appear to be too greedy or opportunistic, they acknowledge that the king is 'holy', greater than any praise that they might conceivably offer, and indeed that they are utterly dependent upon his own generosity over which they can have no real influence. Whatever the effect of the fulfilment of such a 'court protocol' may have upon the 'king', it is a constant reminder to the petitioners of the reality of their own status in the court.

On departing, bowing out backwards from the presence, they request that their petitions be heard favourably, thank the king in anticipation of his customary generous response and leave with a greeting of peace.

Seen in this light, not only is the structure clear, but also the entire psychological and theological underpinning of the prayer. We appear as utterly dependent petitioners before our master who holds the power of life and death in his hands. It is not an easy image to accept in what is essentially a democratic age for us in the West. The word 'king', 'sovereign', *melekh*, that is so central to this entire liturgy is highly problematic for someone living in Britain with an almost powerless constitutional monarch. The image fits better the word 'dictator', but that carries too many images of cruelty and arbitrariness. It is not easy to relate to such prayers if we actually think them through, though for the most part we take them for granted and invest them with our own meaning, particularly as they are usually recited in Hebrew which gives a degree of detachment, not to say mystery, to them.

The point that I really want to make, however, is of a different order. Let us remind ourselves of the structure of this entire prayer:

avot (ancestors)
gevurot (powers)
kedushot (holiness)
Petitions (thirteen blessings)
retzeh (be pleased)

153

modim (thank You)
shalom (peace)

At the risk of appearing somewhat irreverent, I would like to juxtapose this perhaps rather unfamiliar structure with one that will be more familiar from other worlds.

avot (ancestors)	Apologies
gevurot (powers)	Minutes
kedushot (holiness)	Matters arising
Petitions (13 blessings)	Agenda
retzeh (be pleased)	AOB
modim (thank You)	DONM
shalom (peace)	Vote of Thanks

Those with any experience of bureaucracy will recognise this familiar structure of a committee meeting. There is a certain irony about this from a Jewish perspective, in that Jews are convinced that most of Jewish life is bound up with committee meetings – certainly synagogue life is. So much so that people seem to spend more time on committees about, for example, the ritual life of the community than they actually spend in the synagogue itself praying.

But what is the point of making this comparison? Simply that in both instances we are invited through a particular structure to enter a different world, one in which a different logic, or at least set of rules, applies. One is the world of the divine court and the presence of God, the other is that of 'points of order' and votes – nevertheless, they are both self-contained worlds into which we must be ushered by crossing a threshold. Whether it be the ritual blessings we offer God, or the ritual reading of the minutes, these 'rites of passage' between this world and the other, are absolutely essential in preparing us for this new reality which requires a mood and behaviour of its own – and no less for leading us back out into 'real life' afterwards when the prayers or the committee meetings are over.

In a way we have already jumped into the heart of things without paying due attention to some thresholds that have already been crossed. We are standing in the palace of the king – at least in the prayerbook. Though as an old joke reminds us the world of prayer and the world of committees are not that far removed. A rabbi once suggested to his congregation that since they spent so much time discussing their business in the synagogue, perhaps they could set aside an equal amount of time for God during their office hours.

But how did we enter the palace? Again it is helpful to spend a little time looking at the structure of the service within which the *Amidah* is located.

Jews, on the whole, are either unconscious of these structures, because they are so much a part of their prayer life that they feel no need to pay attention to them – or unaware of them because they are so remote from a life of regular prayer. To draw attention to them is already a recognition that I come to them as an outsider seeking entrance. There is a delightful Midrash that compares the great prophetic visions of Isaiah and Ezekiel. The first chapter of Ezekiel is an intensely complex and even confusing description of his mystic vision of vast four-headed creatures on wheels and ultimately of the 'appearance of the likeness of the Presence of God'. On the other hand Isaiah, in chapter 6, gets straight to the heart of things and claims to have seen God seated on his throne with the fiery *serafim* about him. The rabbis asked: 'What is this like? Like a man from the country and a man from the town who come to visit the palace of the king. The man from the country is utterly overwhelmed by the architecture; the man from the town meets the king and hears the message. Nevertheless as visitors from the country we must look a little more closely at the architecture and furnishings.'

We entered the service, if it was in the morning, with two sections of prayers, the 'morning blessings' and the 'chapters of song'. The first, as the name suggests, were originally blessings to be recited on getting up in the morning, some coinciding with the morning ablutions, others, because of their transfer from the home to the synagogue, becoming understood more metaphorically. The blessing of God who 'straightens those who are bowed' must originally have been intended for the moment one stretches in bed. 'Who makes firm the steps of human beings' would have accompanied the first steps of the day. But move them on to a later period in the morning and they take on a symbolic meaning instead. They prepare us for the day, including a blessing on studying Torah, here not just the Pentateuch but all aspects of Jewish religious teaching and thought, since the assumption is that some time should be set aside for study every day.

In that same section, since we have recited the blessing, there are passages from the Bible and later rabbinic writings to study, but also a range of what were originally private prayers and meditations of the rabbis, through which they would indeed prepare themselves for the formal prayers that would follow. Similarly the 'chapters of song', including Psalms and other biblical passages in praise of God, were to set the mood of joyful worship before the service proper began. What has happened in time is that these individual passages which were originally personal aids for preparation, gained a wider popularity and eventually were printed in the prayer books. They thus became transformed into fixed parts of the liturgy which has to be 'got through' before coming to the central prayers. Part of the controversy between Orthodox and non-Orthodox Jews has been in the willingness of the latter to pare these down considerably or at least be selective in which ones were still to be recited.

Perhaps the impression these sections make is best summed up by the remarks of the Jewish novelist Israel Zangwill who chronicled the life of the immigrant Jewish communities in London at the turn of the century.

They prayed metaphysics, acrostics, angelology, Kabbalah [Jewish mysticism], history, exegesis, talmudical controversies, menus, recipes, priestly prescriptions, the canonical books, psalms, love-poems . . . If they did not always know what they were saying, they always meant it.

But all of these sections are merely a preparation for the proper entry into the domain of the King. We have, as it were, straightened our tie, brushed our shoes and rehearsed our mood

so as to be appropriately prepared for the encounter to come –
all of this in the palace forecourt. We now make our formal
entrance into the antechamber of the court. And a herald
announces our coming. The leader of the prayers chants the
command to the congregation:

> Bless (or praise) the Eternal who is blessed (literally, 'in a
> state of blessing' or 'praise').

This is the call to prayer with which the formal service begins,
and for it to be recited at all a quorum of worshipers must be
present – classically a *minyan*, a group of ten adult males, though
non-Orthodox groups either dispense with this necessity
altogether or include women to make up the number. Essentially
what is being asserted here is that for the service proper to take
place, a real 'congregation' must be present, which places great
responsibility on all members of the community to be present,
especially when numbers are few. The congregation, who have
stood for this moment and bowed, respond while bowing again:

> Blessed (praised) is the Eternal who is to be blessed forever
> and ever.

We leave the forecourt and move chamber by chamber inwards
towards our appointed meeting with the King. The various
antechambers are represented by separate blessings rather than
physical rooms, and they lead from wide halls, filled with light,
open to the sky and the outside world, to narrower chambers,
known only to a select few, where the King is waiting.

The first 'antechamber' is a blessing which varies between the
morning and evening, but in both cases speaks of God's power
over the whole of creation. The morning one follows the usual
opening formula, 'Blessed are You, Eternal our God, Sovereign
of the world' with the words, 'who forms light and creates
darkness, makes peace and creates all.' We have met this
formulation in our first chapter on the 'unity' of God. This is a
rabbinic amendment of the text of Isaiah 45:7. The original
phrase concluded 'who makes peace and creates evil'. In the

rabbinic judgment, though such a description of God was legitimate for the prophet and as an intellectual proposition, in a prayer it was too problematic, so the more general phrase 'and creates all' was substituted. Which is a further reminder that the rabbis were not unwilling to amend the texts of their sacred tradition.

In this new context it opens a prayer that, appropriately for the morning, speaks of the light God brings to the world every day. 'How great are Your works, O Eternal; You made them all with wisdom; the earth is full of Your creatures.' Its companion in the evening service similarly talks of God bringing on the evening twilight, separating the darkness from the light and creating and maintaining the regular rhythm of day and night. They are both in effect celebrations of God's creation which is renewed every day – and at the same time great universalistic hymns to the whole of creation, human and animal, cosmic (in its wonder at the sun, moon and stars in God's heaven), and mystic (in its awareness of angelic hosts that likewise perform the will of their creator – though the more rationalistic tendencies of the non-Orthodox movements have rather emptied the latter from the skies). In short in this first antechamber we are still in the open world, celebrating its richness and variety, its regularity and security, the outer court of God's domain. This also establishes the universalistic framework within which our particular Jewish drama is acted out. Thus our prayers constantly remind us of the wider context and ultimate significance of our Jewish task – for the sake not of ourselves alone but for the wider world.

At the end of this chamber is a door marked 'Israel', just as there are separate doorways for other nations and faiths. Through this door we enter the second chamber, the one reserved for us. Again there are variations between the morning and evening, but the message is essentially the same: 'With great love have You loved us, O Eternal our God, with great and overflowing tenderness have You taken pity on us.' Because of that great love in the past, we ask 'our Father, our Sovereign' to 'let our eyes see the light of Your teaching and our hearts embrace Your commands. Give us integrity to love You and fear You. So shall we never lose our self-respect, nor be put to shame, for You are the power that works to save us.'

The thought of the prayer is subtle. Anyone can 'fear' God – the word for fear carrying the sense of 'awe' and 'wonder' as well as real 'dread'. But this is a fear of God that we wish to be 'taught' – it is to be an educated 'fear', one completely intertwined with 'love', an awe and wonder that grow with knowledge and indeed, study, and experience and religious deeds. It is a fear that is to be learned and refined because of God's own participation in the process – in part by the very act of reciting these prayers in the near presence of God.

The end of the prayer is influenced by what follows it, and was presumably composed for precisely this purpose.

> You chose us from all peoples and tongues, and in love drew us near to Your own greatness – to honour You, to declare Your unity and to love You. Blessed are You Eternal, choosing Your people Israel in love.

The heart of this is essentially the chosenness of Israel – those who have access to this inner chamber. But the chosenness is for a purpose – to witness to the special nature of God, to proclaim the divine unity, and above all to maintain our love for God against all the tribulations and sufferings of the millennia. And this in response to a command as old as the Hebrew Bible, which forms the focal point of Israel's witnessing, and which is recited as the next formal part of the service. It is the *Shema*, 'Hear O Israel . . .'

> Hear O Israel, the Eternal is our God, the Eternal is One. Love the Eternal your God with all your heart and all your soul and all your might. (Deut. 6:4–5)

We have loved our God through the millennia, and we have asked for the strength and understanding to make the love continue. The door at the end of this chamber now opens into the corridor that leads to the 'throneroom'.

Oddly enough, at this point in the service we are not standing in anticipation, but sitting. There appear to be good reasons for this – good in the sense of the politics of religion. Various battles were fought in the formative period of rabbinic Judaism which was also the time of the emergence of Christianity and other sectarian groups. One issue over which they fought was what actually constituted the 'Torah', the revealed teaching of God. At one time the regular Jewish service contained the public reading of the Ten Commandments at which point everyone stood up – as indeed they still do when it happens to be read as part of the weekly cycle of readings from the Torah scroll on *Shabbat* morning and during the Festival of *Shavuot*, Pentecost. This daily pattern was stopped when sectarians claimed that the Ten Commandments were the essence of the Torah, hence the respect they were shown. In the rabbinic view the entire Torah was of equal significance and no 'essence' should be isolated and given special public recognition. A similar problem emerged with the recital of the *Shema*, which is indeed often perceived as the 'affirmation' of Judaism, the nearest we get to a dogma. So its degree of prominence was also carefully regulated. In traditional circles it is recited while sitting, but in Liberal and Reform circles, precisely because of its significance, some communities stand.

As is often the case in such matters the rabbis found a good story to justify the maintenance of the sitting position. In Genesis (chapter 18) God visits Abraham in the guise of three men, to proclaim the promise of the future birth to Sarah of a child. But why did God choose this particular time to visit? The rabbis were quick to notice that the previous chapter has described how Abraham, in order to enter into the covenant, has circumcised himself and all the males in his household. So what would God have done on such an occasion? Naturally God would have fulfilled the *mitzvah*, the 'commandment' or 'duty' of *bikkur holim*, 'visiting the sick', and came to wish Abraham a speedy recovery.

When Abraham tried to rise off his bed to greet his guest, God insisted that he remain seated in his presence. Just as Abraham had shown respect and deference to God in performing the act of circumcision, so God too would show such respect and in memory of this allow Abraham's descendants to remain seated when reciting the *Shema*.

I once got into a debate about this matter. It was a new Liberal congregation in the UK, and as is often the case the people who had come together to found it had vastly different Jewish backgrounds. Many came from an Orthodox, or more precisely lapsed Orthodox, background, Orthodoxy being the 'established church' of Anglo-Jewry, while others came from Reform or Liberal Synagogues. Anyway, when the ritual committee got down to discussing the performance of the services a problem arose. Those with an Orthodox tradition wished to remain seated during the recital of the *Shema*. Those with a Liberal or Reform background had been accustomed to standing for what they considered a central and important prayer. In the course of the discussion I told them something of the history of this debate, quoted the story about Abraham and we agreed to remain seated while the *Shema* was said – all except one elderly woman, who introduced herself as someone who was a long-standing member of a Liberal Synagogue. Quite distinctly and with remarkable dignity she pointed out that since she personally had not been circumcised she saw no reason why she should not continue to stand. To the best of my knowledge she does so till today.

To return to more sober matters, with the completion of the recital of the *Shema*, and its two accompanying biblical passages (Deut. 11:13–21 and Num. 15:37–41) we have passed into the final corridor before the entrance to the inner chamber. This is also represented by a blessing. (In the evening service an additional blessing asking that we have a safe night is introduced here in the Ashkenazi tradition, even though it is clearly intrusive here and is located elsewhere in the Sephardi rite.) This blessing is almost a credal statement: 'It is true . . . that the God of the universe is our God – whose Sovereignty is everlasting, whose word is reliable.' It goes on to recite God's past saving acts for Israel, particularly at the crossing of the Sea of Reeds after the exodus from Egypt, where Israel first expressed their faith and trust in God (Exod. 14:31). It concludes:

Rock of Israel, rise up to the aid of Israel, and redeem, as You have promised, Judah and Israel. Our redeemer is the

> Eternal God of creation, the Holy One of Israel. Blessed
> are You Eternal, who has redeemed Israel.

It is as if this corridor has pictures on the walls of those past
moments of God's intervention in our history so as to give us
some kind of reassurance and courage as we prepare to meet the
'King'.

There is to be no interruption between the stillness that follows
the closing words of this blessing and the opening of the *Amidah*.
They are almost one liturgical event, for here at the heart of the
palace, between the redeemed children and the Father, between
the rescued people and the God who saved them, there is now
an ultimate privacy.

Just as there is a final inner journey to be taken within the
Amidah itself, as the petitioners present their requests before the
King, so there has been a similar journey to the threshold, and
indeed we have crossed through many rooms to reach this inner
Presence. Central to that first journey through the courts of the
palace is the dramatic theme of the chosenness of Israel.

As Jewish apologists have had to explain throughout the
centuries it is not a chosenness for power or to rule – rather it is
for a spiritual power and the task of being a model for others. In
fact the vehemence with which Jews have been attacked as the
'chosen people', a term that does not really translate back into a
Hebrew concept at all, must be acknowledged as a problem more
for those who use it in a polemic manner against the Jewish
people than it is a concern of the Jews themselves. The anger
about Israel's particularism is expressed especially by
Christianity and to a far lesser extent by Islam. Both are in some
sense, daughter religions of Judaism, the former having seen itself
as the authentic successor. Both claim to be 'universalistic', but it
could be argued that they display instead an enlarged form of
'particularism' insofar as their doctrines hardly allow for any
access to God or heaven save through them – though in this
respect Islam's respect for the previous prophetic revelations of
Judaism and Christianity is more generous in its relationship to
these 'people of the book'. Judaism, on the contrary, has a
curious sort of élitist universalism – anyone can get to heaven

through their own faith provided they follow seven basic moral laws ('the seven commandments given to the sons of Noah'). It is only Jews who have a harder task because more is expected of them (the fulfilment of 613 commandments to be exact).

Undoubtedly a major part of the resentment has always lain in the refusal of the Jews to accept these daughter religions in their own terms and surrender their autonomy to them, which must imply that these religions are unable to offer Jews anything better than what we have already – which must be particularly galling to faiths imbued with missionising zeal.

However what concerns us here is that Judaism not only acknowledges the reality of the tension between universal and particular concerns within itself, it actually underlines it, spells it out, so to speak, and thus refines and clarifies it, through its liturgical forms. If God is the creator of the entire universe, as the above blessings affirm every day, then there must be a role for all peoples and nations and religions, no more so and no less so than for us. If we have not expressly stated that so far in our inward journey, then we will have cause to do so on the journey back out from this inner sanctum as we return to the outer world.

That return already begins with the recital of the closing words of a short meditation that is appended to the *Amidah*. As we recite, 'May [God] who makes peace in the highest bring this peace upon us and upon all Israel', we physically step back bowing from side to side – as we depart with the final gestures of respect from the presence of the King.

There is still a detour on our journey. Just as we have put our requests before God, so a word comes back to us in return. On *Shabbat*, Monday and Thursday, we take the scroll of the Torah out of the ark and read sections of it in a cycle that allows us to complete the Pentateuch during the course of the year, in a symbolic re-enactment of the revelation at Mt Sinai. It is the response of the King to our petitions, even if the particular passage only addresses our specific needs indirectly.

Other additional passages are also included in the traditional liturgy, but the essential next section is a pair of paragraphs that are jointly known as the *Alenu* prayer, the one that creates a bridge back to the outer world – or to retain our original metaphor conducts us back through another set of rooms to the outer doors of the palace.

The *Alenu* beautifully dramatises the particularistic – universalistic tension, so much so that it was the target of major surgery in the last century by the various Reform Jewish movements. The problem lies in the very strong particularistic statement in the beginning of the first paragraph of which there are a number of traditional versions, some stronger than others:

> It is our task to praise the Master of all, to acknowledge the greatness of the Former of creation, who has not made us like the nations of the earth and not placed us like the families of the world, who has not made our portion like theirs nor our fate like that of their multitudes. [Some traditional texts add here, 'For they bow down to vanity and emptiness and pray to a god that cannot save' – based on Isaiah 30:7; 45:20.] But we bow, worship and give thanks before the Sovereign above all worldly powers, the blessed Holy One, who stretches out the heavens and makes the earth firm, whose glorious dwelling is in the heaven above and the presence of whose strength is in the greatest heights. This is our God, no other exists; truly our Sovereign, besides whom there is nothing. As it is written in the Torah, 'Know and take it to heart that the Eternal is God in the heavens above and on the earth beneath, no other exists.'

In the Middle Ages the accusation was made that the references to others praying to 'vanity and emptiness' were anti-Christian statements, though they may have been composed in Babylon where there was no Christian background. In the eighteenth century in Prussia they were forcibly expunged from the liturgy by the authorities and the prayer had to be read aloud so that their absence could be confirmed. It may be that these memories influenced the discomfort of the Reformers in nineteenth-century Germany who removed them for what they considered more universalistic reasons.

The prayer is a powerful statement of Israel's perceived task of witnessing to God and in the context of the service is a sort of final affirmation of that special relationship as the worshippers move through another of the innermost chambers on their way back to the outer world. But it does not stand alone and the second paragraph of the prayer, the outer chamber, exactly complements it in tone and power and in universal sweep.

> Therefore, Eternal our God, we put our hope in You. Soon let us witness the glory of Your power when idols will be swept away from the earth and false gods will at last be cut off;[4] when the world will be set right by the rule of God and all human beings will speak out in Your name; when You turn to Yourself all the wicked of the earth. Then all the inhabitants of the world shall meet in understanding and know that to You alone each knee shall bend and all shall pledge themselves to You in every tongue. Before You, Eternal our God, they shall bow down and be humble, honouring the glory of Your name. All shall accept the yoke of building Your kingdom and You will rule over them soon forever and ever, for the kingdom is Yours and forever You will reign in glory, as it is written in Your Torah, 'It is the Eternal who shall rule forever and ever' (Exod. 15:18). And so it is prophesied, 'On that day the Eternal shall be One and known as One' (Zech. 14:9).

What seems important with this prayer in its entirety is the assertion of both values, particularism and universalism alike. Unless I am secure in my own identity, unless I know with clarity and confidence who I am, I cannot accept or trust the identity of 'the other'. A one-sided particularism that has no respect for others is no less dangerous than a vague universalism that has no inner self-respect. What the prayer does yet again is dramatise a polarisation within which the Jewish people exists, and calls us to acknowledge both our Jewish task and our common humanity.

We have crossed the spiritual threshold back out of the service, out of the palace of the King, into the outside world. Some closing prayers and songs remain to mark the formal ending of the service. But since we began in the centre and have worked our way to the periphery, perhaps it is worth adding one more detail about the physical aspects of the journey.

To enter the service we first had to enter the building in which it takes place. This is so self-evident that we take it for granted. Yet the physical acts of entering, removing and hanging up our outer clothes that belong to the outside world, and then leaving the lobby to come into the chamber where the service is actually held, are no less a part of the spiritual preparation. Crossing the physical threshold already prepares us for the special nature of the place we are visiting, whether it is an awesome cathedral or a tiny room somewhere with a cupboard for the Scroll of the Torah, a lamp and a few chairs. In this respect the Muslim practice of removing the shoes is an important physical adjunct to preparing to stand before God. Perhaps the Jewish equivalent is the donning of the *tallit*, the prayer shawl, that is worn in the morning services by men and boys after their thirteenth birthday, and increasingly now by women as well in the non-Orthodox communities. For donning the *tallit* is also a way of creating a kind of private space, a physical reminder of the nature of the journey that is about to be undertaken. And the removing of the *tallit* at the end, the clumsy attempt to fold it while shaking hands with fellow congregants, and the general release of tension into movement and activity, are all potent signals that the journey is completed and we are back once more in the outer courtyard with our family and friends. The physical thresholds, no less than the spiritual ones, have also to be crossed and marked. Perhaps some wine and bread to be blessed await us, or a cup of tea and cake. Society is rediscovered after the intense privacy of the journey in the company of others. And outside the world awaits.

Further Reading

On Shabbat

Abraham Joshua Heschel, *The Earth is the Lord's*, and *The Sabbath* (Cleveland and New York, Meridian Books, The World Publishing Company; Philadelphia, The Jewish Publication Society of America, 1963). The second part of this volume is the classic study of the meaning and experience of the traditional *Shabbat*.

On Jewish Prayer

Max Arzt, *Justice and Mercy: Commentary on the Liturgy of the New Year and the Day of Atonement* (New York, Holt, Rinehart and Winston, 1963): classic collection of information and interpretations of the major components of the traditional liturgy of the High Holy Days.

Ismar Elbogen, *Jewish Liturgy: A Comprehensive History*, translated by Raymond P. Scheindlin (based on the original 1913 German edition and the 1972 Hebrew edition edited by Joseph Heinemann *et al.* (Philadelphia and Jerusalem, Jewish Publication Society; New York and Jerusalem, The Jewish Theological Seminary of America, 1993): the classic scholarly history of Jewish liturgy.

Irving Greenberg, *The Jewish Way: Living the Holydays* (New York, Summit Books, 1988): valuable introduction to Judaism through exploring the festivals from the standpoint of a leading contemporary Orthodox rabbi.

Lawrence A. Hoffman, *Beyond the Text: A Holistic Approach to Liturgy* (Bloomington and Indianapolis, Indiana University Press, 1987).

Lawrence A. Hoffman, *The Art of Public Prayer: Not for Clergy Only* (Washington DC, The Pastoral Press, 1988): two fascinating attempts to examine Jewish (and Christian) liturgy in the context of the life of the community.

Lawrence A. Hoffman (ed.), *My People's Prayer Book: Traditional Prayers, Modern Commentaries*, vol. 1, *The Sh'ma and Its Blessings* (Jewish Lights Publishing, 1997): the first in what promises to be an exciting series of detailed commentaries on the Jewish liturgy by leading scholars of all Jewish 'denominations'.

A. Z. Idelsohn, *Jewish Liturgy and Its Development* (New York, Schocken, 1967): scientific compilation of materials on the history and contents of Jewish liturgy.

B. S. Jacobson, *Meditations on the Siddur* (Tel Aviv, Sinai Publishing, 1966), and *The Weekday Suddur* (Tel Aviv, Sinai Publishing, 1973): two superb compilations of traditional Jewish commentaries on the structure and content of the Jewish Sabbath and Weekday prayerbook.

Abraham Millgram, *Jewish Worship* (Philadelphia, Jewish Publication Society of America, 1971): valuable lay guide to all aspects of Jewish worship and liturgy.

Elie Munk, *The World of Prayer*, 2 vols. (New York, Philipp Feldheim, 1963): meditative commentary on the daily and festival liturgies.

Jakob J. Petuchowski, *Prayerbook Reform in Europe: The Liturgy of European Liberal and Reform Judaism* (New York, World Union for Progressive Judaism, 1968), and *Theology and Poetry: Studies in the Mediaeval Piyyut* (London, The Littman Library of Jewish Civilization, 1978). The former is the classic scholarly appraisal of the liturgical innovations of the European non-Orthodox movements, and the latter a fascinating insight into the Jewish liturgical creativity of the Middle Ages.

Some Current Jewish Prayerbooks

Liberal and Progressive (UK)
Siddur Lev Chadash: Services and Prayers for Weekdays and Sabbaths, Festivals and Various Occasions (London, Union of Liberal and Progressive Synagogues, 1995).

Seven are the days of the week

Orthodox (UK)

The Authorised Daily Prayer Book of the United Hebrew Congregations of the Commonwealth (original translation by the Rev. S. Singer – 'Singer's Prayerbook'), enlarged Centenary Edition, 1992).

Reform (UK)

Forms of Prayer for Jewish Worship, vol. 1, *Daily, Sabbath and Occasional Prayers* (7th edn, 1977); vol. 3, *Prayers for the High Holydays* (8th edn, 1985); vol. 2, *Prayers for the Pilgrim Festivals* (2nd rev. edn, 1995) (London, The Reform Synagogues of Great Britain).

Conservative (USA)

Jules Harlow (ed.), *Siddur Sim Shalom: A Prayerbook for Shabbat, Festivals and Weekdays* (New York, The Rabbinical Assembly and The United Synagogue of America, 1985).

Jules Harlow (ed.), *Mahzor for Rosh Hashanah and Yom Kippur: A Prayer Book for the Days of Awe* (New York, The Rabbinical Assembly, 1972).

Orthodox (USA)

Siddur Kol Ya'akov: The Complete ArtScroll Siddur: A New Translation and Anthological Commentary, Rabbi Nossan Scherman (New York, Mesorah Publications, 1984).

Reconstructionist (USA)

Kol Haneshamah: Shabbat Vehagim (Wyncote, The Reconstructionist Press, 1994).

Reform (USA)

Gates of Prayer for Shabbath and Weekdays: Gender Sensitive Edition (New York, Central Conference of American Rabbis, 1995).

Gates of Repentence: The New Union Prayerbook, vol. 2 (New York, Central Conference of American Rabbis, 1978).

Eight are the days to the covenant of circumcision
Aspects of Jewish ritual life

The physical act of circumcision is periodically the subject of debate, and evokes powerful emotions. The Hebrew term for circumcision is *milah*, while the ceremony is called *b'rit milah*, 'the covenant of circumcision', the term *b'rit* (or *bris* in Ashkenazi circles) sometimes standing alone in popular parlance. Which actually makes the point that the purpose of the circumcision is to bring the child symbolically into the covenant with God, the *b'rit*, entered into by Abraham and then the Jewish people at Sinai.

Presumably when Abraham performed it for the first time on himself (aged ninety-nine according to the Bible – Gen. 17:24) and on Ishmael his son (aged thirteen) it was already a familiar ritual in his world. The Jewish practice that was to become the normal time for the act was instituted with Isaac who was circumcised at eight days (Gen. 17:10–14; 21:4). And thus it has been for generations of Jewish males since that time.

It is an extraordinary act that can be perceived as a relatively painless, minor surgical operation or as a massive physical assault on the defenseless child. It does carry certain medical advantages, with less risk of later infection and penile cancer, so that at times it has become a routine surgical procedure for non-Jews as well, famously the British royal family. However fashions change and the swing today is against unnecessary surgical intervention. I remember hearing a Jewish psychotherapist who had practised 'rebirthing' telling us that he had indeed re-experienced the pain of his circumcision, but it is always hard to evaluate the significance of such an adult 'memory'. The truth is that no one knows what the impact is on the child. Empirical observation of the procedure is reassuring. There is a cry at the moment of the act, though this is probably caused by separating the foreskin prior to any actual cutting. But within seconds of the event, with a drop of wine on his tongue, the child falls contentedly asleep.

There are arguments that the nerve endings are not sufficiently developed for there to be real pain. But the number of Jewish jokes that surround the act, the umpteen attempts to analyse Jewish male characteristics in the light of this assault on the penis (a symbolic castration?), and the myths that surround Jewish male sexuality, all point to the edgy discomfort, among Jews and non-Jews, evoked by this physical act. Indeed, if the wish of God was to distinguish a certain people by this action, the ploy has worked. (Such breathtaking self-confidence these Jews have – they are even prepared to chop off the end of the single most prominent male physical attribute!) Though Muslims are also circumcised it is nevertheless seen as a highly specific characteristic of the Jews. And it has been an identifying sign that has sometimes cost Jewish males their lives. In the Hellenistic period Jewish males even had surgical operations to 'restore' the foreskin so that they could perform naked in athletic games without feeling out of place among their Gentile competitors.

All of which overshadows the religious significance given to this ceremony. It is inevitably overlaid with anxiety about the physical act that is taking place, yet is also filled with a deep awareness of bringing the child into an ancient chain of tradition, of handing on a heritage to the coming generation. For the father it is an act of bonding with his son, of sharing a very basic physical characteristic, as well as linking with generations past. Even for Jews with little spiritual attachment to their tradition, the sheer irrationality of the act and its archetypal power, make them wish to perform it – or react strongly against it. It is an initiation rite and as such speaks to a very deep part of our psyche.

At the ceremony the father says:

> Here I am prepared to fulfil the positive command that the
> Creator, may He be blessed, commanded us, to circumcise
> my son, as it is written in the Torah: At eight days every
> male child shall be circumcised throughout your genera-
> tions (Gen. 17:12).

The circumcision itself is performed by a *mohel.* Sometimes the
father does it himself, but generally it is a pious member of the
community who has been trained. Today it is often a doctor who
has learnt the technique. Interestingly the authoritative code of
Jewish law by Maimonides allows for a Jewish woman to perform
this role in the absence of a suitable man (*Hilkhot Milah* 2:1).

The child is first placed on a chair which is designated the
'throne of Elijah'. Jewish communities have often provided a
specially ornate chair for this purpose. The association of Elijah
with circumcision goes back to rabbinic interpretations of a
biblical verse. After Elijah had defeated the prophets of Baal he
was forced to flee into the wilderness to escape the anger of
Queen Jezebel (1 Kings 18–19). In despair he asserted that he
alone was zealous for God and that the entire people had
'forsaken Your covenant'. Since the word *b'rit* is mentioned here
it is assumed that he is referring to the covenant of circumcision
that had been neglected. The rabbis differed then as to what
followed. God decreed that Elijah would in future be a witness at
every circumcision that took place, but it is not certain if this is a
reward for his zeal in insisting that the rite be practised, or a
punishment for impugning the loyalty of the Jewish people!

Elijah is a stormy figure in the Bible and occasionally puts
even God on the spot by proclaiming a famine, or setting a
competition with the prophets of Baal, so that God is forced to
comply with his wishes, witholding the rain or sending fire down
from heaven. His departure from the earth in a fiery chariot is
highly appropriate given his temperament, and in Jewish
tradition he still lives, returning to events like circumcisions and
the Passover evening, as well as encountering individuals on
occasion. Since Elijah is also seen as the forerunner of the

Messiah, yet to come, it is clear that each such birth and event could herald the coming of the long-promised salvation, and this child might be the one who is promised. So the words of the *mohel* open with biblical quotes:

> This is the throne of Elijah, may he be remembered for good. For Your salvation I have waited, O Eternal (Gen. 49:18). I have hoped, O Eternal, for Your salvation (Ps. 119:166) . . .

The *mohel* places the child on the knees of the *sandak* (or *sandek*, 'godfather') who will hold him during the rest of the ceremony. The term may come from the Greek word for a 'patron'. Someone has to hold the child and it became considered a great honour to fulfil this role. Often it is the grandfather of the child.

The art is to ensure that the child keeps still during the crucial part of the operation. So the arms are held down by the *sandek*'s elbows leaving his hands free to move the knees apart, exposing the penis. This can be a significant moment, but not for any particularly religious reason. When I had the privilege of being the technical adviser on the film 'King David', I had to oversee the 'circumcision' of David's son Absalom. I showed the technique to Richard Gere, portraying David, but warned him about what might happen at this moment. And sure enough as the knees were pushed apart the baby peed heavenward, thus confirming my reputation as an authority on the subject.

Before performing the circumcision, and I will spare you the precise surgical details, the *mohel* recites a blessing:

> Blessed are You, Eternal our God, Sovereign of the universe, whose commandments make us holy, and who commands us regarding circumcision.

When it is completed, the father recites:

> Blessed are You, Eternal our God, Sovereign of the universe, whose commandments make us holy, and who

commands us to bring him into the covenant of Abraham our father.

The onlookers also have a role to play and respond to the blessing with the words:

Just as he has entered into the covenant may he also enter into Torah, *huppah* (the marriage canopy), and into good deeds.

A cup of wine is raised and the *mohel* recites a blessing over it and on the event itself, concluding with the naming of the child. The *sandak* drinks the wine, some drops are given to the child and the cup is taken outside to the mother.

Which reminds us that the mother has been significantly absent during this ceremony. In Orthodox circles men alone are present, though it is not restricted in non-Orthodox groups. It might be argued that great sensitivity is being shown in excluding the mother from this act which could be very traumatic for her. However it is always a mistake to make any such assumption about how a woman might react. My impression is that it is women who raise the most objections today to circumcision but there may be any number of reasons behind this as well as sympathy with the child. Certainly in its historical place in Jewish tradition it has belonged to the male 'mysteries', part of the male initiation rites and the defining of separate roles and realms for the sexes. Indeed the ritual itself traditionally reinforces this: the child is taken from the mother by the *sandekit*, the 'godmother', handed over to the *mohel* and thence to the *sandak*, the whole procedure being reversed when the child is returned. He enters the male domain from the domain of birth and women, to return there after the event.

The absence traditionally of a similar 'admission' ceremony for girls has led to considerable creative work by women in recent decades – though obviously without surgical intervention.

The act of circumcision is not itself necessary for entering the covenant. A Jewish boy, or girl, by virtue of being born of a Jewish mother, traditionally becomes part of the Jewish people.

If, on medical grounds, the boy is not circumcised, for example because of the risk of excess bleeding when such a condition is known within the family, he is no less a Jew, despite the emphasis laid on this act by the tradition. Nevertheless it is the norm from which, at least in the past, it has been rare to depart.

But as the words of the onlookers at the ceremony indicate, this is only the beginning of a life within the framework of the covenant, with its many obligations. In the next chapter we will look at some aspects of the life-cycle as experienced in Jewish communities, but use this one to examine something of Jewish ritual life.

If one were to enquire of the average Jewish family living in a middle-class suburb which were the Jewish festivals that still had a direct impact on them, the answer would probably be to name just two: *Pesach*, Passover, and Yom Kippur, not a festival but a fast, the Day of Atonement. Since this is not intended to be a systematic description of the Jewish Calendar, I would refer you to the listing at the back of the book and the suggested further reading at the end of this chapter. Instead let us examine in some detail these two which still impact on the Jewish heart and mind today.

Passover

If the birth of the individual boy is linked to the circumcision, the birth of the people is bound up with the story of the exodus from Egypt and its annual celebration at the Passover. Such is the power of this festival, often the only occasion when the Jewish family comes together outside of life-cycle events, that it deserves to be treated in this context.

From its very beginnings the Passover was a domestic ceremony. The biblical account of the exodus from Egypt envisages a recounting of those events to one's children:

> When you come to the land which the Eternal gives you as promised you shall keep this service. And when your children say to you: what is this service to you? you shall

reply: it is the Passover sacrifice to the Eternal who passed over the houses of the children of Israel in Egypt. (Exod. 12:25–27)

On three more occasions reference is made in the Hebrew Bible to recounting these events to your sons (Exod. 13:8, 14; Deut. 6:20). The second symbolic theme of the Passover period is that of eating *matzah*, unleavened bread, because of the haste of the departure from Egypt.

With the establishment of Jerusalem and the Temple, and the centralising of sacrifices there, Passover became a pilgrim festival alongside *Shavuot* (Pentecost) and *Sukkot* (Tabernacles). Originally harvest festivals, they still retained this character, but gradually acquired a historical overlay as they came to represent three key elements in the birth of the Jewish people. Passover recalled the exodus from Egypt; *Shavuot* the revelation at Mt Sinai and the entry into the covenant; *Sukkot* the period of forty years wandering in the wilderness. Passover retained its power as a domestic ceremony and so was able to continue to be alive for the Jewish people even after the Temple was destroyed.

The four references to questions your 'sons' will ask you in the future provide a key to the entire *seder* evening. (*Seder* is a term meaning 'order', hence it refers to the 'order of service' of this domestic liturgy.) The basis of the evening is a book called the Haggadah, a variation on the word *aggadah* we have seen in chapter 5, which also means 'narrating' and refers to the recounting of the story of the exodus. But the *seder* evening is a paradoxical form of religious service for it consists of a fixed liturgy but one which demands spontaneous questions and answers to accompany it. The very fact that the biblical verses suggest that your children 'will ask you on that day' makes the asking of questions essential. More than that, there is a traditional view that without the spontaneous questioning of the children about the special nature of the festivities nothing can take place at all! Indeed a story is told about a father who took very seriously the need to spark the curiosity of his son, so that at the beginning of the evening he would get up to all sorts of unusual tricks, juggling things, running round the table and so on, so as to prompt his son into asking what it was all about. After half an hour of this, while everyone was getting a bit impatient and still the son had said nothing, his mother finally nudged him and said, 'Don't you think your father is behaving rather strangely this evening?' To which the son replied: 'What's so special about this evening – I know he's crazy.'

If that is taking spontaneity a bit far, the opening of the narrative is a response to questions recited or chanted by the youngest child present, the *mah nishtanah* – 'Why is this night different from all other nights?' Four questions follow, one of which was changed following the destruction of the Temple. Before looking at the questions, it is worth pointing out the central role played by children in the whole evening. They are the ones who are to initiate the questions and whose imagination is to be stimulated. They are characterised as four different types of 'son' in the Haggadah itself. (One has to stress that the tradition speaks of 'four sons' though girls have often read the passage and today's search for equality emphasises that 'daughters' are also eligible. In fact there are emerging 'women's *Haggadot*' which may exclude men from the company.) One part of the *matzah*, the unleavened bread, is hidden during the course of the evening and the children have to seek it out and find it before the formal proceedings can come to a close after the meal. In a variation the children hide it and the adults have to find it – and may be held to ransom for a present by the children if they cannot! Either way it is one of the more subtle ways of keeping the children (and even a few adults) awake throughout the long evening.

The centrality of the children dramatises the sense of the continuity of the generations essential to this celebration of freedom, but it emphasises above all the respect that must be given to them as members of the religious community. It is for them that the ceremony takes place. It is they who perform vital roles within it, and it is their questions (the prerogative of children that is so often dismissed by parents) that must be respected and answered.

Because of the four distinct biblical references to the questions raised by children, one component of the *seder* liturgy evolved – the passage suggesting that there are four different types of 'son' present, each of whom asks a different question during the evening celebration according to their particular character: the 'wise one' who wants to know about the technical details of the festival; the 'wicked son' who is cynical about the whole exercise – though he is not so wicked or else he would not be there at all! the 'simple son' who can only ask: 'what is this all about?'; and the son who is too young to be able to ask at all. These four types open up a variety of opportunities for discussion for they may be seen as ways of accommodating all sorts of different people within the community. They allow for a variety of answers, and levels of answer, to be given. Perhaps more importantly they provide characters at the table, participants in the unfolding drama before us, so that in a quite unselfconscious way we become players in our own historical pageant, identifying with our collective past.

To appreciate the four questions it is worth hearing them in full:

Why is this night different from all other nights? On all other nights we eat leavened and unleavened bread, but on this night only unleavened bread. On all other nights we eat any kind of green vegetable but on this night only bitter herbs. On all other nights we do not dip our food even once, but on this night we dip it twice. On all other nights we eat either sitting or leaning, but on this night we all lean.

While the Temple stood, that final question read instead: 'On all other nights we eat meat roasted, stewed or boiled, but on this night we eat only roasted meat.' This refers to the special Passover sacrifice in the Temple. With the destruction of the Temple and the end of sacrifices this sentence was replaced with the one about 'leaning', part of an astonishingly successful accommodation to this catastrophic change in Jewish physical and spiritual life.

Even within these four questions we can see a number of features of the *seder* itself. First the importance of 'food' – but food given a symbolic meaning, so that the ritual is not confined to words and actions alone, but involves the senses of smell and taste. We experience in our mouths the bitterness of slavery by eating the bitter herbs. We relive the haste of the exodus from Egypt by eating the unleavened bread familiar to our ancestors. We eat a hard-boiled egg dipped in salt water – the tears of suffering. In its origins the egg probably represents the new birth of spring and fertility. But it also, in one interpretation, represents the Jewish people itself: the more you boil the egg the harder it becomes, the more the Jewish people suffer, the more they are strengthened.

On the subject of food, perhaps the best-known ritual part of the *seder* is the drinking of four cups of wine, coinciding with four promises of liberation given by God in the exodus narrative (Exod. 6:6–8). But drops of this wine, the symbol of joy, are removed from our cups at crucial points in the service when we read about the ten plagues that afflicted the Egyptians. Our joy must be diminished when we read of their suffering, so the wine is removed.

Two of the four questions take us into the symbolic reality of slavery central to the themes of Passover – the bitter herbs and the unleavened bread, referred to elsewhere in the Haggadah as the 'bread of affliction'. Conversely, the other two questions seem to reflect on the joys of physical freedom. The dipping of the vegetables seems to be an echo of the *hors d'oeuvres* of a celebratory banquet, and the leaning at the table is reminiscent of the Roman *triclinium*, the couch on which Roman citizens, luxuriating in their freedom, enjoyed a leisurely meal and discussion.

If these questions focus on physical freedom, the parallel aspect of the seder is spiritual freedom. The narrative proper, quoting Joshua 24, reminds us that our ancestors were idol-worshippers before God chose Abraham. Thus the telling of the exodus from Egypt is prefaced by the struggle to be emancipated from spiritual slavery as well. For all that the narrative looks back to the past, it also brings us fully into the present – for each of us is asked to consider ourselves as if we had personally come out from Egypt. And then it looks forward to the messianic future at the end of the dark night of exile. The invisible guest at the *seder*, for whom a special cup of wine is set aside, is the prophet Elijah, the herald of the Messiah. The concluding words of the Haggadah itself look forward to our return to a restored Zion: 'Next year in Jerusalem!' We live this night in a time outside of time.

Though the *seder* predates by two millennia the teachings of liberation theology, and however domestic and ritualistic it may appear to be, its message is deeply subversive, spiritually and indeed politically. The Haggadah narrative records a particular *seder* at Bnei Berak, attended by five famous rabbis of the second century CE, including Rabbi Akiva, who was associated with the Jewish revolt against the Roman Empire and died a martyr's death. It is suggested that when it records that they sat up all night discussing the exodus from Egypt, their hidden agenda was more politically immediate. When their students came to them in the morning to remind them that it was time to recite the morning prayers, they were suggesting to their teachers that talking was not enough and action was also needed. Whether this was historically true or not, the fact of its becoming part of the oral commentary to the Haggadah, reinforces the challenging nature of the ceremonial itself. In every society where Jews have lived, whether as slaves or free people, persecuted by their host society or tolerated, the nuances of the *seder* ritual have acted in and through their lives in extraordinary ways, constantly reminding them of the nature and necessity of human freedom under God.

Like much of Jewish tradition the Passover exists within a tension between its particularistic and universalistic features. Who is to be set free by the events of the exodus recorded and relived on this night? The biblical narrative in the Book of Exodus already displays this twofold nature. It is stressed throughout that the purpose of the exodus is to keep God's promise to Abraham to bring his descendants into the promised land. But no less emphasised is the fact that the Egyptians too will come to know the reality and power of God through these events – the discomfiting of Pharaoh, the 'god' of Egypt, and all of the plagues with their subtle attack on other Egyptian deities, is a major part of the intention. The *seder* is always to be attended by guests who would otherwise be unable to celebrate. In the words of the Haggadah: 'Let all who are hungry come in to eat. Let all in want come to observe the Passover.'

The *seder* celebration is often extended today by readings about contemporary problems of slavery and freedom so as to show solidarity with the oppressed. Special *Haggadot* have been composed and published to express sympathy with the civil rights movement in America, the anti-apartheid movement in South Africa, with women's liberation and the plight of the Palestinians.

Conversely, the celebration of the *seder* has been an occasion for Jews living under oppression to express their own yearning for freedom. I myself conducted a *seder* in Moscow in the late 1970s among 'refusenik' Jews, those who had applied for permission to leave for Israel and been 'refused permission' and were thus stripped of their jobs and rights. Many of them had family members in prison; one of them was later arrested for the crime of teaching Hebrew. During one Passover about that time a strange thing happened in a Moscow school. One of the children turned up with a *matzah* for lunch – at which point a number of other children similarly produced them from their lunch boxes. None of them had known that the others were Jewish; none of their families had ever celebrated the Passover before; few had more than a passing idea about the implications or meaning of the Passover customs and foods. Yet this symbolic act gave new meaning to the unleavened bread as an expression of commitment to Jewish life despite sixty years of suppression at that time.

In the life of a people, religion and politics, spiritual and physical liberation, are always completely intertwined. The text of the Haggadah reminds us: 'This promise has sustained our ancestors and us. For not only one enemy has risen against us; in every generation people rise against us to destroy us. But the Holy One, who is blessed, saves us from their hand.' The Passover has a life of its own and can still generate new meanings and new responses to oppression after more than three thousand years.

To describe the Passover evening in purely theological terms is legitimate and yet something of a falsification. Because on a more fundamental level it is simply a family gathering, one in which the ceremonial often takes second place to the human interaction. And here one does not want to sentimentalise. There is joy at reunion, sadness at people unable to attend, and mourning for those who have died since last year. There is the pleasure of the presence of the children and all too often impatience at the formalities, and even the incomprehensibility for some, of the ritual recital. But it requires enormous amounts of work, often unacknowledged, usually by the women of the household, and puts a lot of strain on people. Apart from which, all family reunions, once the initial pleasure has passed, can be fraught with old resentments and emotions, rivalries and jealousies – in short, all the petty human realities and conflicts of family life. They must have been equally present on the night of that first exodus as well.

We thus celebrate an amazing series of paradoxes. The splendour of the Temple ritual, with its cosmic overtones, has been somehow domesticated into this cosy yet complex ritual and meal. Conversely, this simple family gathering re-enacts a crucial moment in human history, the intervention of God into the life of a people and their rescue from physical slavery. It is therefore a deeply significant event, one that makes real and immediate and urgent God's further promises of an end to all human slavery and the granting of salvation to humanity. The banality of a family reunion takes on universal dimensions without ever losing its all-too-human limitations, its absurdity and warmth and love.

This weaving together of the mundane and the transcendent, the domestic and the cosmic, is the hallmark of liturgy. It is the particular genius of the Jewish people to have achieved this while taking into account also the reality of family life, the value to be accorded to children and the challenge to look beyond one's own self-interest, comfort and complacency. It is also at the same time a public confession of faith in God and of hope in the darkness to which so many Jewish generations have been condemned. As a ritual it is both a recording of a Jewish desire for national rebirth and redemption and an active step towards achieving that end, for sometimes to hold a *seder* has been in itself an act of defiance and it is always a rehearsal of a task yet to be achieved. But it is also at the same time a call for universal spiritual and physical liberation.

All this and more is symbolised by a simple piece of flat, dry bread invested with extraordinary significance and power. As the Haggadah makes clear:

> Behold, this is the bread of affliction our ancestors ate in the land of Egypt. Let all who are hungry come in to eat. Let all in want, come to observe the Passover. This year we are here, next year may we be in the land of Israel. This year we are slaves, next year may we be free.

Yom Kippur – The Day of Atonement

It is a strange leap from Passover to Yom Kippur. The former talks of the liberation of the people, and expresses itself in a domestic ritual in which food, symbolic and *cordon bleu*, is a dominant aspect. If people associate anything with Yom Kippur it is the fact of fasting and a day spent not at home but in the synagogue. Moreover, rather than celebrating freedom in a collective way, we are examining individually the responsibility that comes with that freedom and our failure to live up to all that we have been given. It is a solitary experience rather and a family one. Yet perhaps the secret of its appeal is precisely the sense that it is serious, and that once a year we are able to take a serious look at ourselves, with all the apparatus of prayers and fasting giving the essential background for the task.

Admittedly for many Jews the connection is relatively casual. Some will attend the synagogue only out of loyalty to parents or a vague feeling of unease at staying away. But the sheer richness is overwhelming – provided people can find the bridge between the great mediaeval superstructure of belief and language and metaphor that this entire penitential period contains and our own agnostic, largely secular reality.

The period really begins in the month of *Elul* which precedes

Rosh Hashanah the New Year's day. Throughout the month the *shofar*, the ram's horn, is sounded at the end of the morning service, a call to examine our lives and prepare for repentance. Rosh Hashanah has several designations. It is considered in Jewish tradition as the birthday of the world, and therefore the day in which the whole world is called to judgment before God, hence the title *yom ha-din*, day of judgment. It is also known as *yom ha-zikkaron*, day of remembrance, in which God remembers and reviews the deeds of everyone through the past year. The Book of Life is opened in which our actions are inscribed and God decides who is to live and who die in the coming year. The completely good are written for life, the completely bad for death, but most of us fall into the category of 'in between', and during the next Ten Days of Penitence we have the opportunity to attempt to make up for the harm or damage we have done, and seek reconciliation with those whom we have hurt. The book is then sealed on Yom Kippur. But paradoxically, though the day is solemn, it is known as the 'white fast', a festival occasion, because we know that God will respond to our requests for forgiveness. If these are the underlying motives of the period the details of the services bring out many different aspects.

The best way to give some flavour of the High Holy Days themselves is through the following section which requires a little explanation. It was written originally as an account of the inner journey that takes place on the Day of Atonement and published as such in the *Jewish Chronicle*. A revised form was prepared that was divided up as a series of prefaces to the different services of that day to be included in the High Holyday Prayerbook that I co-edited with Rabbi Lionel Blue for the British Reform movement. It is thus a piece that attempts to speak out of the heart of a Jewish tradition to a community of Jews at prayer. In placing it here you are invited to eavesdrop on that internal discussion. To insert too many explanations within it would be to distort the essence of the piece. So I hope that it may nevertheless find echoes for those who 'listen in'.

The Journey

There is a story that is told in every culture, in every religion, in folk tales, in legends and in our dreams. It is the story of the journey of a hero or heroine in search of a treasure. Every version of it is different, yet every version is also really the same. The hero is called out of his or her usual life – by seeing a burning bush, by hearing a voice saying, '*Lekh L'kha*' ('Go! For your own sake, go!' Gen. 12:1).

Ahead lie many adventures and on the way a meeting with an enemy who tries to prevent the journey and a friend who tries to help. At the end the hero or heroine reaches the entrance to the underworld, or the world of gods – Jonah entering the fish, Moses climbing to heaven to receive the Torah. With luck or skill or aid they cross the threshold and enter this mysterious land, of darkness and beauty, where the treasure is to be found. It is a land where the usual rules no longer hold, where they discover that the enemy and the friend they had met on their journey are really one and the same, and sometimes they turn out to be the guardian of the treasure that this mysterious world conceals. Whether the treasure is given, or it must be stolen, there begins the journey back to the familiar world again.

At the entrance there is a moment of reluctance – why return from paradise, or even the underworld, to a limited human reality? But something pulls or pushes them back through, for this treasure has to be given to humanity, this secret gained by such labour and courage. The journey is completed and life begins again – somehow changed by the experience they have undergone. Whether it is sung as a mediaeval ballad, told as a Red Indian legend, re-enacted in a religious festival or pieced together from the Bible tales and Midrash of Jewish tradition, it is in some way a tale about the journey of each one of us to discover who we are, what our life means.

One day a year we make that journey in the company of the whole community of Israel – all of us together, each of us alone. That day is '*The* Day', the Day of Atonement, the day of death in life. It is the day we wear the *kittel*, the white gown that will one day be our shroud. It is the day when eating, drinking, tasting, excreting cease. It is a day when the world recedes and we are set free to undertake our own personal journey of discovery.

There are five major services to the Day of Atonement – and they are like five movements in a symphony, or five stages in a journey to the place where our own treasure is to be found, and back again to the world of everyday.

The journey begins with a call. It has not the drama of Moses' burning bush, nor the clarity of God's appeal to Abraham. It is more of a nagging discomfort triggered by irritating New Year cards or sudden family invitations, or perhaps the drawing in of the season, or the reminder notice from the synagogue about booking our seats for the services, or a rash of appeals from Jewish charities, or any one of a host of formal and informal hints that the High Holy Days are here and that it is time for the annual visit, or at least a brief awareness of the season. Since Jews still turn up, for some reason or other, at some time over this period, then in its own disguised way the call out of daily life still has the power to move us, however briefly, however marginally, however reluctantly.

We are called to a court of law. We stand in the dock under oath. And God is 'the judge, Who is the witness, Who is the plaintiff and Who will summon to judgment'. In God's court 'there is no fault and no forgetfulness', for 'God shows no favour and takes no bribe'. We are called out of our daily routine of compromises and half-truths, of evasions and hypocrisies, of fighting to survive in the pecking order or to preserve some sort of values in a confused and confusing world – and for one brief moment we have the chance to tell the truth. Without fear of being mocked or misunderstood, without having to apologise or pretend to be what we are not, we can begin to face ourselves.

Kol Nidre, the title of the evening service of the Day of Atonement, is derived from the opening prayer, a strange mediaeval formula whereby all vows made to God in the previous year are formally annulled. It tells us that the words of our mouth do not always agree with the meditations of our hearts. It reminds us that this gap between our inner selves and our outer words and deeds is significant beyond our own private concerns, for it reflects a basic tension within the whole fabric of our society. Our private denials of the truth about ourselves spill over into public hypocrisies. Before we can ask for God's judgment on society, we must seek if for ourselves. At the start of Yom Kippur we take the first step towards stripping ourselves of the layers of indifference, and callousness, and self-defensiveness that we learn to wear day by day.

How important is the night of Yom Kippur, the time of silence between the chants and prayers? It is a strange period when time hangs heavy. All the usual distractions, coffee with friends, television, some other entertainment, are ruled out – either by conviction or by a sort of uneasiness about breaking the rules, or possibly the mood. It is the first moment of that acute discomfort of being thrown on our own resources and reserves – an unfamiliar experience in crowded lives. It is the moment of temptation on the journey – to fill up the time or be filled by it, to turn back in impatience or to go on, past the strangeness, the boredom, the silence.

At the morning service we move deeper into the inner language of the day. This is the place where our own individual personality blends with the personality of Israel. The outside world recedes further. We are experiencing and acting out the drama of our people on its day of meeting with God. We stand in judgment. But it is a strange language that we hear: of sacrifices, of goats, of priests, of rituals, of white clothing and red blood. It is the language of symbols of a world far away – and yet it contains a secret about our existence as a people, our values, our purpose and the renewal of our task.

Abraham was called to become a model for a new humanity: caring, compassionate, righteous. As he was tested and refined, so were his descendants who were to grow to become a people, themselves an example of God's will in an indifferent or hostile world. They were given a land, a microcosm of the earth, with responsibilities to serve it and protect it, to care for it and for each other and for all who lived there.

If we succeed, we save the world. If we fail, the world itself is at risk. On this day the record is set straight. So what is asked of us this day is very simple, and yet the hardest task of all – to be honest about ourselves as a people: how far we live up to this task, how well we treat each other, how well we treat our friends, how far we seek to win over our enemies.

Our history seems to have been one of continuous surprises. Each time we have pinned down God's will or location, it is something completely different, something new, God demands of us. When the pillar of cloud moved on, we had to follow – whoever remained behind was lost in the desert. The cloud was in the Temple, but the cloud moved on. The cloud was briefly in Jerusalem, but Jerusalem was destroyed. So we are always chasing after the cloud, only aware after the event that we have failed to see the new task demanded of us. And for this we ask forgiveness – for being trapped by habit, for being pious in everything that does not matter, for forgetting who we are.

So we chant poems and sing hymns and recite confessions, with or without meaning, trying to break through the defensive layers we have built around our souls. For these are our daily protection against a dangerous world – only sometimes the defences become more real to us than the soul within. So if we confess to things we have never done it is not enough to say that we speak as all Israel, and maybe another has done these things.

For we say too many words on Yom Kippur – thousands, perhaps hundreds of thousands, of words rise up from our lips. And the more we say, the less they mean. For just as the language of the Temple ceremony is a mystery to us, so do the words of Yom Kippur become deadened of meaning. It is as if we are trying to reach a point beyond words, when something within us speaks in its own tongue to God. All the ritual and recitations are there only to push away the barriers of habit and convention and fear that stand in the way.

In *Musaf* (the 'additional' service that follows the morning one) we reach the deepest part of the day. It is the centre of the mystery into which we have been journeying. There are many indications of this. It is here that we read of the actions of the High Priest in the past, of his prayers on behalf of himself and his family, the priests, and the whole of the family of Israel. It is here that the name of God was said aloud – the holiest name recited by the holiest man on the holiest day in the holiest of places.

That event seals its importance – but there are personal

indications that echo within our own private experience and lives. For with some of the prayers we confront our own mortality in its most direct and unequivocal form.

> We come from the dust, and end in dust. We spend our life earning our living, but we are fragile like a cup so easily broken, like grass that withers, like flowers that fade, like passing shadows and dissolving clouds, a fleeting breeze and dust that scatters, like a dream that fades away.

And in utterly uncompromising language even the ways of death are spelled out: 'who perish by fire or water, by the violence of human beings or the beast, by hunger or thirst, by disaster, plague or execution'. We who hide from death, lock it away in a hospital ward, who cannot speak about it and have no words for the dying, we are told to face our own end.

But that, too, is not all. Again the symbolism of the ritual nags at us. The two goats, chosen at random, one going to the desert, one going to God, one to death, one to life. The hands laid on their heads mean that they stand for us, represent us, remind us again and again that we are called to choose. By facing our death, we are asked to justify our life. The excuses are now left far behind us. The achievements and the failures have been recorded and noted; they stand or fall now on their own; they are history. What remains is the soul alone.

And that is still not all. Since the Middle Ages a poem has entered the Ashkenazi liturgy that speaks of the death of ten martyrs, who died at the times of Roman persecution, for teaching Torah. It is a great cry of anguish and bewilderment at the savagery of Jewish fate during the Crusades. It is a reminder of the price paid by countless generations of Jews for their stubborn clinging to their faith. It is a commemoration of, and perhaps also a cry of protest against, the fate of six million who died in the Shoah. It is an uncompromising reminder that there is a price we may ourselves have to pay for this strange vocation, even if it only summons us once a year to this time and place. For here is the ultimate question that pierces to the heart of our life and its meaning – for what are we prepared to die?

The day is turning. The moment cannot be sustained and we move slowly back from the mystery to the world outside.

The memory of death is not quite left behind, for at *yizkor* (the memorial service) we will remember our own family who are no more. But the trend of the service is now different. For we will shortly celebrate the magnificent stubbornness, the wilful blindness, the childish tantrums and consummate selfishness of the greatest Jewish prophet, Jonah. Greatest because he is the only one who actually succeeded in making his contemporaries repent! Greatest because he is the most familiar, most absurd, most human and most Jewish – he is us!

'Go to Nineveh,' says God, and he is off to the other end of the world. Tell your greatest enemy that God's love can reach him – Jonah argues God's right to be so generous. He emits a grudging five words of warning from God – and worlds are overturned. Things get uncomfortable when his shade disappears and suddenly he is concerned about nature, preservation and ecology. He is exasperating and impossible and splendid – and he is us!

Why is the Book of Jonah read at *minchah* (the afternoon service)? One answer lies in the lessons Jonah brings concerning the power of the decision to return to God. And there are warnings that fasting alone is meaningless unless there is also the intention to change our ways. But Jonah also tells us about the world outside to which we are soon to return – with its Ninevehs, those we fear from afar, those we help to create. He wrenches us out of ourselves to the world for which we bear responsibility. If we have burrowed into our Jewish consciousness in the morning, by evening we must re-experience what we share with all humanity, for we are called to live with two identities and two faces to our vocation.

It is not easy for us to hold these two poles of our being together, to be true to our identity as Jews and our feelings for our fellow human beings. All too often we choose one at the expense of the other – either leaving behind our Jewish identity, perhaps out of convenience, perhaps out of a feeling of a constraint that limits our humanity and concern in some way; certainly a narrow Judaism can seem that way. Or else we climb into a physical or mental ghetto, partly in response to a hostile outer world, but partly as a measure of our own inner insecurity.

Holding the two ends together in the middle is a great Jewish art, and one that we practise in so many parts of our existence – holding together the tensions between our individual desires and the needs of our community, the demands of our tradition and the equally urgent call of today's reality.

At *minchah* we are summoned back to face again that supreme balancing act that marks us as a people – ever marginal, inside and outside at one and the same time, ever torn, and yet ever seeking an inner security that does not come from outer success in the world or acceptance within the ghetto. Somewhere within us is the place where we have met God, and it is to that reference point that we return on this day. It is the fulcrum that can topple worlds, it is the still centre that sustains and nourishes a universe.

The world with its tasks awaits us. Now is the time to find that still centre before we enter it again. It is time for reconciliation.

At *neilah* (the concluding service – literally, 'the closing of the gates') there are so many images of finality: the gates that are closing, the book that is sealed, the judgment that is handed down on Israel and the world. All the outward images are of urgency, of decision, of the last chance to escape to safety, as if we see thousands of souls streaming towards the closing gates, desperately trying to get in before they slam to.

That is part of the truth of these last moments – and yet there is also another, an inner dimension. For there is also present a feeling of relief and calm and certainty. For if Israel has done its task this day, then God too will do what He has promised us again and again throughout the centuries: 'I have forgiven according to your word.' For this is the white fast, not the black fast (the day of mourning for the destruction of the Temple on the Ninth Day of the month of Av). It is a time of joy at the certainty of reconciliation, of returning home.

For how many is there no relief, no alleviation of suffering, no feeling of a journey safely undergone, of returning home? We are so estranged from our inner life, from the inner life of our tradition, that this annual drama brings too little and comes too late. Perhaps it is true that what you bring is more important than what you carry away – but the assumption often is that what you should bring are the formal measures of observance and practice, of commitment to Jewish forms, and that these alone make the journey possible.

It is true that they are the path for many, but no life is without its commitment, its struggle for values, its search for meaning. In today's fragmented world, when we live off the remains of our tradition amid the remnants of our people, it is not easy to know where the truth of our Jewish task lies. But we should not be fooled by the feelings of the moment – or even the absence of such feelings.

For the journey through Yom Kippur was a real journey – one to be measured not by what we feel when it is over, but by how we lead our lives in the days and weeks and years afterwards, when the final *shofar* blast has pierced not only the highest reaches of the heavens, but also the deepest reach of our souls.

Further Reading

Michael Strassfeld, *The Jewish Holidays: A Guide and Commentary* (New York, Harper and Row, 1985): a comprehensive guide to the festivals with valuable comments by leading American scholars.

Richard Siegel, Michael Strassfeld, Sharon Strassfeld, *The Jewish Catalog: A do-it-yourself kit* (Philadelphia, The Jewish Publication Society of America, n.d.): an extraordinary compilation of material on Jewish customs with 'hands-on' practical instructions.

Yaacov Vainstein, *The Cycle of the Jewish Year* (Jerusalem, The Department for Torah Education and Culture in the Diaspora, The World Zionist Organisation, 1953): for those who like their traditional Jewish explanations 'neat', a detailed account of the liturgy and festivals.

9

Nine are the months of childbirth
Life-cycle moments

There is a persistent belief that the Jewish family manages to hold together as a unit in a special way, somehow resisting the trends in modern society to break it apart. It is a comforting myth, for others as much as for Jews. But like many other myths it has to be questioned in the light of dire statistics. Divorce in Jewish families is almost as high in the UK as the national average – and has long been so in the United States. Matters such as wife-beating and child abuse that 'could never happen in a Jewish family' have now been shown to be as likely as with anyone else. It is simply that such things were concealed or not discussed or were tolerated out of fear at 'what the neighbours . . .' or 'what the *goyyim*, the gentiles, might say'. Jews live in the modern world with all the opportunities and strains this presents to the individual and family. It still takes nine months till childbirth, but everything that comes afterwards is open to reassessment.

According to Jewish tradition the first law given to human beings is in Genesis 1:28, 'be fruitful and multiply'. It is understood to be a law incumbent upon a man, though not upon a woman, to have children – at the very least one boy and a girl – so as to 'replace' the parental unit with a new generation. In the biblical period the number of adult males within your own family or tribe helped determine your power to survive. Able-bodied men worked the land and protected your property or tribe or nation. When battles were fought, largely as hand-to-hand combat, physical numbers could be decisive. Moreover, since infant and child mortality was high, the more pregnancies and the more births the greater the chance that some, at least, would survive to help ensure the family's future. By the same reasoning, a barren wife was viewed as a personal tragedy within that society – that a man might be sterile was rarely considered! In biblical times a man could always take a second wife, but as that option became less acceptable in the rabbinic period, the rabbis went so far as to require that a man whose wife produced no children after ten years should divorce her. However, a man who had already fulfilled his obligations to reproduce the family unit but who was subsequently widowed could marry a woman even if she was known to be incapable of producing children – in this case it was recognised that marriage was for the sake of companionship.

Incidentally polygamy, though rare anyway, was only abolished among Ashkenazi Jews in the tenth century by a ban attributed to Rabbenu Gershom. It never applied to Sephardi Jews, and, since such a legal ban could only last for a thousand years, it is by now officially no longer applicable, though few are likely to take up the option.

Part of the pressure to reproduce in the biblical period was connected with ensuring the physical continuity of the family name, which was in turn closely linked with the possession of specific allocations of family and tribal areas within the land of Israel. Thus a whole range of social, territorial and religious factors contributed towards ensuring a large family.

The continuing reality of high-risk births, together with the other factors listed above, created a psychological mindset that persisted into the time of Jewish exile from their land and through a wide variety of differing social conditions. Until a century ago in Eastern Europe, the large family with ten or more children was the norm. It was part of an intuitive strategy for survival shared with the surrounding culture.

Social realities in the West have changed in the last few centuries. Industrialisation led to vast migrations to urban centres, leaving behind the traditional closed societies that continue the 'old ways'. New factors that have affected Jewish, no less than other, lives have included the emancipation of women; their entry into the job market, a process promoted by the labour needs created by the two World Wars; improvements in health care leading to a dramatic reduction in infant mortality, plus, of course, the advent of new contraceptive techniques, particularly the 'pill', with the consequent freedom to make choices; the gradual appearance of a new leisure and freedom ethic to challenge the work ethic of previous generations. All these have contributed to the lowered birthrate and the more self-conscious planning of family growth to match financial, social and individual needs and desires.

The only group within Jewry to buck this trend are the ultra-Orthodox who continue to have a high birthrate. In part this is even seen as an ideological task, to rebuild the numbers of a Jewish world destroyed by the Shoah. This trend was once expressed somewhat triumphalistically by a former Chief Rabbi of Britain as proof of their eventual victory over progressive and secular Jews. A Reform Jew, he argued, might have three children, of whom one will convert to Christianity, one will marry a non-Jew and disappear as well, and only one will remain in the Jewish world! However the Orthodox Jew with ten children, even if one converts and one marries out, the rest will continue to be 'Torah-true'! (Of course Reform Jews are descended from Orthodox Jews, so he might be feeding both markets.) Time alone will tell if his prediction is correct.

A number of issues arise out of this new situation. Is the command to be fruitful and multiply without any limiting factor still operative in today's society? Is large-scale family planning acceptable in religious terms? Is it still a male responsibility to decide on such matters when there is no question any more of passing on the name or land of the male line? Moreover, it is no longer possible to consider women as merely chattels, as passive figures, dependent on male support and authority.

All these, and many other issues, such as those arising out of genetic research and surrogate motherhood, challenge today's Jewish world no less than all other religious communities. Moreover the women's movement has forced us all to re-examine the roles played by women and the degree to which the family unit we know today is an inevitable, biologically controlled relationship or actually something enforced by male power. Such issues are dramatised by the question 'Whose body is it anyway!' and the debate about the respective rights of the pregnant woman and her as yet unborn child, given the ready availability of safe medical abortions.

To what extent do these and related issues represent 'secular' challenges to the tradition which must be combatted in the name of religion, and to what extent are they merely part of the inevitable tension between differing stages of the development of our human society? To take the case of birth control, is it an anti-religious phenomenon, an assault on a divine charge to be fruitful and fill the earth, or is it merely a new variation on an old theme that the rabbis have explored in the past and that requires no more than a reinterpretation or rediscovery of older options and answers? Certainly in the specific case of birth control, when the life of the mother is endangered contraception and abortion are permitted by Jewish tradition. The Talmud has no problem discussing contraceptive devices. However, they must be used by the woman rather than the man since he is still under the obligation to be fruitful. From the earliest times rabbis have debated how widely to interpret the issue of endangerment of life. But today the boundaries are wider. The risk of severe psychological disorder to the mother is now accepted by some rabbinic authorities as grounds for termination. But what if the concern of the woman is more social than psychological, or even a matter of personal choice or convenience? And who should have the right to decide the matter, religious authorities or the actual woman herself as the autonomous person most directly concerned? Here Orthodox and Progressive Jewish movements tend to differ, with the latter more open to individual choice.

Each of these particular cases needs to be explored by the teachers of the tradition, but deeper than the specific question is the unease felt in traditional societies about all these new, or newly expressed, problems against the background of a secular society. Is any change to be seen as threatening to religious values, so that the label 'secular' becomes a way of demonising the new? Or do we think of a neutral universe, part natural, part by now a human artefact, within which we are to try to discover and express the will of our Creator in the new as well as in the old? And anyway, in today's divided Jewish world who has the authority to make such decisions and for which part?

If the earth is now 'filled' in accordance with God's command, so that serious questions arise about the feeding and sustaining of whole societies, should we control global population growth as a religious responsibility, if not as a religious duty? At what stage does quality of life replace quantity of life as an imperative? Here too the Jewish world may offer a highly particular argument – namely that we have to make up the losses we suffered by the Nazi onslaught on the Jewish people. In such a context, the argument can be put forward that birth control may be all right for the rest of the world, but clearly not for us!

So what happens when ideological religion encounters pragmatic human solutions? How long does it take before the heretical new becomes the conventional tradition? In the past, unless faced with a major onslaught from outside, religious communities adapted to changing situations so gradually that they often had little perception that they had even changed or that what they did was new. Today we are too historically conscious, too knowing, to be able to pretend to ourselves that we are not in command of change.

It has become increasingly difficult to differentiate the 'religious' from the 'secular' in these vital areas. In part this is because avowedly secular humanist, life-preserving and life-enhancing values have come to occupy so much of the ground formerly occupied by religion. The 'caring professions', almost by definition, are religiously agnostic but committed to improving the quality of human life. Conversely religions that feel under threat in a secular, materialist society have tended to retreat into tradition or else lack the inner security to accept the new even when it expresses a religious or spiritual impulse, because they cannot see beyond its secular expression. We all need to learn how to refine our perception.

Within the Family

If the above complex of questions look at the broader issues of contemporary challenges to Jewish religious family values, I want to look also at a far more domestic version of the same issue.

This is the mundane question that affects all families, namely what sort of schooling you expect for your children. As parents with two young children this was something that we had to address in our own family and the particular solution we found illustrates the complexity of the issues under the surface for any of the minority communities co-existing within the open society today.

The religious movement to which I belong, the Reform Synagogues of Great Britain, is one product of a variety of religious responses to the Enlightenment and the Emancipation of the Jews. In their varied forms all these movements have tried to synthesise the best of the traditional religion as they saw it with the best of contemporary values. While in an earlier period these movements had been highly critical of the tradition and rejected much of it, since the Second World War there is a growing conservatism noticeable in them, paralleling the similar movement to the 'right' apparent in traditional communities right across the religious spectrum.

One feature of the early Reform was its stress on those elements in Judaism that were universalistic – in part this was a form of assimilation that enabled Jews to take their place in the society around them and emphasise those values within Jewish tradition that most resembled those of the Christian societies they inhabited, thus leading to greater acceptance. One consequence of such a view was a rejection of any separatist schooling for their children. In many ways they accepted the contemporary humanist, secular ethic of Western societies trying to establish both national unity within their own countries and democratic forms that were tolerant of individual and group differences.

Within Britain, which remains a nominally Christian society, the Jewish minority felt particularly constrained to conform to the norm of society rather than emphasise their differences and particularlity. (Whether this was or is a good strategy remains constantly open to debate.) However the influx of other immigrant minorities in the post-war period and a growing acknowledgment of the realities of pluralism and the right to ethnic expression have encouraged Jews to 'come out of the closet' in recent years and demand more public recognition of their specific differences and accompanying needs.

It was nicely illustrated for me by the 'Prayer for the Royal Family' which is recited in Orthodox synagogues throughout the country. The version I grew up with, which was to be found in the 'authorised' *Singer's Prayerbook*, reads:

> May He [God] put a spirit of wisdom and understanding into her [the Queen's] heart and into the heart of all her counsellors, that they may uphold the peace of the realm, advance the welfare of the nation, and deal *kindly and truly* with all Israel.

The latest edition however reflects the change in self-consciousness of the community so that the final phrase now reads: 'and deal *kindly and justly* with all Israel' – we were not to be the objects of some particular 'kindness' anymore, but to be treated with the 'justice' available equally to all citizens!

However, to return to our topic, in the years since the war a number of Jewish primary and secondary schools have been created in Britain, frequently under Zionist sponsorship but increasingly today with encouragement from successive Chief Rabbis, under Orthodox Jewish auspices. The Reform movement has been very slow to move in this direction, reflecting the kind of ideological reasons given above. But some years ago they too founded their first Reform Primary school, called Akiva, and others are now in the pipeline.

For us, as a family, the existing Jewish day schools had little attraction, but the creation of Akiva school dramatised the issue. I myself am the product of a British public school and, before that, a private prep school. Though my parents were nominally Orthodox, the idea of sending me to a Jewish school seems never to have occurred to them. Public school meant a better education and the entry into wider opportunities in later life, even though it meant going to school on Saturday and thus breaking the *Shabbat*. The quest for material success, security and establishing a 'British' identity and place were overriding concerns for such second-generation immigrants, to which traditional Jewish religious values took a back seat. But, and it was a large but, now was a different time. The Jewish community immediately after the war felt particularly insecure and vulnerable and there was a certain paralysis within the religious Jewish world, then primarily Orthodox, when it came to dealing with these real situations of choice. Many of my generation saw these split messages, nominal Orthodox synagogue affiliation coupled with secular and as-similationist aspirations, as hypocrisy, and in later years made absolute choices – for Judaism or for nothing. It takes a lot of inner security to recognise the legitimacy of compromise.

In the end, as far as our children's education was concerned, it was the discussion with a young Jewish couple that helped determine our decision. He was a British Jew, she a Jewess from South Africa. He had been brought up in much the same sort of assimilated existence as I had, with no Jewish education other than the Sunday morning classes leading to barmitzvah, and abandoned as soon as that rite of passage was passed at the age of thirteen. He was uncomfortable with his Judaism and it had no relevance in his daily life. She had been through the South African Jewish Primary and Secondary school network, was well educated Jewishly, and, more importantly, was comfortable in her Jewish identity. Now to some extent that is a reflection of the different nature of South African society and the Jewish experience there, at least until recent years. But in conversation with them it became clear that giving our children a primary education in a Jewish environment might give them a security of identity, as well as the beginnings of a Jewish education, that would be essential for their later development. If they went on to a secondary school within the State system, they would become integrated into the wider society, but they would at least enter with a degree of self-confidence in the Jewish part of their life, a self-confidence I never experienced as a child.

But I must here point out the questions surrounding this

particular solution, those that have repeatedly recurred in our discussion of Judaism today. A Jew cannot be defined anymore in a purely religious sense. Jews have national, cultural, ethnic, religious and other sources to their identity and to their motivations as Jews. So are we strengthening a religious consciousness by this choice of a Jewish school, or are we rather concerned with the human issue of a minority group within a Western democracy trying to maintain its personal identity in a positive rather than a neutral or even negative way? Are we preserving a culture or a faith – and can they be separated? As a professional religious Jew myself I have a fairly clear perception that to have a whole personality we must attempt to integrate all of these components – and indeed this particular school seems to be successful in doing so, and was excellent for my children. But is it so clear or so successful with the average Jewish family? As the grandson of immigrants to Britain am I merely seeking to rediscover a cultural identity from the past, to find again the values, beliefs and practices that my own parents largely shed – or is this a genuine attempt to provide a *religious* set of values for my own family in a secular world, trusting that the tradition of Judaism will still be effective in our time?

Traditionally Judaism has been an all-embracing way of life which saw no separation between the spiritual and mundane aspects of our life. We have lived through two centuries of splitting and fragmentation of that integrated Jewish identity. Are we now able to resynthesise such a unity by assimilating these various cultural elements into a new whole, but including also the values, particularly that of tolerance, that derive from our secular cultural life?

Essentially Jews today, like so many others, have to recognise and acknowledge the different components in our intellectual and spiritual identity and find the way to hold them together despite, or even because of, all their tensions.

Closures

But let us look at another aspect of the 'life-cycle' and the way in which Judaism addresses it.

There is a statement in Ecclesiastes that obviously puzzled the rabbis: 'A good name is better than precious oil and the day of death [is better] than the day of one's birth' (Eccles. 7:1). It is the latter statement that they found challenging, perhaps because of its seeming pessimism for a religious tradition that is so life-affirming. So they found a parable to explain it.

> When a person is born all rejoice; when they die all weep. It should not be so.
>
> It is as if there were two oceangoing ships, one leaving the harbour and the other entering it. As the one sailed out of the harbour all rejoiced, but none showed any joy over the one which was entering the harbour. Someone who was present said, 'I take the opposite view to you. There is no reason to rejoice over the ship that is leaving the harbour because nobody knows what will happen to it, what seas and storms it may meet on its journey. But when it enters the harbour all should be rejoicing since it has come in safely.'
>
> In the same way, when a person dies all should rejoice and offer thanks that they have left the world with a good name and in peace. (Ecclesiastes Rabba 7:4)

Perhaps it is just human nature to want to celebrate beginnings and somehow neglect or ignore or even shy away from endings. And yet endings are as important as beginnings, and in many ways more important. Like those stories that finish with the words 'and they lived happily every after', one wonders what really happened when the curtain came down on Cinderella, when the beautiful girl married her handsome prince. Did they have problems with their children, with keeping up the mortgage payments, with the prince's occasional infidelity – maybe the 'ugly sisters' were not so ugly after all. Real life intrudes the moment after the beginning is celebrated and we have to cope with that ongoing reality. Worse, when something in our life comes to an end, for example through a divorce or a death, those who have undergone such a loss may be caught up in a myriad unresolved questions, great waves of anger or guilt or feelings of failure, on top of all the material problems and anxieties about the future that immediately intrude.

A proper 'closure', a ritualised acknowledgment that something is over, cannot remove these problems but may, in the short term, help the one who is in pain cope with the time of transition, and in the long term help give some meaning to, and perspective on, what has happened.

The problem is often that our discomfort with ritual in general, our lack of familiarity with it in the rest of our life, may mean that precisely when we have need of it, it is remote or unavailable. It may even serve to increase our insecurity in the face of unknown or troubling customs and practices. Perhaps the most pathetic experience a rabbi has to witness is the son or near relative of someone who has died struggling to read an English transliteration of the Aramaic *Kaddish*, the prayer that is recited at the funeral and has come to play a major symbolic role in acknowledging the fact of death and honouring the memory of the dead. In their hesitations and reading mistakes, often standing among family or friends of an older generation who know the *Kaddish* by heart, such moments can be exquisitely painful. Not just because of the clumsiness of what is being performed, but because of what it says about the state of Jewish knowledge and experience in the contemporary Jewish world.

Earlier this century the Hafetz Hayyim (Israel Meir Ha-Kohen Kagan, 1838–1933), an influential contemporary Jewish Orthodox thinker, could write in a comment on Deuteronomy 8:14:

'[B]ut your heart becomes proud and you forget the living God'. But if, heaven forbid, it gets to a stage where Torah is forgotten, when the people grow up without Torah and no one takes it to heart and they are merely satisfied with barmitzvah celebrations and reciting *kaddish* – that is 'forgetting Torah'.

If today's average, vulgar, barmitzvah celebration and the uncomfortable recital of the *Kaddish* just described are anything to go by, we have moved beyond even the Hafetz Hayyim's pessimistic prophecy.

With today's greater awareness of the psychological stages of bereavement, much has been written about the value of Jewish mourning customs. There is a graded series of rituals – seven days of *shivah* (the Hebrew word for the number seven), seated at home with daily visits from family and friends: *shloshim,* thirty days of gradual return to normal life; eleven months of the daily recital of the *Kaddish.* Subsequently a memorial candle is lit on the anniversary of the death and during various of the annual cycle of festivals. The grave is visited during the High Holy Day period. The mourner is thus overwhelmed with activity and support during the crucial first few weeks of shock, but at the same time is curiously cut off from the responsibilities and indeed the realities of daily life. It has even been suggested that the bereaved thereby shares in some ritual sense the 'otherness' of the deceased, and experiences a small death of their own. The gradual return to life with its continuing ritual obligations marks and acknowledges the reality of the loss but offers a formal way of discharging one's duty to the dead. Finally the formal limit set upon the mourning period allows, indeed forces, the mourner to pick up the pieces of normal life again. To mourn beyond the eleven months is in some way to be complaining to God that the loss has taken place. At the same time Jewish folklore has the deceased living in purgatory during this period, examining and being corrected for their previous life. But thereafter all go to their place in heaven. To mourn longer is to suggest that they do not deserve to go there!

How far any of these rituals are practised today, and whether in full traditional or modified forms, is hard to assess, and indeed the extent to which people find comfort and support in them. What is important, though, is that another rite of passage is being formally marked by the liturgy, once again in a private and collective way. The reality of our human needs, to mourn and eventually to cease from mourning, have been acknowledged by the tradition and an appropriate response created. We have to bury our dead. We have to go on living afterwards.

However we are also given the possibility during the liturgy of the Day of Atonement to acknowledge at least once a year the implications of our own death. The Day itself is a total fast and traditionally we wear white garments that will later be used for our own shroud. Symbolically, during the twenty-five hours of the day, we are dead and are invited to examine our life from the detachment that comes from the grave. In such a controlled, well-defined, context it is possible to do some of the work of preparation that may help us when facing the death of those we love and indeed our own death. Once again the estrangement of so many people from their religious traditions, irrespective of any belief in God that they may have, can cut them off from a source of help and strength in difficult times. Perhaps the worlds of therapy and counselling opened up for us this century by Freud and his myriad successors are ways of allowing us to re-enter these sources of human experience and wisdom through a more acceptable and less weighted route.

Marriage and Divorce

If death is the ultimate 'closure' on a life, there are a myriad other losses and transitions that need to be marked by an appropriate rite of passage. Not all need or indeed could be marked by a liturgical procedure, though a great deal of ingenuity has been expended in recent years, particularly in America, and most creatively in feminist circles, to find a collective religious expression to mark many such transitions, including, for example, the onset of menopause. However there is one ancient Jewish ritual that belongs in this category. It comes about not through some expressed psychological need, but the practical legal requirements of a society that has to regulate the marital status or otherwise of its members. And though there is no prolonged 'mourning' ceremony to mark it, the procedures of a traditional Jewish divorce do acknowledge the need to mark the closure of a relationship and thus open up the way to something new.

Jewish marriage is both a legal contract made between two consenting adults and a religious act that celebrates the continuity of Jewish life and even looks forward to Messianic redemption. In terms of the central series of seven blessings, the *sheva b'rakhot*, the couple become almost submerged in the theological references to creation, the Garden of Eden and the promised restoration of Jewish life in the land of Israel. All but two of the blessings begin with the standard formula 'Blessed are You, Eternal our God, Sovereign of the Universe'. They then continue in sequence:

> ... who creates the fruit of the vine.
> ... who has created all things to Your glory.
> ... Creator of Adam, human beings.
> ... who created human beings in the divine image, in the image of the form of God's likeness, and prepared for human beings out of themselves an eternal fabric. Blessed are You, Eternal, who forms human beings.
> Let the barren one (Zion) truly be glad and rejoice in the ingathering of her children within her in happiness. Blessed are You, Eternal, who gives joy to Zion through her children.
> Give these companions in love great happiness, the happiness of your creatures in the Garden of Eden long ago. Blessed are You, Eternal, who rejoices the bridegroom and the bride.
> ... who created joy and gladness, the bridegroom and the bride, love and companionship, peace and friendship. Soon, O Eternal our God, may the sound of happiness and rejoicing be heard in the towns of Judah and in the streets of Jerusalem, the voice of the bridegroom and the voice of the bride. Blessed are You, Eternal, who causes the bridegroom to rejoice with the bride.

Significantly the religious aspect of the marriage ceremony carries none of the irrevocability associated with the Christian, particularly Catholic, marriage ceremony. In Judaism it remains a contract between two people, duly signed and witnessed in a public ceremony. If the two partners to the contract wish to separate by mutual consent, they must be free to do so – and indeed the quicker and more efficiently the whole operation is carried out the better so that both can go on with rebuilding their lives.

Whereas biblical law allows the man to dismiss his wife seemingly at will, rabbinic law enacted a number of provisions to safeguard the situation of the woman. However they were unable (or unwilling) to reverse the basic premise that it is the man who initiates divorce proceedings. Thus though 'mutual consent' is the ideal, the man must take the formal action, and if he refuses for whatever reason, the woman is in many ways trapped. Should she subsequently live with someone, even following a civil divorce and re-marriage, she is technically an adulteress and any child would be a *mamzer*, unable to marry other 'normal' Jews but only another *mamzer*. (Surprisingly this did not create a caste system within Judaism in the past, because of the absence of records and the possibility of simply moving elsewhere and being discreet. Today, with computer records, the issue has become a problem it never was in the past for Orthodox communities, though Reform ones do not recognise the category – which, naturally, further distances them from Orthodox Jews.)

Within closed Jewish societies of the past, divorce procedures were regulated by the rabbinic courts. But enormous complications arise today from the openness of society where Jews can marry each other in civil ceremonies, as well as intermarry with those of other faiths. So Jewish religious divorce has acquired not only religious but also subtle political overtones, given the current struggles for authority between Orthodoxy and the non-Orthodox religious movements.

The actual divorce procedure is a remarkable ritualised way of formally marking the end of a relationship and a stage of one's life. While there is still a chance that the marriage can be held together the rabbis who function in the Beth Din, the Jewish law-court, are duty-bound to try to bring about reconciliation. Once it is clear that the breakdown is irretrievable, then things are carried out with remarkable dispatch. The following description of the beginning and end of the procedure by Jenni Frazer is based on her observation of the workings of two cases at the London Beth Din which serves the major sector of Anglo-Jewish Orthodoxy:

> Mr A . . . is told exactly what is going to happen and how to appoint as his proxy a member of the Beth Din staff. 'Your hands should be like my hands,' he is instructed to tell his emissary.
>
> The proxy, referred to as the *shaliach* ('emissary'), is obliged to drop the sheet of Aramaic writing that is the instrument of Jewish divorce into the open cupped hands of Mrs A.
>
> Mr A grants the *shaliach* permission to appoint a deputy if he is unable to deliver the *get* (divorce certificate) personally. The deputy is himself permitted to appoint a deputy, and so on up to 100 deputies.
>
> Then Mr A addresses the witnesses, two other Beth Din employees: 'You witnesses, be witnesses for me before the Beth Din.' Turning to the *sofer* (the scribe who has written the document), he says: 'You scribe . . .'
>
> Mr A, the *dayanim* (judges), the scribe and the witnesses vanish before Mrs B enters. She has come to receive her *get* from the Beth Din-appointed *shaliach* . . .
>
> The contents of the *get* are explained to Mrs B. Each document names the husband and wife, their fathers, and London, 'on the river known as Tamesis.' . . .
>
> The *dayan* (judge) tells Mrs B that her husband has appointed a proxy to deliver the *get*. Turning to the *shaliach*, he asks: 'What brings you here in this chamber this afternoon?' 'I am the *shaliach* of Mr B, known as . . .'
>
> The *shaliach* is then interrogated as to the manner in which he was appointed as Mr B's proxy. Did Mr B give instructions to the scribe? Was the *shaliach* present when the *get* was written? Was he present from the beginning of the signatures to the end of the signatures?
>
> If all these questions are answered satisfactorily, the *get* is then translated for Mrs B.
>
> Mr B [the *dayan* tells her] has given instructions 'to set

you free, to release you and to divorce you, that you should have mastery over your own destiny in the future. It is a letter of release, a bill of freedom.'

Mrs B is instructed to take off her rings – so that there should be no separation between her hands and the *get* – and to cover her hair. The document is folded and dropped into her open hands by the *shaliach.*

'Take the *get* and put it under your arm,' says [the *dayan*], 'to show that it belongs to you.' Mrs B then moves a few symbolic steps away from the *shaliach.*[1]

Though it is clear that the above is a legal procedure, and indeed in many ways a formalised ritual, it has its place within the overall spirituality of Judaism. It reminds us that Judaism is a 'way of life' that seems to address all aspects of our existence. For a community bound together and bound to God by a covenant, all human behaviour, all relationships, all ritual actions, all piety, flow into and out of each other with no clear distinction between them. The correct carrying out of such a procedure is a religious act in the broadest sense no less than it is a legal act of the dissolution of a partnership, itself created by a religious/legal act in the past. Just as the marriage was validated by the presence of two witnesses, so too is the divorce. The symmetry of opening and closure is maintained even if the mood and circumstances are utterly different.

Does such a procedure help either partner in coping with all the leftover emotions of the breakdown of their lives together? Probably not. It marks the formal end and release to a new beginning, but nothing more. The mourning for such a loss, the feelings of failure and inadequacy, the anger and bitterness of the period of breakdown and dissolution may well remain. They need the passing of time, or the aid of counsellors or therapists, or a far deeper dimension of faith, to be resolved.

It is here that much work has been done in creative liturgy for addressing these kinds of issues, largely by women's groups, as we saw in chapter 4. In the past, Jewish tradition must have served some of these supportive goals, even if the rabbis did not set out consciously to do so. Traditions grow through practical wisdom and their personal and social effectiveness, whatever the ideological underpinning. Today we start from the identification of needs and only then turn to the tradition to answer them when it can. When it cannot we look instead to resources available in the surrounding culture and our own imagination. Time alone will tell which of the 'liturgies' created for new situations will gain wider acceptance or remain private and personalised. Certainly there is enormous experimentation going on precisely at the points of transition or loss in our lives which will play its part in whatever forms of Judaism are evolving at this time.

Further Reading

Blu Greenberg, *How to Run a Traditional Household* (A Fireside Book, New York, etc., Simon and Schuster, 1993).

Morris N. Kertzer, *What is a Jew? A Guide to the Beliefs, Traditions, and Practices of Judaism that Answers Questions*, revised by Lawrence A. Hoffman (New York, Touchstone, 1993).

Debra Orenstein (ed.), *Life Cycles: Jewish Women On Life Passages and Personal Milestones*, vol. 1 (Woodstock, VT: Jewish Lights Publishing, 1994).

Hayyim Schauss, *The Lifetime of a Jew Throughout the Ages of Jewish History* (New York, American Hebrew Congregations, 1950).

10

Ten are the divine commandments
Jewish law and Jewish life today

The story could be apocryphal except that to the best of my knowledge it is true. (Since it involves the synagogue of my youth, alas long since knocked down, I am inclined to believe it.)

It is Yom Kippur, the Day of Atonement, the holiest day of the year. The synagogue is packed with people present for their annual visit. Sometime during the morning the police send in a message that they wish to talk urgently with the rabbi. Obviously he is disturbed to be called out on such an occasion, but the service is in the safe hands of the *chazan*, the Cantor. What do they want? Could the rabbi please explain something puzzling to them. In front of the synagogue is a carpark which is totally empty. Yet the entire High Street is filled with the cars that belong to his congregation, so much so that they are blocking the traffic.

Of course the rabbi can explain, though he may hardly have wished to. We are encountering here a curious phenomenon that I remember from my childhood and which I regarded then with considerable scorn. Jews are forbidden to drive on the *Shabbat* or the main festivals – they are technically 'days of rest', and driving, with its use of energy, constitutes work. When Jews lived in small towns or villages, within easy walking distance of the synagogue, walking there on the special day posed no problem. But living in London, few people live that close unless they consciously choose to do so. (When I was Barmitzvah, and formally entered the covenant at the age of thirteen, my *bubba*, my father's mother, visited us from Canada. She was genuinely pious of the old school and insisted that we walk to the synagogue, perhaps a couple of miles. Unfortunately she had very bad feet and we had to leave a good hour early to allow her to limp there, with frequent pauses, on time.) So a lot of people, unless *frum* (pious), drive there by car, but so as not to be seen as desecrating the *Shabbat,* park 'around the corner'. Or if, as in this case, there was clearly no corner to park around, block up the High Street.

I do not know how universal this phenomenon is. Perhaps with the increasing polarisation in the Jewish world between those who are more rigorously adhering to the tradition and those increasingly ready to acknowledge how lax they are, the phenomenon is decreasing. If you belong to a Reform or Liberal synagogue you happily drive there on the *Shabbat* and park in the carpark, though perhaps an older generation brought up in an Orthodox *shul* will still feel a twinge of guilt. There was an incident when a British Chief Rabbi made some unfortunate remarks about the religious honesty of the newly emerging Masorti or Conservative Jewish movement in the UK. As a result their phones were inundated with people asking for more information and seeking to join. They were defectors from the United Synagogue (the middle-of-the-road Orthodox movement) who were themselves hardly practising but who felt the need for a change while still keeping to the forms of worship to which they were accustomed. I did suggest at the time that though they may be happy to join, their new-found enthusiasm might not last as they would miss the feelings of guilt.

The above remarks, though a bit unkind, actually reflect a curious phenomenon that is particularly a trait of Anglo-Jewry though not entirely absent elsewhere. Again it finds its expression in a Jewish joke. A Jew is shipwrecked on a desert island and left alone for five years. Finally a ship discovers him and he shows the landing party round the island pointing out all the things he has achieved. He takes them to a building and proudly announces that this is the synagogue where he prays. 'So what's that building over there?' asks one of the visitors. 'Oh! that's the synagogue I wouldn't be seen dead in!'

Ten are the divine commandments

Such attitudes belong to a kind of religious hierarchic thinking that grades people and institutions by their degree of adherence to some kind of assumed norm. In today's fragmented Jewish world people adhere to, and not always consistently, their own anthology of Jewish practice and values, sometimes individually, sometimes as part of a particular community. In some places a kind of *laissez faire* attitude allows Jews to live alongside each other despite quite major differences. But all too often, and it seems increasingly so today, there is a kind of polarisation and a demand to 'take sides' within particular formulations of Jewish practice. Hence, there are synagogues one simply does not belong to.

Of course, such opinions and feelings may simply be the result of personal pique, but it is always better to dress up our feelings in some kind of ideological justification. Such differences, whether because of genuine religious disagreement or simply *broigas* (a marvellous Yiddish word meaning 'anger' or 'upset') are often the way in which new synagogues get created. After all, you do not need a rabbi to conduct services, nor even a special building. Any room will do; you just need a few others (ten adult males in Orthodox circles) prepared to join you when you leave in a huff. (I once thought there ought to be a Jewish board-game called 'Trivial Disputes' – but it need not be confined to Jews.) Actually it is also rabbis who create new congregations on such personal grounds, perhaps leaving after a dispute and taking their supporters with them. Theories about Jewish life often break down when they encounter the human irrationality that determines so much of what we actually do.

But the problem facing the Jewish world today is not the multiplication of synagogues, rather the reverse. Whether regarded as an amusing idiosyncrasy or as a sad and threatening matter about the future of Jewish society, there are many Jews who continue to belong to a synagogue to which they have little or no intention of going, because they neither understand nor value the service. What is strange is that they stay rather than simply leaving it or joining a Reform or Liberal synagogue where at least they could understand what is going on and may even enjoy it. Moreover they would be hard-pressed to explain why they stay, but the argument would be something about the presumed 'authenticity' of the Orthodox synagogue in which their grandfather prayed. And though it is damaging to Jewish self-respect, and the morale of liberal religious groups, one can understand the deep emotional pull of such arguments, even though at times they ring a bit hollow.

The same phenomenon on a grander scale applies to the State of Israel where a vast secular majority have given not only a *de facto* political power to extremely right-wing Orthodox Jews but even a kind of grudging approval. 'They may be impossible but at least they are authentic,' they argue, 'whereas "reform" kinds of Judaism are not.' This loyalty to the myth of tradition, if not to the tradition itself, has been used by Orthodox leaders as a kind of self-justification. It is argued in the case of non-observant but nominally Orthodox congregants that even though they are sinning they know that they are sinning and this shows their ultimate respect for the tradition. Perhaps more honest is the recognition that as fee-paying but undemanding members they do help keep the structure going. And with a resurgence of more 'right-wing', that is to say 'ultra-Orthodox' groups, which appeal to young people in particular, it may also be argued that despite the weakness of the system, at least something is in place for those who genuinely want it. It does seem, though, that at some point the gap between theory and practice is so great that a newer generation simply finds it intolerable and departs without even really knowing what they are saying goodbye to.

In Britain the Liberal and Reform movements have grown since the war, a growth in large part due to their willingness to 'tidy up' the unresolved problems of the Orthodox community (intermarriages, conversions, feelings of being Jewishly disenfranchised). They remain a minority compared with the majority 'United Synagogue', 'middle-of-the-road' Orthodox congregations. In America the opposite is the case, where the Reform and Conservative movements serve the majority of the Jewish community, with a small, but growing, Orthodox minority. Because there is a *de facto* pluralism in America it is easy for people to mix between the various synagogue movements there and for considerable interaction between them. This is not the case in Britain where Orthodox attempts to delegitimise the Liberal and Reform movements are met by equally critical ripostes and self-justifications. Off-stage relationships are often somewhat better but the two major religious groupings feel themselves in competition with each other. Nevertheless it is sometimes the case that an Orthodox rabbi will privately advise someone with a status problem that he cannot resolve within his own system to 'go down the road' to the Reform or Liberal synagogue. Sadly this private acknowledgment of the need for different criteria for different circumstances is often accompanied by a public disavowal of the non-Orthodox movements and all their works. What should be seen as complementary parts of a complex Jewish life today are perceived as competitors for Jewish souls.

The sense of belonging to the Jewish community, however minimally, but without any commitment whatsoever to its religious forms, is nevertheless understandable because of the dual nature of Jewish identity itself: peoplehood together with religious belief. In a technical sense Jewish identity is largely determined by our parents, particularly the mother's Jewish status. That is to say, most Jews are born as Jews, and can be happily (or miserably) Jewish without any religious element ever affecting them.

That says nothing about what, if anything, of Jewish heritage they will pass on to the next generation. Indeed that has been used in Orthodox circles to attack those who feel that their 'cultural Judaism' is enough to sustain them. And indeed some Jewish educationalists feel that their task, in the absence of a rich Jewish ritual life at home for so many young people, is to use the opportunities of Sunday school or informal Jewish education, to create positive 'Jewish experiences' that they will carry into their adult lives. Logically the absence of such a background must inevitably make it harder to feel part of the Jewish people and even more to wish to partake in its religious life. Nevertheless there are also cyclical patterns of moving away to be followed by a younger generation wishing to move back.

One consequence is the phenonemon of vicarious Judaism. Those who do practise the religion – and the more visibly they do it the better – offer those who do not practise it the reassurance that it continues even if they are not actively engaged in helping the process. Religion itself, on this reading, has become a kind of sacred cow. We pay respect to the institution, the buildings, those who adhere to them, and especially the spiritual leaders, even though it is not for us. They substitute for us and assuage our guilt at the fact that we ourselves do not practise.

It follows on from this that those who convert to Judaism are often seen by those who are only nominally Jewish as threatening in some inexpressible way. Clearly the primary interest of converts, except those who are marrying a Jewish spouse, is Judaism itself as a religious way of life, and even those converting so as to marry can become gripped by Jewish traditions, values and ideas if well taught. After all, this may be their first experience of religious education as adults instead of the fairy stories they learnt as children. But this religious commitment of the convert can be felt as a kind of challenge for those who are themselves insecure in their religious identity and do not want to be forced to address certain questions. Nowhere is this more clearly seen than in the case of a convert, usually a woman, who wishes to marry a Jewish man who has himself little Jewish knowledge or interest. For the sake of the family, or some vestigial feeling of loyalty, he expects that she will convert, and she may often come to accept that as a reasonable and intriguing option. Such an arrangement is not acceptable within the Orthodox community, but is often recognised as a realistic and legitimate reason in non-Orthodox synagogue movements. The important thing is not where one starts on the journey to Judaism but where one ends up. However the non-Orthodox movements tend to insist that the Jewish partner has to undertake the same course of preparation as the convert – namely regular attendance at synagogue and a full course of study in Judaism. Here the 'non-Jewish Jew' may find himself in a very uncomfortable situation, often protesting: 'I'm Jewish, I don't need to know all this stuff!'

Given these kinds of attitudes it is not surprising to find the familiar paradox: the more the Jews who 'do our praying for us' dress and behave in a traditional manner, the blacker their hats and the greyer their beards, the easier we can dismiss them as 'not really us'! We could never behave in such a way, so if this is Judaism it is not for us. Such thinking is of the type that composes an image of God as an old man with a beard. Since it is clearly impossible to believe in such a childish picture one can comfortably dismiss religion as being nothing more than fairy tales. Moreover, since Jewish males may have had nothing to do with religion since their Barmitzvah, they tend to be still saddled with a 'thirteen-year-old' God.

Those who convert to Judaism, and those who find a middle way of adhering to it through some kind of Conservative, Reform or Liberal Jewish movement, threaten these comfortable fantasies. Normal people can be Jewish!

There is a new dimension to these issues because of the particular political structure of the State of Israel, where minority Orthodox religous parties have been able to exert an influence far beyond the size of the constituency they represent, simply because they were needed to keep coalitions in power. But the more they seek to impose their will on the population at large, the more angry avowedly secular Israelis become. Which leads to more disenchantment with Judaism as such. There should theoretically come a time when the political impositions of the Orthodox outweigh the psychological gains from the vicarious religion they provide – which could prove an explosive turning point, certainly in the political make-up of the State. The more extreme the positions of some of the ultra-Orthodox become, the more there arise voices from more moderate Orthodox individuals and groups who see here the damage being caused to the traditional values they hold dear. It remains a highly complex and changeable situation.

I want, at this point, to move away from generalities into a more autobiographical mode, because I think it illustrates some of the tensions which we confront today as Jews. I experience myself to be the product of a number of different Jewish worlds. I feel as much at home praying in the Italian synagogue in Jerusalem as I do in St Johns Wood Liberal Synagogue. I enjoy struggling to understand a comment of Rashi or Ibn Ezra on the Torah, but I experience the same value wrestling with a biblical parable of Kafka or a scholarly article on Bible by a secular professor from the Hebrew University. I find religious truth and challenge in discussions with Orthodox rabbinic friends just as I do with Reform and Liberal ones. But the same is also true of secular Jewish psychotherapists or committed Christian or Muslim religious teachers. They are all in some way part of my religious landscape and it would be crazy to deny their importance to me. Therefore I am by temperament and personal history a pluralist, the product of a multiplicity of Jewish and non-Jewish worlds and experiences. And I have to live with, acknowledge and value them all. Most of the contradictions that exist in the Jewish world exist within me. To deny this would be to deny the truth about my life and to cut off any part of this would be an act of self-mutilation.

Let me mention some of the contradictions that arise from this pluralism. I am by intuition and experience a religious believer but at the same time I am intellectually secular and critical. I am the child of two thousand years of Jewish rabbinic tradition, and an even older biblical one, but I am equally the child of two centuries of the Enlightenment. To deny the truths of that Jewish religious tradition and the martyrdom of the Jewish people to preserve it, would be for me a great betrayal. But it would be no less a betrayal to deny the intellectual and scientific insights of the past couple of hundred years, including the critical challenges they raise to the foundations of Jewish tradition. In this sense I am deeply schizophrenic. But I think that all of us committed to Jewish life today are schizophrenic in the same way – it is just that we find different strategies for coping with this deep inner conflict.

I cannot be an open-minded intellectual seeker in my professional or academic life, and switch off a part of my mind when I enter Jewish studies. I cannot be a liberal democrat in my social and political life, yet accept autocracy and authoritarianism in my Jewish religious life. I cannot live in a society which claims to be, or at least seeks to be, open, pluralistic and multicultural and at the same time reduce the pluralistic Jewish world that I know and experience to a narrow monolithic one, whether the particular label is 'Orthodox' or 'Progressive'. To quote Rabbi

Dr Leo Baeck, Judaism is my home, not my prison. As a man, I cannot value the things I have learnt from the struggles of the women's movement, and then deny these hard-earned perceptions in my Jewish life. I cannot set aside the insights of a century of depth psychology into the nature of prejudice and projection, into the sexual fears and insecurities of human beings, and then shrug off the attitudes towards sexual and social minorities in our own tradition. I cannot celebrate *Pesach* and support Jewish causes, yet ignore the suffering of Palestinians at the hands of Jewish power. I cannot acknowledge the enormous religious growth I have experienced through interfaith dialogue, with Christians and with Muslims, over much of my adult life, and then accept the narrowness and even prejudice against others I find in many parts of the religious Jewish world today, my own no less than others'. I may be schizophrenic but at least I can try to be consistent.

I have to explore further one more polarisation as well. Instead of the God-centred universe that was inhabited by my great-grandparents, today I live in a human-centred universe, where human values and achievements seem to take centre stage. The very existence of a Jewish secular, democratic State is a measure of the degree to which the Jewish people was prepared to take its destiny into its own hands and challenge the messianic hopes of the tradition that assumed we must wait for God's own good time. If Judaism is a curious complex interaction of a religious faith and peoplehood, a *mamlekhet cohanim v'goi kadosh*, 'a kingdom of priests and a holy nation' (Exod. 19:6), then these two aspects are also split in our time – split from each other, and each in turn subject to enormous questioning and re-evaluation.

This conflict between tradition and modernity is well expressed through the words of one of the leading Orthodox Jewish thinkers of our time, the late Rav Joseph Soloveitchik, writing about 'the lonely man of faith'.

Let me spell out this passional experience of contemporary man of faith.

He looks upon himself as a stranger in modern society which is technically minded, self-centred and self-loving, almost in a sickly narcissistic fashion, scoring honour upon honour, piling up victory upon victory, reaching for the distant galaxies, and seeing in the here-and-now sensible world the only manifestation of being. What can a man of faith like myself, living by a doctrine which has no technical potential, by a law which cannot be tested in the laboratory, steadfast in his loyalty to an eschatological vision whose fulfillment cannot be predicted with any degree of probability, let alone certainty, even by the most complex, advanced mathematical calculations – what can such a man say to a functional utilitarian society which is *saeculum*-orientated and whose practical reasons of the mind have long ago supplanted the sensitive reasons of the heart?[1]

However, there are a number of strategies for dealing with these deep contradictions since we do have to maintain our sanity. There are extreme positions: for example, denying the tradition entirely and attempting to live a totally secular, uncommitted Jewish life; or denying the secular and creating a religious world as if the secular challenge did not exist. And there are any number of shades of accommodation between the two. In the religious area we recognise them under a continuum of synagogues and movements labelled as Progressive, Liberal, Reform, Reconstructionist, Conservative and 'modern' or 'central' and 'ultra' Orthodox. In the area of peoplehood we do have a plurality of ways of identifying as Jews in the Diaspora. It may be that in terms of classical Jewish parameters of identity we are seeing a falling away from previous norms – but in a situation of such radical ferment no one can predict what new patterns might actually emerge in time. And what is the State of Israel if not an alternative option for asserting Jewish peoplehood without necessarily having any religious identity whatsoever? From certain religious perspectives that may appear to be a bad thing, but from the limited perspective of ensuring Jewish continuity and indeed of redefining Jewish unity in an entirely new way, Israel is clearly of enormous significance.

I have approached this topic so far from a somewhat personal viewpoint, and perhaps it is time to put it into a more formal historical and cultural context. We have looked at the nature of the 'covenant' between God and Israel. If 'law' is a central element in Judaism, it is because it is the basis of our constitution as a people, regulating our behaviour towards each other, to others and to God. The essential term in this regard is *Halakhah*, from the root *h-l-kh*, meaning 'to walk', which we have encountered in chapter 5. *Halakhah*, translated usually as 'Jewish law', is actually 'conduct': how the individual and community are to conduct themselves. But the nature and role of *Halakhah* has changed in our time.

I would venture to suggest that there is a relatively small number of Orthodox communities throughout the world who, by their own lights, adhere strictly to *Halakhah*. There are considerably larger movements that consider that they are Orthodox, though a better term would be 'orthoprax' since it is their behaviour that defines their position more than their system of belief. Some have shown remarkable resilience and regeneration in the post-war period. Nevertheless they accept that many of their members are only partially observant or even non-observant. There are Conservative, Reconstructionist, British Reform and Continental European 'Liberal' communities that claim, in varying degrees, to be *Halakhic* in ideology, but nevertheless insist on their own, sometimes radical re-interpretation of *Halakhah*. Even American Reform, and to some extent British Liberal and Progressive, Jews that have taken ideological stands against *Halakhah* in the past, feel the need to measure themselves against its practices and assumptions, if only to criticise or contradict them. *Halakhah* is discussed, avowed, gossiped about, flaunted, flirted with and exploited for political ends. It is in a very profound way a unifying force in Jewish life. Certainly it was the cement that held together Jewish society in exile, from the time of the destruction of the Second Temple until the period of the Emancipation. But it is also today a divisive force of devastating power, and a weapon for some Jews to use against others. And for vast numbers of Jews around the world it is an irrelevancy that almost never impinges upon their lives.

Let me make it clear that I am not challenging the primacy or legitimacy of *Halakhah*. Nevertheless the conventional view of

Halakhah is a very narrow legalistic one. I prefer the broader perception given in the following passage by Rabbi David Hartman, an Orthodox rabbi originally from Canada who settled in Israel and has fought to assert an open-minded Orthodox Jewish position on a number of issues. The tension he sees *within Halakhah* is not unlike something we have seen above described by A. J. Heschel as the relationship between *Halakhah* and *Aggadah*:

> *Halakhah* revolves around two poles: the legal, that is, specified and detailed rules of behavior, and the relational, that is, the yearning to give expression to the intimate covenantal relationship between God and Israel. Both these poles have shaped *halakhic* thought and practice. The legal pole, the tendency to fix formulations for conduct, may reflect the yearning and need of human beings for order and predictability in relationships. The way is given. The task of the covenantal Jew is merely to respond. On the other hand, the covenantal pole emphasizes that *halakhah* is not only a formal system concerned with rules of procedure but also an expressive system grounded in the love relationship symbolized by God's invitation to Israel to become his covenantal community. The understanding of *halakhah* as a covenantal relational experience guards against the mistaken notion that a dynamic living relationship with God can be structured exclusively by fixed and permanent rules. The need for order must not be at the expense of spontaneity, personal passion, novelty, and surprise. One committed to the *halakhic* system can meet God in new ways. The perennial problem that one faces in living by *halakhah* is how to prevent the covenantal relational pole from being obscured by the massive, seemingly self-sufficient legal framework.[2]

Yet the paradox remains – why is *Halakhah* so important and at the same time so marginal to the lives of so many Jews?

The problem seems to lie in the difference between theory (or ideology) and reality. *Halakhah* as a legal system today, is one almost without legal sanctions. Jews once shared unquestioningly a common system of belief and practice, lived in relatively closed societies and administered their own courts that judged all aspects of public and private life and could enforce their decisions, either by law or by public pressure. All these factors have radically changed in an open society. If you cannot enforce law, however significant it may be in theory, it ceases to have power or reality.

If a Jew today does or does not keep *kashrut*, the dietary laws, or *Shabbat*, conduct business in accord with Jewish teachings, obey the laws of family purity or the sabbatical year, or indeed any of the 613 *mitzvot*, it is a matter almost entirely for his or her own conscience. No one else is going to do anything about it. The sanction of divine displeasure is only a reality for those with religious faith; the community sanctions (of ostracism or public criticism) only work when a group of people volunteer to form their own community, agree values and rules, accept certain authorities to guide them and punish those who do not conform – whether they are a Chasidic group in North London or a Liberal Synagogue in Holland or a Conservative congregation in New York.

Until the Emancipation, *Halakhah* provided the primary source of Jewish cohesion. Since the Emancipation we have yielded the authority of large areas of *Halakhah* to the legal system of our host societies, and we are still seeking alternative ways to find a common basis for Jewish identity and unity. That is why *Halakhah* is seen as important whether we belong to a group that adheres to it strictly, one that pays lip service to it, or one that rejects it entirely. It is the classical touchstone for a shared Jewish identity despite the limited extent to which Jews adhere to it or even accept it. The question is whether it can again be made the functional agent for establishing Jewish unity or whether we are actually in a transitional period towards something different.

Nevertheless there is one area of *Halakhah* that still has public significance because it carries sanctions. It is the area of 'status': who is 'in the club' and who not; who is a Jew and who is not; who may marry whom; and hence who has authority to decide in such matters. This is therefore the area over which Orthodox and non-Orthodox groups fight each other and, incidentally, over which both groups fight internally when one subdivision questions the legitimacy of another sub-division. Moreover it is here, and only here, that rabbis have power over other Jews. So it is in this area that the bitterest quarrels take place. And since this is the last area where the power of *Halakhah* in Jewish life is tested, it is very easy for the struggle to shift from the values and authority of *Halakhah* itself to the power and authority of the particular ecclesiastical authorities who wield it.

The question of the correct *Halakhic* procedures for conversion is one issue over which this larger 'political' struggle is fought because *Halakhah* reflects policy as much as it enacts law. Which is why the most *halakhically* correct non-Orthodox conversion to Judaism cannot be accepted by Orthodox authorities, and why every compromise solution offered, even by Orthodox rabbis, has been shot down by others. The issue is not really 'Who is a Jew?' but 'Who is a rabbi?' (It has been pointed out that in America, since there is no 'Chief Rabbi' to determine such things, it is sociologists who decide 'Who is a Jew'!)

Issues like conversion to Judaism and Jewish status have become major divisive matters in Jewish life today. Concern has been expressed about Jewish individuals being unable to marry each other because of these 'sectarian' divisions. Ultimately, in the view of a celebrated article, will there be two Jewish peoples by the next millennium, or, as expressed in the title of a book: *Will We Have Jewish Grandchildren?* Why are such matters surfacing now? They have been ostensibly triggered by concerns at the American Reform decision to introduce a patrilineal policy instead of the traditional 'matrilineal' one – the view that someone who has a Jewish father, but not a Jewish mother, provided they have been brought up and educated as a Jew, should automatically be accepted as a Jew. But any look at the Jewish world today will immediately show the extent to which different Jewish societies have moved away from the traditional *halakhic* criteria for identifying someone as a Jew for a multiplicity of different reasons.

Just add up the ways in which this has come about: a century of intermarriage, divorce and remarriage in Western societies; seventy years of State control over Jewish identity in countries of the Soviet Bloc, whereby you were Jewish if that was stamped in your passport and so were your children irrespective of whether your wife was Jewish; the different criteria for conversion to Judaism adopted by the many forms of non-Orthodox Judaism worldwide; the 'black-market' commercial availability of Orthodox conversions; the unresolved status problems of refugees and survivors after the Shoah; the adoption of patrilineal status by the American Reform movement, which has incidentally been on their books for most of this century; and the gap between religious and civil authorities in the State of Israel in determining who belongs to the Jewish people in terms of the Law of Return. All of these contribute to a massive challenge to the *halakhic* basis of Jewish identity.

There are today growing numbers of people who sincerely believe they are Jewish and contribute as Jews to Jewish life, but who simply do not fit into the classical categories of Jewish law. Individual cases can be adjusted by at least one of the different branches of Judaism even if not accepted by others, but the collective cannot. Nor is the will there, for all the protestations on all sides, to solve the question in a unitary way.

What seems to be bringing matters to a head is the increasing centrality of the State of Israel in all matters Jewish and the inner power struggle there between Orthodox and civil authorities that has its ramifications throughout the Jewish world

With its creation the State has become potentially the new unifying factor for the Jewish people. It signals the reversal of two thousand years of Jewish diaspora existence. We are *en route* back to a biblical model so that those living in the Diaspora will, as the generations pass, be increasingly regarded as expatriate Israelis, part of a Jewish nation resident for the most part abroad. Every time Jewish politicians or rabbis talk about the 'centrality' of Israel, we take a further step towards that possible reality. Jews today readily acknowledge the enormous influence Israel has on our lives in the Diaspora. We are moving towards a situation where it might have authority over our Jewish identity as well.

This can already be seen in the area of status and particularly of conversion. The power of Israel to determine things for the Jewish people as a whole has given the issue of 'identity' new significance. Under the Law of Return, created as a response to the desperate plight of Jews during and immediately after the Second World War, any Jew has automatic right of citizenship of the State of Israel. This right extends to their immediate family, even if they are not Jewish. It also applies to people converted to Judaism through any Jewish religious authority recognised in their own particular Diaspora society, including 'non-Orthodox' movements. This right for their converts to be accepted does not apply to such movements within the State itself – a matter, along with other 'disabilities' constantly being fought over in the Israeli courts. Since 1958 Orthodox groups in Israel have tried to change the Law of Return so as to take control of the issue of 'status' for themselves, this being, as they see it, an essential element in their commitment to 'Torah-true' Judaism. In this they are clashing, sometimes violently, both with the civil authorities and the long-established religious pluralism of Diaspora communities such as that of the United States.

We are clearly in a process of realignment as a people, with exclusivist and inclusivist solutions being offered at different ends of the religious spectrum. We have known for a long time, but never quite believed the implications, that you can be ethnically Jewish and not have a religious bone in your body, and spiritually identify with Judaism one hundred per cent but not be accepted in significant parts of the Jewish world. Pluralism on a vast scale is now the reality across a wider spectrum than ever before in Jewish history. So what is the factor that actually holds this diverse people together?

It is possible that the State of Israel, which is as much a part of the problem as the solution to it, will become in time the focal point of a newly emerging 'Jewish' identity. Certainly on demographic grounds within a few generations it will be the largest Jewish society, provided nothing drastic happens. So we should be more concerned with the quality and content of that coming identity than with quarrels that still only harp back to a past that is effectively no more.

What stands in the way is another belief, no less a fantasy, held by both Orthodox and Progressive Jewries, that in the end one of them will win and defeat the other, the Progressives through ideology and the Orthodox by outbreeding everyone else. Both believe that they have 'the truth', whether they express it assertively or diffidently, with proof-texts or qualifications. (Rabbi Lionel Blue points out that he has never met anyone 'crazed with liberalism', which is why the 'traditionalists' seem more strident and the 'progressives' more muted in these quarrels. The leadership of both sides seem equally stubborn.) The real quarrel is about authority and pride, and who has control over a diminishing Jewish cake. While movements and ideologies go on squabbling the Jewish people vote with their feet and leave, or make their own anthology of Jewish practice or do surprising new things and leave it to the various 'authorities' to catch up as they wish.

When it comes down to the basic issues of status, who belongs to the Jewish people, and who is married to whom, it is something very non-traditional that tends now to determine the result. As Peter Oppenheimer points out in his thoughtful paper,[3] it is the civil law, not the religious law, that actually helps hold the Jewish people together.

> Today in the presence of multi-denominationalism, rabbinical judgements (in the plural) are liable to be divisive. So the civil law is called in aid: both the civil law of gentile states and the civil law (the Law of Return) in Israel itself . . . It is . . . the creation of Israel, and the mutual interdependence (or exploitation) between the civil law of Israel and of Diaspora countries, which has given the civil law its new prominence as the last-resort unifying mechanism for the Jewish world. The question is whether this situation will prove durable in the decades and centuries ahead.

But perhaps it is not enough to leave the matter in quite such an open-ended way. Because there are issues that the Jewish community has to address, whether willingly or unwillingly, that pinpoint exactly the area where the tradition is helpless but the demand for action is present. Most particularly and obviously there is the question of homosexuality and lesbianism, and the acknowledgment that a proportion of the Jewish community, perhaps more than 5 per cent, are disenfranchised by their sexual alignment, a minority within a minority.

The biblical strictures on male homosexual activity occur in two passages in Leviticus. 'You shall not lie with a man as with a woman, it is an abomination' (Lev. 18:22), the punishment for which is the death penalty (Lev. 20:13). But there is no recorded instance in Jewish history of such a punishment, and only one doubtful case of the death penalty for adultery, though it is equally condemned in Leviticus.

Interestingly the rabbis found quite different ways for handling these two laws. In the case of adultery they so hedged it in with conditions that it became virtually impossible to punish – even if it actually took place. For example, there must be two witnesses to the adulterous act itself who have previously warned the offending couple of the consequences of what they are about to do – enough to put the most lusty adulterer off his stride one would have thought. But homosexuality was given a quite different treatment, through a curious rabbinic formula that effectively put the issue on the back-burner till recent times made it necessary to re-examine attitudes. 'Israelites are not suspected of either sodomy or bestiality' (b. Kiddushin 82a). Does this mean that Jews do not do it, or are not to be suspected of doing it? Whichever interpretation the principle was effective, even in the 'Golden Age of Spain' when Jewish poets wrote love songs to their male lovers in imitation of Arabic models, alongside hymns to the glory of God.

Lesbianism is not explicitly acknowledged, let alone condemned, in the Hebrew Bible, but the rabbis forbade it under the heading of 'deeds of the land of Egypt' (Lev. 18:3) which were not to be imitated. Being a lesser offence it incurred the lesser punishment of 'rabbinic beating'.

With the emergence of Gay Liberation the issue has entered centre stage and led to predictable responses. From strict Orthodox circles the matter remains anathema. Indeed they add it to the catalogue of sacrilegious horrors perpetrated by 'progressive' Jewish movements that they have sought to address the issue or accommodate gay people. Within modern Orthodoxy attitudes have varied from outright condemnation (sometimes linked with discussing AIDS as a divine punishment) to an interesting *laissez-faire* approach – Jews sin all the time but that does not prevent them from being essentially good Jews and being permitted to come to the synagogue, so why is being gay any different from not observing *Shabbat* or eating kosher food? Some treat it simply as a wilful sin that should be controlled. Others see homosexuality as a kind of sickness, whether of physical or psychological origin, that should be treated or else suffered in silence, the best advice being to lead a life of celibacy.

Non-Orthodox communities, which may be no less intuitively homophobic than Orthodox ones, have nevertheless tried to accept homosexuality and lesbianism as lifestyles that are beyond the control of the individual and which have to be accommodated on their own terms. This approach has been slow to develop, with the West Coast of America being the trend-setter. Rabbis who have taken the lead have been largely motivated by a basic concern for social justice. But how far can one go in such a radical direction, and at what cost of disapproval from 'normal' fee-paying members of congregations? An early response to the slowness of change was the creation in America of Gay Temples ('temple' being the American Reform term for synagogue) that were subsequently admitted for membership of the Union of American Hebrew Congregations, the 'Reform' movement. Not surprisingly, once created, they were seen as indicating a failure of the mainstream communities to integrate their own gay members, so a greater openness has developed.

The existence of rabbis who happened to be gay has long been known, though either the legal strictures of their society or personal caution meant that they remained 'in the closet'. Incidentally they existed, and exist, in all the different religious denominations of Judaism, Orthodox and non-Orthodox, with different degrees of difficulty and downright suffering as they effectively led a double life. With the rise of Gay Lib the possibility of their coming out, and of self-proclaimed gays being accepted for rabbinic training, became a challenge to the seminaries. The Reconstructionist Rabbinic College in the United States, and the Leo Baeck College in the United Kingdom, both, incidentally, institutions created in the post-war period, have taken the lead in a quiet, unheralded way, to be followed only by the Hebrew Union College in America of the 'classical' seminaries born in the nineteenth century. Known homosexual and lesbian rabbis have since been employed by congregations in the USA and UK but as yet there are few other Jewish societies elsewhere secure enough in their ideology or membership to take such a step. Here society's norms and openness clearly determine the direction taken by the Jewish community.

A major debate has erupted over the question of whether there could be a religious ceremony to mark the desire of a gay couple to live in a permanent relationship with each other. Can it be permitted within a Jewish framework, given the strongly antagonistic line of the tradition? If so should such a 'commitment ceremony' be similar to the heterosexual wedding or should it be of a completely different order. And should there also be provision for a *get*, a document of divorce, if the 'marriage' comes to an end? There are individual rabbis in the USA and the UK who willingly perform such ceremonies, convinced of the justice and human value of them, though it remains a highly charged subject. It is hard to see any way in which *Halakhah* could accommodate itself to such an act at this time. It is one more example of the challenge faced by Judaism as a whole by the Enlightenment and Emancipation. No human issue can be avoided or set aside any longer. Indeed such was the openness, courage and perhaps curiosity of the rabbis who created the Talmud that they were willing, within the limitations of their time and tradition, to address the most intimate of human questions. Today, if it is possible within the Orthodox world (or better, worlds) to discuss such issues sympathetically, there is little they can do to help, and it is largely left to the non-Orthodox movements to deal with them, whether they wish to or not.

I would like to add a further nuance to what a contemporary

approach to *Halakhah* might mean. It is based on my experience as Principal of the Leo Baeck College. Having been created from new in the post-war era, the College has been able to look with fresh eyes at Jewish needs and the skills required for a new generation of rabbis, and address some of the problems we examined at the end of chapter 6. Thus our training has expanded on classical studies of Jewish tradition to include a formidable programme throughout the five years in 'Pastoral Care and Community Skills'.

This includes a year-long introduction to basic counselling skills, as well as short-term external courses, for example in bereavement. Increasingly students undergo a prolonged period of personal psychotherapy as a part of the training. This programme has its origins in an awareness by many of our earliest graduates that they were poorly equipped to deal with the sort of problems that people actually brought to them, so that some skills in this area became crucial. Today's rabbinic students learn to listen to what the congregant is actually bringing to them, and are able to respond with professional understanding, including recognising when they need to refer someone on to those with appropriate skills. In place of the authoritarian image that still clings to the 'rabbi', we are attempting instead to empower people to take responsibility for their own lives. But such training also helps meet the needs of the rabbi him/herself. As we saw earlier, enormous demands are made upon them in their work. They must cope with everything from the fantasies projected upon them by congregants, to working with the deep hurt experienced by survivors of the Shoah and their sometimes traumatised children. There are pressure on the rabbis' families and family life and they need to gain considerably more insight into their own functioning and limitations, learning how to establish appropriate boundaries for what is a limitless task and create the kind of support system they themselves need.

There does seem to be one particular consequence to this emphasis on training, now over twenty years in its development. It seems to me that in the way our Progressive rabbis examine contemporary issues they do bring these new insights and skills to bear. The combination of an openness and sympathy for human realities, together with a greater awareness of their own motivations and, indeed, prejudices, do have a long-term impact on the way decisions are made about a whole variety of community issues. In this sense a new dimension is being brought to what are essentially *halakhic* issues in a new guise. We see here something of the legacy of Freud and all his many and varied followers being reintegrated into a classical Jewish consciousness. Whether it proves to be significant or not in the long run, here at least is something that contributes a new dimension to the old tension between Jewish law and Jewish life.

Further Reading

Arthur A. Cohen and Paul Mendes-Flohr (eds.), *Contemporary Jewish Religious Thought: Original Essays on Critical Concepts, Movements, and Beliefs* (New York, The Free Press, a division of Macmillan; London, Collier Macmillan, 1972): a remarkable collection of essays covering most areas of contemporary Jewish thought.

Jonathan Magonet (ed.), *Jewish Explorations of Sexuality* (Providence and Oxford, Berghahn Books, 1995). As well as examining traditional and contemporary attitudes to sexuality in general, this volume offers a comprehensive look at attitudes to homosexuality.

Eleven are the stars of Joseph's dream
Jewish dreams and visions

Joseph is the dreamer. We first meet him in the Hebrew Bible as a young man, the favourite of his father and consequently isolated from his brothers. He does not help matters by telling them about his dreams in which he sees himself as the leader of his people before whom his brothers and even his father and mother have to do obeisance.

Dreams for the biblical writers were as mysterious as they are for us today. With their curious mixture of the familiar and the surreal they hint at possibilities and experiences both within and beyond our grasp. But they can also be cruelly misleading.

> As when a hungry man dreams he is eating and awakes with his hunger not satisfied, or as when a thirsty man dreams he is drinking and awakes faint, with his thirst not quenched . . . (Isa. 29:8)

Dreams can be the expression of hopes that might nevertheless be realised:

> . . . your sons and your daughters shall prophesy, your old men shall dream dreams, and your young men shall see visions . . . (Joel 3:1)

But they can also be exploited to seduce people into false hopes:

I have heard what the prophets have said who prophesy lies in My name, saying, 'I have dreamed, I have dreamed!' ... they think to make my people forget My name by their dreams which they tell one another. (Jer. 23:25, 27)

Inevitably it is Ecclesiastes, though in a suitably obscure verse, which points to the untrustworthiness of dreams:

For just as a dream comes in the midst of much business, so the voice of a fool comes with many words. (Eccles. 5:2)

That dreams reflect waking ideas was recognised, and even exploited, by the rabbis:

The Roman Emperor said to Rabbi Joshua ben Chanania: 'You profess to be clever. Tell me what I shall see in my dream.' The rabbi answered: 'You will see the Persians take you to do forced labour, robbing you and making you feed unclean animals with a golden implement.' The emperor thought about it all day and at night he saw all this in his dream. (b. Berakhot 56a)

In the Middle Ages Abraham Ibn Ezra, a rationalist, as well as being a physician, philosopher, grammarian, Bible commentator, etc., took a more pragmatic view: 'When a dream is confused with many contents, it is known that it comes from mixing foods, one of the four "roots" being overpowering. There is no "solution" to the dream, nor can you learn from it good or ill, for it is vanity.'

Whether dreams are evidence of divine revelation or simply indigestion, across the millennia 'old Jewish men and women' have dreamt dreams and young Jewish men and women have seen visions of a better world. In the past these have been linked to the hope of the end of exile, the return to the land and the coming of the Messiah.

This latter term needs a bit of explanation. Literally the Hebrew verb *m-sh-h* means 'to anoint', and refers to the practice of pouring oil on the head of people appointed to special office – including priests, prophets and kings. David was anointed by the prophet Samuel to become king in place of Saul, and he became seen as the first successful ruler of the Jewish nation, and hence the prototype of a future king who would one day restore Israel to its former glory. (The many personal failings of David were explained away or justified by later rabbinic tradition, which also made him into a Torah scholar after their own likeness, otherwise the formulation below by Maimonides of what the Messiah should be like could prove problematic.)

Actually the rabbinic tradition knows of two 'Messiahs', one designated as 'Ben Yosef', the 'son of Joseph' and one as 'Ben David', the 'son of David'. The former will fight a war against the forces of evil and be killed in the struggle, to be succeeded by the latter who will usher in the messianic age. The existence of two messianic figures probably follows from the biblical fact of the anointing of Saul as well as David. The patriarch Jacob had two wives, Rachel and Leah, who between them, with the help of two concubines, bore twelve sons. The division between the 'Rachel' tribes and 'Leah' tribes is a recurrent theme in the biblical account. Saul descended from the Rachel tribes (to which Joseph belonged) and David from the Leah tribes (Judah). Thus two messianic lines were started, though the first was aborted. Nevertheless a descendant of Saul's family, 'ben Joseph', will still have a role to play in the Messianic drama.

As always in Jewish tradition such yearnings and expectations find their expression in concrete *halakhic*, legal, form. Maimonides formulates it as follows in his Code:

Should a king arise from the house of David, one who is learned in Torah and performs the *mitzvot*, commandments, like David his ancestor, according to both the written and oral Torah, and he ensures that all of Israel follow the Torah and adhere to it, and he fights the wars of the Eternal – behold this one is under the presumption of being the Messiah. If he does this and succeeds and is victorious against all the nations round about and rebuilds the Temple on its place and gathers in the exiles of Israel – then this is certainly the Messiah! But if he does not succeed in such a manner, or is killed, then it is clear that he is not the one promised by the Torah. (*hilkhot m'lakhim* (Laws of Kings) 11:4)

The messianic visions in the Bible are full of other dimensions, but of these Maimonides is very wary:

It must not be imagined that in the days of the Messiah any of the laws of nature will be set aside, or that creation will become new in any way. The world will continue just as it is. As to what is written in Isaiah (11:6) 'The wolf shall dwell with the lamb, and the leopard lie down with the kid', this is just a metaphor which means that Israel will dwell in security among the world's evil nations which are likened to the wolf and leopard. (*hilkhot m'lakhim* 12:1)

So, too, according to Maimonides, are all such images to be explained.

If you will excuse a slight aside, the story is told that the Jerusalem Zoo has a cage in which a leopard and a kid do indeed lie down together. A tourist who saw them was quite astonished and asked the keeper how this miracle was performed. 'It is quite simple,' he replied, 'you just have to replace the kid every day.'

What will the Messianic world be like? Again Maimonides:

The prophets and the sages did not long for the days of the Messiah in order to dominate the nations of the world, nor to rule over them, nor to be exalted over them, nor simply to eat, drink and be merry, but rather in order that they should be free to study Torah, with no one to oppress or prevent them, so that they would be worthy of the life of the world to come . . .

In that time [of the Messiah] there shall be no famine, no war, no jealousy and no strife. Prosperity shall be spread everywhere and all luxuries will be as common as dust, and the whole world will only be engaged in knowing the Eternal. Therefore Israel will be great sages, and all things

that are now mysterious and deeply concealed will be
revealed to everyone, and they will acquire the knowledge
of their Creator to the fullest human capacity, as it says:
'The earth shall be full of the knowledge of the Eternal as
the waters cover the sea' (Isa. 11:9). (*hilkhot m'lakhim* 12:4–
5)

Such Messianic dreams began in the Bible itself and were part of
the complex ever shifting situation of Jewish life in the centuries
following the closing of the biblical canon. Out of this turmoil
emerged rabbinic Judaism and Christianity, which was itself a
stunning inversion of the messianic hope. Jesus, the 'king of the
Jews' died on a cross, like so many thousands of other Jews killed
by the Romans at the time, but his apparent failure in worldly
terms became transformed into a spiritual success. Judaism has
known both the 'evolutionary' approach of Maimonides and
more apocalyptic versions. The 'temptation' of the latter kind of
messianic thinking was very powerful, especially in times of
hardship. Reality demands a careful relationship to messianic
expectations because of the danger they themselves could pose
to the ordering and continuation of society. Rabbi Yochanan ben
Zakkai, living at the time of the destruction of the second Temple,
when Messianic hopes abounded, could advise: 'If there be a
plant in your hand when they say to you: "Behold the Messiah!"
Go and plant the plant, and afterwards go out to greet him' (Avot
d'Rabbi Nathan II version 31 q).[1]

The yearning for the Messiah led many to attempt to fulfil
that role over the centuries, the most successful in terms of
attracting many followers inevitably leading to disastrous
consequences for the Jewish world. The great Rabbi Akiva
supported Simeon Bar Kokhba whose uprising against the
Romans in 132–5 CE led to the loss of Jerusalem and massive
destruction. Warlike self-proclaimed Messiahs followed the rise
of Islam in the seventh, eighth and ninth centuries. Rumours of
a coming Messiah followed the Crusade of 1096 and figures
proclaimed themselves in Baghdad and Fez in the twelfth
century, one of them even gaining the approval of Maimonides,
though he strongly criticised a similar figure who arose in Yemen.

I have no patience with people who console themselves with the thought that the Messiah will soon appear and lead them to Jerusalem. They who remain in the country, expecting the Messiah, are causing others to transgress the Law. Besides there is no definite time for which the appearance of the Messiah is foretold. It is not known whether his coming will be in the near future or at some remote period. A sincere wish to observe the Jewish law has no relation to the appearance of the Messiah.

At the end of the thirteenth century in Spain the kabbalist Abraham ben Samuel Abulafia saw himself in this role and the philosopher Hasdai Crescas announced that the Messiah had been born in the kingdom of Castile. Jews forced to convert to Christianity, who nevertheless retained their Jewish loyalties, believed that Messianic intervention was about to come to save them. Preachers in the sixteenth century foresaw his imminent arrival, while the seventeenth century saw perhaps the most infamous claimant to the role, Sabbatai Zevi. Enthusiastic Jews from all over the world left their homes to follow him on his march to Constantinople to claim the Sultan's throne – only to convert to Islam to save his life! He based himself on kabbalistic teachings and after his apostasy it seems that the Jewish world reacted against such apparently dangerous overt mystical activity. Some argue that the rise of Chasidism, a popular pietistic movement led by charismatic teachers, was itself a kind of introverted response to Sabbatainism, the struggle to redeem the world for God no longer being conducted in the outer world but within the individual soul.

In the nineteenth century the Reform movement turned away from the idea of a messianic figure and instead concentrated on the prophetic promises of universal harmony, a 'messianic age'. After the Emancipation many Jews translated the range of messianic hopes into their secular equivalents. Thus Zionism, with its central theme of the rebuilding of the Jewish people on their own land, can be seen as an attempt to fulfil the messianic promise, but through our own human efforts rather than waiting for God's own good time. There are similar equations of the sort: messianic idea minus God equals ... (I learnt this kind of messianic maths from my colleague Rabbi Lionel Blue.) Thus the biblical ideas of universal justice, 'brotherhood' and peace become translated into socialism and communism which Jews wholeheartedly embraced. Instead of a lifetime dedicated to studying Torah, Jews lent their precocious intellectual abilities to every field of academic and intellectual life.

How far this equation is a legitimate reading of what has happened in the Jewish world is hard to say. Certainly issues like freedom, so familiar from the powerful Passover ceremony, have led Jews to embrace movements for liberation. It was American-Jewish teenagers in disproportionate numbers who came to Alabama to march with Martin Luther King – two of them were killed for it. When asked, most of the young Jews who had marched denied that being Jewish had anything to do with participating. Some argue that the Jewish campaign for the right to leave the Soviet Union did much to trigger the break-up of that power. Some South African Jews were at the forefront of the political struggle against Apartheid. That is not to say that individual Jews do not also belong to reactionary groups and movements – though they are less likely to be welcomed.

Nothing illustrates the fascinating divergences of ideology and activity that can co-exist within the Jewish people than the story of two pioneers of 'modern' languages. In 1859 in Bialystok, Poland, was born one Ludwik Lazar Zamenhof. He did some early studies in Yiddish, but then pursued the idea of creating a universal language so that all peoples could communicate directly with each other. His research was made public in 1887 with his book *Lingvo Internacia* which he published under the name Doktoro Esperanto – Doctor Hope. The language, Esperanto, took its name from this publication.

One year earlier, 1858, in Luzhky, Lithuania, was born Eliezer Yitzhak Perelman. From early on he became a Zionist and came to the conclusion that the ancient language of Hebrew should be revived so as to serve as the language of the Jewish people in their new nation. He took the name Eliezer Ben Yehuda, edited a sixteen-volume Hebrew–Hebrew dictionary, and became known as the father of modern Hebrew. Between Zamenhof and Ben Yehudah lie the parameters of the universalism and particularism of the Jew entering the world of modernity.

Moshiach Now!

Though one would have thought that we would have learned the lesson from so many disasters in the past, the idea of the Messiah is not dead. In any generation he (today we should add 'she') might come and any pious sage might be qualified to fill the role. In our time, after the horror and destruction of the Shoah, it was inevitable that messianic hopes and speculations would arise, and the resettlement of the Jews in the land of Israel has added fuel to the flame, even if Zionism itself was avowedly non- if not anti-religious. (Incidentally, Christians are no less susceptible to such expectations with groups, mostly from the USA, enthusiastically supporting the State of Israel in anticipation of the second coming of Jesus now that the Jews are back on their land. It is a somewhat uneasy alliance for Jews, since the Christian expectations include the assumption that the Jewish people will then convert *en masse* to Christianity.)

However it has been among the Lubavitch Chasidim, the most active and missionising movement within Judaism, missionising in terms of trying to win Jews back to their tradition, that messianic hopes have been most prominent. They saw in their leader, the incumbent Lubavitcher Rebbe, Menachem Mendel Schneersohn, a man of extraordinary authority and charisma, all the hallmarks of the Messiah for which the world has been waiting. During the long period of his terminal illness the rumour spread throughout their world – and they have emissaries virtually wherever a community of Jews is to be found – that he would soon reveal himself. Car stickers promised, and advocated, '*moshiach* now!' Even his death seems to have left undimmed the enthusiasm of some (possibly many) Lubavitcher Chasidim, who argue that his resurrection is imminent, quoting one of the Thirteen Principles of Faith of Maimonides to back their claim. An advert from a group within Lubavitch calling themselves 'Project Moshiach Awareness' reads in part:

> We eagerly await the fulfilment of the Rebbe's clear statements, made with the clarity of prophetic vision that Moshiach is coming immediately. It is apparent that, in our times, there is no one more fitting to assume the role of leading us to the redemption as Moshiach than the Rebbe. We therefore join in an expression of commitment and faith in the coming redemption.[2]

The solemnity of this message is somewhat undermined by the concluding paragraph, though the combination of piety, appeal to Jewish 'intellect' (provided certain questions are ignored) and extraordinary public relations, sums up the appeal and success of the movement with a certain public:

> Faith causes problems sometimes. The intellectual person questions and needs help in this area of Judaism. The Rebbe taught us how to GIVE YOU A 'FAITH LIFT'. With over 50 years of experience, we guarantee you satisfaction.
> If you need a 'Faith Lift', call on us. Our doors are open – so are our minds. Satisfaction guaranteed. Try us, you'll like us!

The concept of the 'resurrection of the dead' is an ancient Jewish belief that precedes the post-biblical battles for power between the Sadducees and Pharisees. But it refers to a collective physical revival at the end of days, the nature of which has been hotly debated over the centuries. The only religious offspring of Judaism till now to apply it to an individual, and a Messiah at that, has been Christianity. So however understandable their loyalty to the memory of an extraordinary man, this does seem to represent a bizarre assimilation of Christian beliefs into ultra-Orthodox Jewish faith, something that earlier generations of Lubavitcher Rebbes, including the recent incumbent, would have found grotesque. (A joke currently in circulation suggests that guards have been posted at the Rebbe's grave to prevent assassination attempts!)

Kabbalah and Jewish Mysticism

Once again we have stepped into a contemporary issue that has its origins in the remote past. The Chasidim are the latest, populist inheritors of a Jewish mystical tradition whose origins are obscure precisely because of the restrictions placed on access to it in the past. Kabbalah is currently undergoing something of a revival, in a popular form that would have been anathema to earlier generations of practitioners. That texts are even available for study in Western languages is, ironically, the result of the highly rational, anti-mystical work of the 'Science of Judaism' movement which began in the last century with the aim of exploring the whole of Judaism as a historic phenomenon. At the beginning it was highly judgmental in what it considered belonged to the 'pure' essence of Judaism and what were superstitious or corrupt accretions from outside. It required someone of the genius of Gershom Scholem (1897–1982) to establish an entire discipline devoted to the study of this significant if hidden tradition within Judaism. Since his pioneering study, *Major Trends in Jewish Mysticism*, whole libraries of scholarly research reflect the breadth and complexity of this tradition, and indeed the difficulties of interpreting it both in its own terms and within its historical context. Here we can only look at a few of the 'trends' and figures and refer the reader to the suggested reading at the end of this chapter.

There are considerable problems about defining the term 'mystical'. The desire to serve God, be heard by God and come near to God, are all part of mainstream Judaism, so where does the 'normal' end and the 'mystical' begin?[3] How far is the 'mystical' actually an attempt to go beyond, and hence contradict, the normative forms of Judaism that everyone else practices – the 'surface' appearance being for the masses while initiates penetrate beyond? The term used to describe this activity, Kabbalah, derives from a word meaning to 'receive', hence the secret 'tradition' that is handed down orally from master to pupil. Thus alongside the 'revealed' Torah, the Hebrew Bible, the Talmud, Jewish philosophy and legal Codes, there was the 'concealed' tradition based on the Zohar and subsequent Kabbalistic works. Not all of Kabbalah is necessarily of a mystical nature. Moreover unlike the parallel traditions in Christianity and Islam, Jewish mystics rarely left behind descriptions of their experience.

For some its study was a purely intellectual exercise. For others, however, such knowledge was pursued because it was felt to carry the power to change the material universe itself, for after all the Torah was a blueprint for the creation of the world. This sense of power, which had its expression in later practices like alchemy, further reinforced the idea that only certain people, appropriately pure in their motives, should be allowed access to it. Moreover it was precisely this aspect that could fuel the kind of disastrous messianic activism just mentioned.

Mystical experience can exist at any time. The first chapter of the Book of Ezekiel with its mysterious description of the Chariot ridden by the 'likeness of the appearance of the glory of the Eternal' is itself the record of such an experience. Understandably this chapter became the basis of early mystical speculation, as did the creation story in Genesis 1. As early as the second century CE the Mishnah warns about precautions that need to be taken in studying these passages:

The 'work of creation' (Genesis 1) may not be taught in the presence of two students, nor the 'work of the chariot' (Ezekiel 1) in the presence of one, unless he is a sage and can follow with his own understanding. Whoever speculates on four things, it would be better if he had never been born. What is above, what is beneath, what before and what after. (Hagigah 2:1)

The Talmud knows wonder-working rabbis and those with a special relationship with God. But a particular story attests to the attractions and dangers of mystical activity. It tells of 'four who entered Pardes'. 'Pardes' is a Persian loan word meaning 'orchard' which appears once in the Hebrew Bible in the Song of Songs (4:13). From it will come the word 'paradise', but here it seems to be a term used for mystical speculation. All four rabbis named were important teachers of the second century, Ben Azzai, Ben Zoma, Elisha ben Avuya and Rabbi Akiva. Ben Azzai looked, and died; Ben Zoma looked, and went mad; Elisha ben Avuya 'cut down the shoots' – he became an apostate from Judaism and was afterwards known as 'Aher', 'the other one'; only Rabbi Akiva entered in peace and departed in peace.

Though various movements and writings can be traced across the centuries the one 'book' that transformed the nature of Kabbalah and had the greatest influence was the Zohar, which became virtually another 'Scripture' to put alongside the Hebrew Bible and the Talmud. The word means 'light' or 'splendour'. It is an esoteric commentary on the Torah, that purports to be composed by Shimon bar Yochai, a rabbi of the second century, and his circle. Nevertheless the style and content reveal it to have been written in the thirteenth century by Moses de Leon, someone steeped in the already existent mystical literature of his time.

Again there is no space here to examine its contents or influence in any depth, but the following passage shows something of its emotional appeal:

> It is like a girl, beautiful and gracious and much loved and she is kept closely confined in her palace. She has a special lover, unrecognized by anyone and concealed. This lover, because of the love which he feels for her, passes by the door of her house, and looks on every side and she knows that her lover is constantly walking to and fro by the door of her house. What does she do? She opens a tiny door in the secret palace where she lives and shows her face to her lover. Then she withdraws at once and is gone. None of those in her lover's vicinity sees or understands but her lover alone knows and his heart and soul and inner being yearn for her and he knows that it is because of the love that she bears him that she showed herself to him for a moment, in order to awaken love in him.

So it is with the Torah. She reveals herself only to her lover. The Torah knows that the wise man walks to and fro every day by the door of her house. What does she do? She shows her face to him from the palace and signals to him and she withdraws at once to her palace, and hides herself. None of those who are there knows or understands but he alone knows and his heart and soul and inner being yearn for her. And so the Torah is revealed and then is hidden and treats her lover lovingly, in order to awaken love in him. (Zohar Mishpatim 99a)

At the heart of the Kabbalistic enterprise was the question of how to resolve the paradox of God as an infinite being outside the world of time, space and causality, utterly 'transcendent', who could at the same time be present in a material universe and available to mere human beings, fully 'immanent'. The former perception of God is known as the *En sof*, 'without end', that aspect of the divine of which nothing could be known or said. In order for there even to be a material universe, God becomes manifest through ten successive 'emanations', the *sefirot*, 'spheres'. 'When [the *En sof*] first assumed the form [of the first *sefirah*] He caused nine splendid lights to emanate from it which, shining through it, diffused a bright light in all directions' (Zohar Idra Zuta on Haazinu 288a).

Another image is that of water poured into different coloured bottles, each representing a different one of the *sefirot*, which are named: 1. *Keter* (crown); 2. *Hokhmah* (Wisdom); 3. *Binah* (Understanding); 4. *Hesed* (Loving kindness); 5. *Gevurah* (Power); 6. *Tiferet* (Beauty); 7. *Nezah* (Victory); 8. *Hod* (Splendour); 9. *Yesod* (Foundation); 10. *Malkhut* (Sovereignty). Innumerable different interpretations are placed on each of these 'emanations', and the pattern of their relationship becomes itself the source of further speculation.

A major development in Kabbalistic thought took place in sixteenth-century Palestine in the circle of mystics who lived in the city of Safed. The most important of these was Isaac Luria (1534–72), the *Ari*, 'lion', an ascetic who reported teachings that came to him from the prophet Elijah. He introduced the concept of *tzimtzum*, 'withdrawal', that God 'withdrew from Himself into Himself' to leave room for the material world to exist. Into this 'space' entered the *sefirot*. Louis Jacobs summarises this highly complex system as follows:

> Into this 'empty space' a thin ray of light from *En Sof* emerged. This is the sustaining power of all that subsequently emerged. From this there emerged what is known in the Lurianic Kabbalah as *Adam Kadmon* ('Primordial Man') ... Subtle lights then emerged from the 'ear', 'nose' and 'mouth' of *Adam Kadmon*. These produced *in potentia* the 'vessels' with which to contain the light of the *Sefirot* which were later to emerge. Lights then proceeded from the 'eyes' of *Adam Kadmon* and while the 'vessels' of the three higher *Sefirot* – *Keter*, *Hokhmah* and *Binah* – were able to contain these lights the 'vessels' of the seven lower *Sefirot* were unable to do so. The result was the cosmic catastrophe known in the Lurianic Kabbalah as *shevirat ha-kelim*, 'the breaking of the vessels'. Ultimately this was necessary in order for the 'other side' (*sitra ahara*) to emerge. This is the demonic side of existence, necessary if the world was to become an arena in which man could freely choose the good and reject the evil. Only in this way could he make the good his own ...
>
> As a result of the breaking of the vessels the light of *En Sof* became, as it were, fragmented. 'Holy sparks' from the Infinite light were scattered to form the vital power to sustain the Sefirotic realm and the 'worlds' beneath it. But now that the vessels are broken everything is in a state of disarray. Nothing is in its proper place. The gigantic task allotted to man is that of reclaiming and releasing the 'holy sparks' by restoring them to their Source. This is the process known as *tikkun*, 'putting right', 'perfecting'. When the task of *tikkun* is complete, redemption will come not only to Israel and not only to mankind as a whole but to the entire cosmic process, in fact, to God Himself in His aspect of manifestation.[4]

One consequence of these ideas is to make every human activity part of the quest for redemption, the 'redeeming of the sparks'. In a popularised form this became part of the teaching of the 'Chasidic' movement, started by Rabbi Israel ben Eliezer, the Baal Shem Tov, the 'Good Master of the Name (of God)', the Besht (1700–60). The movement spread rapidly throughout Poland in the eighteeenth century, despite, or because of, opposition to it from traditional rabbis. The movement continues today and though relatively small, and full of internal rifts and rivalries, occasionally leading to punch-ups on the streets of New York, it is certainly the most visible aspect of Jewish existence if only because of their garb which is a version of the clothing of eighteenth-century Polish gentry. Legends surrounded the leaders, *tzaddikim*, the 'righteous' ones (*chasidim*, the 'pious', being the term for their disciples) and these had an impact on Jewish thought through the popular writings of Martin Buber. In fact Buber has been criticised by Gershom Scholem for focusing on these folkloristic aspects and seemingly ignoring the complex philosophical and theological writings that stand behind them. But the appeal of the early movement was to an impoverished, suffering Jewish population, poorly educated Jewishly, who found in the popular mysticism of Chasidism a way of expressing their spiritual needs in a simple and direct way.

A famous story has a Jew standing at the back of the synagogue on Yom Kippur, the Day of Atonement, desperately unhappy because he cannot read the Hebrew prayers. So finally he starts reciting the Hebrew alphabet over and over again and prays to God – 'here are the letters, I have to leave it to you to put them together in the right way'. In a variation, a boy in a similar situation, equally despairing, suddenly starts to whistle aloud at the end of the day of fasting and prayer. The other congregants turn on him in anger at disturbing the piety of the day, but the Rebbe admonishes them that only his prayer had the simple sincerity that God desired and it had pierced the highest heavens. A teaching attributed to the Baal Shem Tov illustrates something of the power of such teachings.

A king had built a glorious palace full of corridors and partitions, but he himself lived in the innermost room. When the palace was completed and his servants came to pay him homage, they found that they could not approach the king because of the devious maze. While they stood and wondered, the king's son came and showed them that those were not real partitions, but only magical illusions, and that the king, in truth, was easily accessible. Push forward bravely and you shall find no obstacle.

Chasidism found its opposition both from traditional circles and those entering modernity through the 'Haskalah', 'enlightenment' movement. The Chasidic masters were often regarded as miracle-workers by their followers and even as intercessors on their behalf with God, a kind of personality cult that was regarded with disfavour by those outside the circle. It has to be remembered that in the early days their emphasis on joy, their spontaneous prayers, their use of the *niggun*, a melody, as ways of reaching God outside of the conventional religious forms, made them very suspect, particularly since the memory of the Sabbataian debacle was still very fresh. The Chasidim we see today, usually of the Lubavitch movement, have come full circle so that paradoxically they are seen as the upholders of 'authentic' Orthodox Jewish practice. Jews have a very selective historical memory.

Buber's *Tales of the Chasidim* and other collections helped create an interest in the movement in Western circles and his selection and retelling has great spiritual power. They introduce us to extraordinary figures like Nachman of Bratslav, the great-grandson of the Baal Shem Tov, the only major master not to have founded a dynasty of his own. Instead his followers study his writings and particularly a series of stories he wrote shortly before his death – since they have no 'living' teacher they are known as the 'dead Chasidim'. The Chasidic world is yet another vast area of Jewish spiritual exploration that needs to be given a far fuller treatment, so I would refer you once again to the reading list at the end of this chapter.

Precisely because of the popularity of the Chasidic masters

and the rivalry between their followers about the relative merit of their *Tzaddik*, numerous tales arose about their respective abilities. While some are pious compositions others clearly belong to parodies written by opponents of the movement, so it is not always easy to tell what was meant sincerely and what was a parody. I have no idea about the source of the following story, but in a curious way it suggests both the apparent absurdity and utter self-confidence of those who feel themselves under the direct protection of the divine.

Two Chasidim are travelling on a train. When the guard asks them for their ticket they say that they do not need one. 'But everyone needs a ticket!' says the guard. 'No,' one of them replies, 'you do not need a ticket and neither does the driver of the train.' 'But without the driver the train would not go!' 'Precisely!' answers the Chasid.

There is another story that sums up the tension between the values of the early Chasidic movement and the traditional rabbinic world. I have also heard it as a Sufi story from the late Umar von Ehrenfels, a German anthropologist convert to Islam with whom I shared some early Jewish–Muslim dialogues. I will give first the Chasidic version in the form in which I heard it – inevitably there are other ones as well.

A rabbi is walking along a country lane and sees a Jewish peasant in the field. The man is praying: 'Dear God, thank you for giving me this marvellous life. If I had the chance I would work for you for nothing, because I love you.' The rabbi is horrified at these words and admonishes the peasant. 'This is not how we address God! It is the time for the afternoon prayer.' He sets about teaching him the *Amidah*, the standing prayer, and all the other parts that belong to the afternoon service. At the end the peasant thanks him, and satisfied, the rabbi goes on his way. That night he has a dream in which God appears to him and is very angry. 'Look what you have done! The peasant has already forgotten the prayers you taught him, so he cannot pray them. But he also knows that the prayer he said before is not acceptable. So I have lost one of my prayers!' In one version the rabbi is so horrified that he drops dead! In another, he returns to the peasant the next day, apologises for interfering and gives him permission to resume praying as he had in the past.

The Sufi version has a different conclusion, and it is one that I think is also far closer to an appropriate Jewish conclusion today. Let's stay with the rabbi and the peasant.

When the rabbi returns to the peasant and explains, the peasant thanks him but says, 'Now that I know what the tradition is and how I should be praying, I cannot go back to what I used to say. Instead I have to learn to recite the traditional prayers but with the same sincerity that I felt before.'

The Dream of Jerusalem

Nowhere have Jews invested more dreams than in the land of Israel and in particular Jerusalem. In exile from our land for almost two thousand years, the promise and hope of return has been constantly present in virtually every aspect of our religious life. Three times a day we recite the blessing in the *Amidah*:

> To Jerusalem, Your city, return in mercy, and dwell within it as You have spoken; and rebuild it soon in our days as an everlasting building, and establish speedily the throne of David. Blessed are You Eternal, who rebuilds Jerusalem.

At every mealtime the closing grace speaks of the restoration of Jerusalem. At every traditional wedding ceremony, as we have seen, we recite:

> Let the barren one (Zion) truly be glad and rejoice in the ingathering of her children within her in happiness. Blessed are You, Eternal, who gives joy to Zion through her children.

At *Pesach* and the end of the New Year celebrations we say: *l'shanah haba'ah birushalayim* – Next year in Jerusalem! In each house Jews are instructed to leave a part of the ceiling unplastered, as a reminder and sign of mourning that the Temple is destroyed. There is no part of our religious ritual or calendar or even physical life that does not contain some echo of Jerusalem, some yearning for our return and its rebuilding. And all our prayers, wherever we live throughout the world, are directed towards Jerusalem, a tradition that goes back to the Hebrew Bible itself (Dan. 6:11).

But this Jewish return is always linked in our tradition to events of universal, even cosmic, significance. For Jerusalem in rabbinic and later mystical thought is the centre of the world. The Temple site is where creation began, where heaven and earth meet, where divine energy flows into the world, and where the messianic age will be ushered in. The physical Jerusalem has its spiritual counterpart in the divine realm: what happens below has consequences above; the Temple, with its sacrifices, sustains the cosmic order. The fate of Jerusalem and the fate of the Jewish people and the fate of the whole world are completely intertwined in this deepest strand of Jewish thought and experience. And this must account on some level for the depth of feeling for Jerusalem in even the most secular Jew.

The Jewish longing for the restoration of Jerusalem with all its wider implications is beautifully illustrated in the story told of the Chasidic master, Nachman of Bratslav, we met above. When he sent out invitations for his daughter's wedding the wording was as follows: 'The wedding of my daughter will take place on such and such a date in the holy city of Jerusalem.' There was a mark beside the word Jerusalem indicating a note at the bottom of the invitation which read: 'If, in the meantime, the Messiah has not come, the wedding will take place in Bratslav.'

But the spiritual in Judaism is always wedded to the physical, the real, the tangible. Jewish law makes it a priority on Jews to return to the land and settle there. And throughout history, except for a couple of centuries immediately following the Roman destruction of the Second Temple, when Jews were banned by official decree from entering Aelia Capitolina, the name given the city by the Romans, Jews have returned to Jerusalem to visit and live. There are documents from almost every century recording this, poems of longing, letters home and travellers' tales.

I once tried to capture in a poem something of this longing and the extraordinary fact of the ingathering of Jewish exiles from every part of the world since the creation of the State of Israel. It was written in the late 1960s when the Post Office used to auction off lost property.

AND THE WORD OF THE LORD FROM JERUSALEM

Such, indeed, is the holiness of Jerusalem
that the Post Office auctions it off
at regular intervals in bulk.

'Holy books'
that by some oversight of divine providence
(and the aforementioned Post Office)
have strayed from their destined path
can be redeemed in anonymous packages
by those with a feeling for the sacred
or facilities for re-marketing
at a price more suited to their worth.

Scattered among crates
of assorted underwear
of twenty identical parts to an unidentified machine
of shoes and tubes of toothpaste
of sardines, children's games and one coffee tin
of endless clothing
of an incomplete set of Shakespeare in French
of a complete set of something in Polish,
are these jewels of religious wisdom
of perceptive commentary
of refutation and polemic
of saintly dreams
of pious admonitions
– prayers of the holy people
tossed about in the familiar indignity
of yet another temporary exile.
Going for the first time.
Going for the second time.
Gone!!

For most of the past two thousand years, Jews have lived in the city under sufferance, as successive empires and religions have ruled it. In the two and a half thousand years since 587 BCE when the Kingdom of Judah fell, the city has been conquered more than twenty times. The historian Sir Martin Gilbert points out that it has been ruled from Babylon, Susa, Thebes, Alexandria, Antioch, Rome, Byzantium, Damascus, Baghdad, Cairo, Aleppo, Constantinople, London and Amman. It is in some ways the ultimate paradox, a place called, according to one interpretation, *ir shalom*, 'the city of peace', which has probably witnessed more bloody conflict than any place on earth.

An Orthodox rabbi friend once asked the rhetorical question: Why is Jerusalem filled with so many crazy people? – something that anyone who has visited there can easily verify. His answer was that Jerusalem is like a spa, a place renowned for the healing properties of the waters. If you visit a spa you expect to find healthy people, but instead you find it full of sick people hoping to be cured. In the same way Jerusalem, because it is known to be a holy place, attracts those seeking holiness, or some magical cure to their spiritual ills. But while they wait they display and act out the sicknesses they have brought with them

It is as if on a personal level, and sometimes on the level of religions or great empires, people seek to own Jerusalem, to find there an ultimate spiritual healing. But rather than seek God within it, they settle instead for the physical place, and get caught up in, and inevitably lost in, the power games of ownership. The struggle should be to find God. Instead we squabble over God's real estate. The greater the spirituality to be found, the greater the dream to be dreamt, the greater the blood that can be shed, the greater the greed and hubris that is evoked. That is the tragedy and disgrace of Jerusalem, but that indicates always its potential greatness. If conflict and struggle is intrinsic to the place, the true issue should be not a struggle for ownership, but the struggle to outdo each other in deeds of goodness and generosity.

Nevertheless there are innumerable records of a greater spirituality being expressed where Jerusalem is concerned. Israel Abrahams reports the following delightful anecdote:

'Next year in Jerusalem.' So have we all said since childhood. I heard a grey-beard repeating it in Jerusalem itself.
'What?' I said, 'you are here and I am here. Let us say:
Next year also in Jerusalem.' 'No,' replied the cheery
nonagenarian, 'next year in Jerusalem the Rebuilt (*Ha-
benuya*).' The old man firmly hoped that by the following
spring the Temple would be restored, and he would go up
with a joyous throng to the Mount of the House. Two
Passovers have gone since then. The old man still lives,
still hopes. He wrote to me last week: 'I am in no mood to
hurry God; I am only 92.'

Today, as always in the past where Jerusalem is concerned, the
political, social and spiritual, the deeply religious and the
equally deeply secular, issues are hopelessly intertwined. Too
many truths, too many legitimate cries for justice, too much
greed and too much narrowness of vision, are inevitably in
collision with each other. Each strand needs its clarification and
resolution, each claim needs to be acknowledged and met by
negotiation and compromise. Given the history of the physical
Jerusalem, the chances of a peaceful resolution to current
conflicts seem very slim. Given the history of the spiritual
Jerusalem, Jews, Christians and Muslims alike must work
together in hope.

It had been a while since I had visited the city and returned to
a place considerably enlarged, even more politicised and full of
emotions and tensions. But I found myself writing:

AGAIN JERUSALEM, AND AGAIN

Nevertheless
it is still possible to fall in love with
Jerusalem
all over again.
Despite everything.
Despite the fear in the streets of the old.
Despite the anger in the streets of the new.

Eleven are the stars of Joseph's dream

For any hidden courtyard
any vista
any crowded corner
can snatch away your breath
by its sheer . . .
density.

It is not the holiness,
too compromised,
nor its age alone.
It is something else:
a sad mocking at our pretensions
and a wonder at our dreams.
To have invested so much
in a couple of hills and valleys,
to have suffered so much to possess them
and done such harm to hold them
in the name of so many gods,
so much hope and greed.

So boast not of unity,
promise no eternity,
where Jerusalem is concerned,
for she will outlive our rhetoric
and lose even the memory of our passing –
another relic
for antiquarians to ponder
and archaeologists tenderly to reconstruct.

No,
better to tread softly,
woo her with tender care
and give the love we feel
to all her many children.

There is in the Hebrew Bible a prophetic vision that in a restored
Jerusalem, a rebuilt Temple, all peoples who believe in God can
meet together. That is a dream worthy of Joseph.

ki veiti beit t'fillah yiqqarei l'khol ha'amim
For My house shall be called a house of prayer for all
peoples. (Isa. 56:7)

Further Reading

On Kabbalah, Jewish Mysticism and Chasidism

Martin Buber, *Tales of the Hasidim,* vol. 1, *Early Masters;* vol. 2,
Late Masters (New York, Schocken Books, 1961); *The Tales of
Rabbi Nachman* (London, Souvenir Press (Educational Academic), 1956); *The Origin and Meaning of Hasidism* (New York,
Harper & Row, 1966): a subtle and powerful retelling of tales
of the Chasidic masters, as well as an introduction to their
world.

Louis Jacobs, *Jewish Mystical Testimonies* (New York, Schocken
Books, 1976). Any of Louis Jacobs' books on Jewish mysticism
and Chasidism, or indeed his popular collections on Jewish
law, ethics, thought or Bible exegesis are excellent value. I
would single out in their area *Hasidic Thought* (New York,
Behrman House, 1976); *Rabbi Moses Cordovero: The Palm Tree of
Deborah* (London, Valentine, Mitchell, 1960).

Gershom Scholem, *Major Trends in Jewish Mysticism* (London,
Thames and Hudson, 1955). This is the classic study of the
field. For a more popular introduction to the Zohar, see
Scholem's *Zohar: The Book of Splendour: Basic Readings from the
Kabbalah* (New York, Schocken Books, 1949). Two books
examine messianic thought and experience: *The Messianic Idea
in Judaism: And Other Essays in Jewish Spirituality* (London,
George Allen and Unwin, 1971), and the major study of the
false Messiah, *Sabbatai Sevi: The Mystical Messiah 1626–1676*
(The Littman Library, London, Routledge and Kegan Paul,
1973).

Adin Steinsaltz, *The Thirteen Petalled Rose: A Discourse on The
Essence of Jewish Existence and Belief* (New York, Basic Books,

1980): the spiritual exploration of a contemporary master of the Jewish rabbinic and mystical tradition.

Herbert Wiener, *Nine and a Half Mystics: The Kabbalah Today* (New York, Macmillan, 1969, 1992): an account of meetings with contemporary mystics living in Israel.

On Jerusalem

Karen Armstrong, *Jerusalem: One City, Three Faiths* (New York, Alfred A. Knopf, 1996): a balanced account of the history of the city from the perspective of the three faiths.

Martin Gilbert, *Jerusalem: Illustrated History Atlas* (New York, Macmillan, 1977): a helpful overview of the history of the city using very clear and well-chosen maps.

Miron Grindea, *Jerusalem: The Holy City in Literature* (London, Kahn and Averill, 1968): an anthology that captures the city in different literary forms.

Dennis Silk, *Retrievements: A Jerusalem Anthology* (Jerusalem, London, New York, Israel Universities Press, 1968): a delightful anthology of travellers' tales, legends, poems, etc., that paint a poet's portrait of the city.

Twelve are the tribes of Israel
The Jewish people today

It is strange to have reached this stage in the book without yet describing who the Jewish people is, or are, today. In part this relates to the pattern of the song which serves as the basis for the chapters of this book. But it is not without other advantages. It is one thing to discuss theoretical possibilities about the nature, characteristics and qualities of a particular people. But it is quite another to meet them in flesh and blood, to share a meal with, to visit a home of, to have a raging quarrel with, or even fall in love with, a flesh-and-blood person. We have met a number of Jews on our journey through this book, shared some of their most intimate experiences, certainly eavesdropped on some of their quarrels, and if it is too much to talk of love, I hope that some have proved attractive and intriguing.

Now as to who the Jewish people are today, and certainly tomorrow, that is anybody's guess. We have seen that there are two components, at least, to Jewish identity, the ethnic and the religious. To that we must add today the 'national' – of which more later. We have looked at the classical definitions used to decide who is a Jew – someone with a Jewish mother or someone who has converted to Judaism through an accepted religious authority – which begs the question of which authority and into which part of the Jewish world they can admit you. We have seen something of a historical perspective of the past and present ideological divisions among Jews, some of which led to permanent separations, some of which were resolved in time.

Twelve are the tribes of Israel

Too often today we are struggling with myths from the past that still haunt us. Are the Jews a race? The very term today is anathema after the Nazi period and the defining of Jews by this label as part of the softening-up process that led to genocide. The Bible speaks of seventy nations descended from Noah, a convenient round number, which points to human diversity and a common ancestry. Common sense identifies different racial groups by virtue of the colour of their skin and shared facial and occasionally more subtle biological characteristics. How far one can differentiate within each group sufficient characteristics to lump them together is outside the remit of this book. Nevertheless it is evident that groups that remain in a fairly bounded locality and intermarry over long periods, will come to share certain characteristics. But this is precisely not the case with Jews, or rather different Jewish groups have had extended periods in a particular locales while at the same time other Jews have had extended periods elsewhere. Such occasions have seen extensive degrees of assimilation to the local population through inter-marriage and conversion to Judaism, sometimes on a large scale. The gene pool has also been extended by less voluntary means – marauding soldiers have never been fussy about the women they raped and it has been left to the victim and her society to assimilate the children. Some argue that this is the kind of reason that matrilineality has been the norm for Jewish society, since the second exile. You always know who the mother is even if not the father.

Of course the traffic of assimilation has always been two-way with the odds more in favour of the disappearance of the Jewish community into its surrounding populace than the other way. But that too has odd consequences, for Jews long since lost can return a few generations later – the classic example is the Marranos, those forced to convert to Christianity in Spain at the time of the Inquisition who nevertheless maintained their Jewish identity in secret. Some converted back as soon as it was politically possible, others, over the centuries, have drifted back when they discovered, often by accident, that their roots were elsewhere. It might be triggered by the discovery that grand-mother's custom of lighting candles on a Friday night and insisting that the family dine together, was not a Catholic rite but the preserved memory of *Shabbat*.

Even more astonishing has been the mass reappearance of 'lost' Jewish groups because of the creation of the State of Israel and the Law of Return. The most dramatic, and in some ways, the most controversial, are the 'black Jews of Ethiopia', the Falashas, who claim an ancestry going back to the legendary affair between King Solomon and the Queen of Sheba. Controversial, because though much of their tradition is recognisably Jewish, much is not, and a cautious Orthodox rabbinate in Israel wanted to insist on 'converting' them according to more conventional *halakhic* criteria, which was felt to be deeply insulting to Falashah traditions.

But if some Jews reappear after a time, many do not. Perhaps most famous, because in many ways the most remote from what is normally considered to be Jewish are the Chinese Jews of Kai Feng. Jews arrived there at the end of the eleventh century, probably from Persia or India to work with cotton fabrics. Their synagogue was destroyed on two occasions over the centuries through natural disasters. But after the seventeenth century the community gradually disappeared so that by the nineteenth century few were left, with little knowledge of Judaism. Over the centuries they had adopted Chinese names, and with little contact with other Jewish communities, intermarried. A photograph of a 'Chinese Jew' can be seen in the *Philo Lexikon* which we will be discussing below.

How many Jews are there in the world? It is a question I often ask groups when I lecture and the answers tend to range from fifty million upward, which is an interesting reflection on the perception people have of this vast Jewish community. Before the Second World War, the total number of Jews is estimated at about seventeen million. Though the figures are not exact, and are subject to attack by apologists for the Nazi regime, about six million Jews were murdered in the years between 1933 and 1945, just over one-third of the population, mostly those living in Eastern Europe. The Jewish population today is estimated just under fourteen and a half million, of whom five and a half million live in America, just over three and a half million in Israel and about three and a half million in Europe, of whom about two million are in countries of the former Soviet Union. The figures throughout Central and Eastern Europe are somewhat uncertain since people often hid their Jewish identity under the communist regimes for safety's sake. Conversely, many people today claim to be or wish to identify as Jews who do not fit the traditional *halakhic* criteria.

This latter fact is a reminder that the whole exercise of deciding who is Jewish today is fraught with complications. Where do you begin and end when it comes to 'counting' Jews, something which is anyway frowned upon in the tradition? (In order to determine if a *minyan*, quorum, of ten adult males are present, thus enabling the traditional service to take place, people sometimes recite a verse from the liturgy containing ten words as they glance around the number of those present. It is sometimes a consolation for a rabbi on a Saturday morning when he sees just how few of his members have attended synagogue to recall that God does not *count* the faithful but *weighs* them.)

Spotting Jews among the famous or infamous is an old Jewish pastime, movie stars being fair game. The London *Jewish Chronicle* is great for such an exercise, discovering how many of the MP's newly elected to the British Parliament after an election have 'Jewish ancestry'. Unfortunately this rarely brings any benefit to the Jewish community, since their entry into Parliament is as often as not a mark of their assimilation to British life as it is an expression of their wish to bring Jewish values into the public arena or address Jewish issues for the sake of the community.

Incidentally, the *Jewish Chronicle* occasionally gets it wrong, and I remember a dignified letter from the jazz pianist Dave Brubeck explaining that he was flattered that they might think him Jewish, presumably because of his reputation for charitable work, but actually he was the son of a Christian clergyman.

But if Jews are fascinated about where hidden Jews can end up, so are non-Jews. Sometimes this is an uncomfortable reflection of anti-Semitic attitudes, but it may simply be an illustration of the old adage: Jews is news! In a novel, *Les Juits*, that was as much a telephone directory of names, Roger Peyrefitte set out to prove that most members of the French aristocracy today had Jewish blood – impoverished aristos of the past marrying into Jewish money. I do not know how far that enters the realms of fiction, but in a delightful book Philip José Farmer explored the history of Lord Greystoke, more commonly known as Tarzan,[1] and inevitably discovered a Jewish family connection. He also managed to find a family link with Sherlock Holmes which is much more likely, and certainly more acceptable to the Jewish community.

The science fiction writer Harlan Ellison located a blue-skinned, multi-eyed, eleven-armed, Yiddish-speaking Jew on the planet Theta 996-VI, studying the story of Abraham.

Survival

What motivates Jews today? The simple answer given in thousands of variations wherever Jews exist is 'survival'. In part this belongs to an ingrained Jewish value so as to fulfil the role set for us by God; in part to the habits acquired through existing over millennia as a minority, struggling to preserve our unique traditions, values and identity under constant siege from others. The way Jews have survived in the past is itself the stuff of fantasy, as well as theories ranging from Darwinian selection to divine intervention. But Judaism also operates on the basis of a 'reality principle' that time and time again has led us to discover appropriate survival policies or techniques.

This 'reality principle' has two aspects to it. The first lies in the power of *Halakhah*, at least in the past, to regulate Jewish life in a pragmatic way, altering itself to fit new situations. Thus a legal decision was needed about such realistic problems as the limits of compromise with the ruling powers. In what circumstances and to what extent, was it permitted to Jews to break the laws of their faith when faced with the alternatives of forcible conversion or death? The principle that underlay the rabbinic decision was their reading of Leviticus 18:5, 'You shall keep My statutes and My ordinances, which if a person do so, he shall live by them.' God gave the laws so that people should live by doing them and not die because of them. At times, for example during the persecutions following the failure of the Bar Kokhba revolution against Rome, it was necessary to check the zeal of those wishing to die in witness to their faith. The verse in Leviticus was made the authority for limiting martyrdom to situations where one was forced by the ruling power to commit one of the three cardinal sins: murder, idolatry and forbidden sexual unions – and idolatry was further qualified to depend upon whether the act would be private, and therefore permitted, or public when it was not permitted since this would cause others to be led astray.

The sheer common sense of the Jewish approach to such matters is beautifully illustrated in the following story.

When the Temple was destroyed, the number of Nazirites (those who took special vows) increased who would neither drink wine nor eat meat. Rabbi Joshua went to them and asked why this was so. They said, 'How can we eat meat? It was the altar that made meat holy through sacrifices to God, and now it is destroyed! And how can we drink wine, since wine was poured out in the ritual, and now the Temple is destroyed!'

Rabbi Joshua replied: 'In that case how can you eat bread, since the Temple's meal offerings are no more?'

They said: 'Perhaps we shall live on fruit.'

Rabbi Joshua replied: 'In that case we cannot eat fruit for the offerings of the first fruit (on *Shavuot*) are no more.'

They said: 'Perhaps we can manage on fruits that were not used in the Temple ritual.'

Rabbi Joshua then said: 'But we may drink no water, for water was used as a part of the Temple service.'

Then they were silent.

But Rabbi Joshua added: 'My sons, not to mourn at all is impossible for us; but to mourn too much is also not possible for us. No religious duty is placed upon a community which the majority of the community cannot endure.' (b. Baba Bathra 60b)

This concern with reality had a second aspect which worked on an even deeper level – that of the intuitive will to live, to carry on, to survive, come what may. How many times were communities decimated, their possessions lost, forced to leave as refugees to find yet again a temporary haven elsewhere. And how often on settling down again did the normal pattern of life reassert itself. Jews must have somewhere to pray, a classroom in which to study and a place to meet – the three constituting the synagogue; they need a kosher butcher and a ritual bath, welfare for the living and a cemetery for the dead. If the community grows to any size then welfare organisations, hospitals, schools will appear. Thus, organically, the community grows – without asking why, or how – after all, life must go on.

Perhaps the strangest thing to Jews and gentiles alike is the existence of a Jewish community in Germany today after the Nazi experience. Certainly for many decades, and still today, Jews outside were disturbed at the existence of organised Jewish life there – and every argument from theological to emotional, might be brought to the subject. But reality is reality. Some returned after finding it too difficult to settle elsewhere; others stopped off in Germany while fleeing from persecution elsewhere, and decided to stay; a few survived the war hidden somehow from the Nazis. Jews have been present in Germany and a community exists. If even a few years ago it would have been written off as a community of old people with no possible future, a younger generation has begun to take responsibility for their own Jewish future. Moreover, since the break-up of the Soviet Union, the community has doubled through the influx of Jews from that region. Life must go on and no one knows what may happen in the future. An elderly Jew once told me: 'I suffered under the Nazis. I suffered under Stalin. Here in Germany I have found a home. Don't tell me where to live!'

But this stubbornness, this will to survive as a people is also of a different order today than it was before the Emancipation – the theme that must inevitably recur in any analysis written today. The assumption that all of our Jewish existence was in God's hands could exist in a world without a modern kind of historical hindsight when Jews still had a clear sense of a divine vocation. It was in God's hands to do with us according to the divine will. Judaism, like the State, would wither away when its purpose had been fulfilled. What was important, when troubles came, was less the survival of the Jewish people, than the survival of Torah, the word of God. Of course, one presupposed the other, but elements of national and ethnic identity were subsumed under the religious – Jews were only the vessel whereby the message would be transmitted. If the messengers did their best, God would take care of them.

But we are two centuries on from the secular revolution which came with Emancipation – not merely from the physical ghettos but from the confines of the old tradition and from the faith that underpinned it. Then came the Holocaust, the Shoah, which utterly changed the physical make-up of the Jewish people, one-third being destroyed within a decade. Over fifty years later we are still struggling to understand the event itself and the impact it has had on Jewish life and self-understanding. We have seen echoes of this question throughout the rest of this book, for it is at the heart of the deepest of Jewish concerns: our survival as a people. Alongside it is the question of what trust we can place, if any, in other peoples when our security is at stake – something which goes to the heart of positions taken by the State of Israel.

If I may interject a personal note here, I remember the feeling of utter abandonment in the weeks leading up to the Six Day War after the United Nations withdrew. I was in Jerusalem at that time and shared the feeling that the nations of the world were simply waiting to see Israel destroyed so that they could weep salt tears at the familiar sight of a Jewish tragedy. How far this was simply a paranoid delusional state, shared by many Israelis at the time, I cannot tell. But the incredible military success of that war, from Israel's point of view, should not hide the real concerns that it raised at the time.

A third concern raised by the Shoah, which should not merely be a Jewish one, is a terrible doubt about the very nature and future of Western civilisation. Jews had wholeheartedly embraced it, only to find it turning on us with murderous savagery and efficiency. To what extent, if any, have we addressed the underlying issues that could allow such a thing to take place? All these factors combined have produced in our time not one but many Judaisms, from the most pious traditional to the most cynically dismissive. Yet underlying all of them is an atavistic feeling that survival itself is the one shared value, with or without God.

Emil Fackenheim, the Canadian/Israeli Jewish philosopher and theologian postulated the need for a 'six hundred and fourteenth commandment' for the Jewish people (613 commandments being the traditional number of positive and negative laws Jews have to obey):

> Jews are forbidden to hand Hitler posthumous victories. They are commanded to survive as Jews, lest the Jewish people perish. They are commanded to remember the victims of Auschwitz lest their memory perish. They are forbidden to despair of man and his world, and to escape into either cynicism or otherworldliness, lest they co-operate in delivering the world over to the forces of Auschwitz. Finally they are forbidden to despair of the God of Israel, lest Judaism perish.[2]

In this 'manifesto' Fackenheim clearly has in mind more than mere survival for its own sake. But of all these sentiments the only one that is ever remembered and quoted, to his personal frustration, is that Jews must survive so that Hitler is not granted a posthumous victory. Somehow it is that view that truly echoes the gut feelings of a generation.

The State of the State of Israel

But there is a new factor in Jewish existence today that radically changes our situation. The State of Israel exists. The exile is over. Jews have re-entered history. Rabbi Dow Marmur elaborates on the need for a new model of Jewish existence:

> The old way of perceiving Jewish existence – Jews relating to God while dreaming and hoping about the land and reading about it in books – is obsolete. One of the

confusions in contemporary Jewish life originates in the myth – nurtured by propagandists seeking to harmonize diaspora piety with Zionist reality – that the new Israel is a mere consummation of the old yearnings. Much of the unwarranted criticism of Israeli actions and Israeli life comes from that confusion. The truth is that Israel today is in many ways a negation of the old yearnings. That is why it has given rise to a new paradigm in Jewish life that cannot be adequately appreciated when judged by the criteria of the old.[3]

The State exposes Jews to the need to address modernity in all its aspects. Moreover, within a State of our own there is no aspect of life we can avoid, there is nowhere we can hide from our mistakes and we must accept full responsibility for what we do. Some implications of this are spelled out by Moshe Greenberg.

To this day it is only in the State of Israel that Jews have to deal as a people with the problems, institutions and temptations of power – economic, political, and military. These issues, which are at the heart of mature societies, can be dealt with Jewishly only here; Diaspora Jewish communities leave them to the secular, gentile political order . . . I give three such examples:

1. **The problem of a democratic political system**, endowing the people with power and responsibility and protecting the minority from the tyranny of the majority . . .
2. **Pluralism**, accepting the co-existence and legitimacy of a variety of life patterns and values . . .
3. **The challenge of equality under the law** of sexes and creeds, including varieties of the Jewish religion and, of course, ethnic groups among its citizens.

The great value of the Land and the State is that they allow the ultimate experiment with Judaism, testing whether Judaism can supply the ideology and wisdom to engage modernity.[4]

Greenberg adds one particular warning about the temptations of the new situation, for the creation of the State has evoked messianic yearnings. Greenberg calls for

> a severe restraint on messianism, that is, on the view that the State of Israel is the beginning of the eschaton, the beginning of the final age . . .
>
> This messianic view of the State in effect is a mandate to pursue national egoism, because all rules are suspended if we are living at the beginning of the final age – all normality, rationality and common morality are suspended if we are living in the eschaton . . . We cannot say what current history means, we cannot interpret it in terms of reward and punishment, in terms of the covenant idea literally understood. Military victories are not simply portents of divine approval or a license to do what national egoism would lead us to. Defeats are not simply portents of divine disapproval or warnings to be more single-minded, not to say fanatical, in observance of the rituals of Torah . . .[5]

Israel and the Diaspora(s)

But what happens in Israel has implications for Jews elsewhere. Rabbi David Hartman calls for the Diaspora participation in all aspects of Israel's existence.

> It is a total evasion . . . of Israel's larger responsibility to the Jewish world to offer the Diaspora only one message: 'Come to Israel to save your grandchildren from assimilation.' . . .
>
> Israel is rather the major vehicle for Judaism's confrontation with modernity. The moral and spiritual issues that surface in Israeli society challenge the basic foundations of Judaism and possibly provide new opportunities for the renaissance of Judaism. The quality of Jewish society that we build in Israel will be paradigmatic for the manner in

which Judaism develops everywhere in the modern world. Involvement and concern for the direction of Israeli society should not, therefore, be restricted to those living in Israel. The whole Jewish world must become involved and have an important say in the major moral and political issues that surface daily in Israel.[6]

But such a view of the interrelatedness of Israel and Diaspora is matched by a contrary position, one that is more sanguine about the political realities of the State. Thus Jacob Neusner:

Where we cannot as foreigners enter into the formation of Israeli policy, we should support what we can when we can and otherwise, let the Israelis make their own mistakes. Their political process, democratic and just, or clumsy and corrupt, must be free to do its work and will do its work. We who live far off must give up our prophet's cloak, ceasing to leap to condemn the slightest Israeli infringement upon our heightened and selective sensitivity to the requirements of justice. The calling of Israel as holy has too long been confused with the conduct of the State of Israel in its worldly tasks and the rhetoric of self-righteous – and selective – indignation at the flaws of Israeli public policy bespeaks a misunderstanding of the category, Israel . . .

[T]he Israelis must now recognise that the cost of the special relationship with world Jewry exceeds the benefit. Insisting that they form the centre of world Jewry, proposing to utilise Jews throughout the world in the achievement of their national goals subject the State of Israel to politics it cannot accommodate . . . Just as the Israelis have built a normal State, so they have now to rethink the requirements of the normalisation of relationships with, even, Jews outside the State.[7]

Neusner's view is disturbing. Israel as a State has its own interests, national and international, and Diaspora Jews who do not live there have no right to interfere directly. Conversely, Israel in setting its agenda has to make the needs or views of the Diaspora secondary to its own.

But in Judaism can one divorce *realpolitik* totally from broader issues of ideology and religious values? David Elazar has argued that Zionism remains the ideology of the State, but notes certain limitations.

> It is not far-fetched to suggest that, *de facto*, Zionism has become another branch of Judaism, parallel in its own way to Orthodoxy, Conservatism, Reform or Reconstructionism in the Diaspora. Like Communism, it is a secular rather than a theistic religion in its fundamentals . . . [which] serves as the basis for the Jewish self-definition of a majority of the Jewish population of Israel . . .[8]
>
> With a few exceptions, classical Zionist theory suffers from some very real deficiencies, stemming from the fact that it arose in the late nineteenth century out of a particular milieu of that period. It suffers additionally from the fact that it was primarily a polemic against assimilation, designed to restore political awareness to Jews; but it had little to say about political life once a Jewish political self-consciousness existed. Both of these deficiencies make it difficult today to build upon classical Zionist theory. We need a true political theory, not a nationalistic polemic, and it must be a theory that accords with Jewish tradition in the broadest meaning of the term . . .[9]

For Elazar an authentic Jewish political vision must also have a theological basis.

> First there must be a renewed sense of the Jewish Covenant (*brith*) . . . [which] sets forth the dimensions of consent which originally transformed the family of tribes into a people. Further, it continually transforms simple kinship into pursuit of a commonly agreed vision . . .
>
> Leading out from the concept of *brith* is a second part, *hesed*, or the loving sense of obligation which true partners

must share with one another and which is created by convenantal ties ... *Hesed* in the Zionist dimension of the Jewish vision is concerned with the survival and unity of the Jewish people ...

A third path is their constant necessity, as Jews, to wrestle with God ... thus the religious dimension of life for Jews is not a matter of finding some orthodoxy but of wrestling with God in the proper way.

The responsibility of freedom leads to the fourth and fifth paths, *zedek u-mishpat* (justice and law), which oblige all Jews to strive for the creation of a just society.[10]

Elazar is here using Hebrew (biblical) terminology and structures in seeking the inner nature and priorities of a renewed Jewish political thought. The temptations to be avoided in our new situation are listed by Louis Jacobs:

1. God alone is to be worshipped, not the Jewish people
2. Jewish nationalism is no substitute for religion
3. God is the father of all mankind
4. There should be no crude interpretation of the notion of 'sacred soil'.
5. Hebrew culture is not Torah.[11]

If these are the classical theological issues, there are certain overriding problems which the State confronts that require immediate and urgent attention. With these Jewish 'theology' enters the public arena. The most direct and uncompromising challenge is expressed in the writings of Marc Ellis who focuses on the plight of the Palestinians as the testing ground for authentic Jewish values.

If one believes, as do I, that the concrete act of solidarity with the Palestinian people – which includes among other things the immediate end of the occupation, the creation of a Palestinian state alongside Israel and a repentance for past and present transgressions against the Palestinian people – is not just a matter of political expediency but a necessary element of contemporary Jewish faith, then an explicit theological statement regarding the intertwined destiny of Jews and Palestinians is of absolute importance . . .[12]

Ellis's views have not been welcomed in Jewish circles, in part because as an academic who has spent most of his time in non-Jewish contexts his Jewish 'credentials' are questioned. Moreover he uses a theological language, borrowed from 'liberation theology' that Jews have problems assimilating. Nevertheless, though the terminology may be different, his views coincide with many within and without Israel who see the necessity for a just solution to the Israel–Palestinian conflict, even without a religious imperative to guide them. In this respect the constant sense of siege under which Israeli life has been lived since well before the creation of the State has hindered the kind of dialogue thinking that is growing more common in our pluralistic Western societies.

In a shrinking world of greater mutual responsibility the concept of 'dialogue' becomes a new potential mode for relating to others, one in which both partners in the enterprise grow inwardly through the encounter. Though Jews in the West inevitably perceive our natural religious partner in dialogue as Christianity, it is self-evident now that we must also meet with Islam.

Dialogue is not without its own difficulties, but it helps us challenge our own inner Jewish temptations and traps: of an unfettered Jewish nationalism; of a perception of ourselves as victims only, with no responsibility for our situation; of the idolatry of a new Jewish self-worship, one born of a deep instinct to survive but too readily becoming a denial of relatedness to the rest of humanity. In rediscovering our particularity as a nation and State, we risk losing sight of the universalism that is the complementary part of our religious vocation. Perhaps with our new political base we can now become equal partners with other nations and faiths in a new experiment in human sharing and mutuality.

There are any number of other issues to be addressed when considering these new configurations of the Jewish people. What do we make of the large number of Israelis who choose to live outside the State yet feel alienated from the Jewish communities of the West? And what indeed is the meaning of a Jewish 'Diaspora', when the State is only a plane ride away and those who remain outside are there by choice? As Zwi Verblowsky expressed it, 'Life is a struggle. The question is: what arena do you pick to struggle in?'[13]

What is the responsibility of Progressive, non-Orthodox, Judaism within the State of Israel itself? Can it help provide an ideological middle ground within the extreme polarisations that happen in all aspects of life in Israel? To find a major place in Israeli life, the Progressive movements (Reform and Conservative) may have to enter the political arena itself. Does this mean a loss of innocence and authenticity in the inevitable compromises that would be required, or is this too a necessary testing of its aspirations and values in the hard reality of national life?

The questions are easier than the answers. But whether we speak of the 'centrality of Israel' in Jewish life today as an ideological value or as a simple and obvious fact, all of Jewry is increasingly affected by and challenged by our 're-entry into history'. As David Elazar puts it: 'Israel is the only State we have or are likely to have. Therefore it is the focus of our vision. As in the case of any other experiment based upon a vision, it is not at all certain that the Jewish State will succeed, but without trying to make it succeed, we are not complete as Jews.'[14]

The Boundaries of Jewish Life

The Jewish world is hopelessly divided between religious and secular Jews, between religious Jews of different ideological persuasions, between Zionists and non-Zionists, between committed and indifferent Jews, as well as suffering a myriad private areas of discord.

From the religious perspective, the issue of *Halakhah* is still dominant as we have seen. From it flow the conflicts resulting from different competing rabbinic authorities: which converts are acceptable and to whom – in the Diaspora and in the State of Israel; the difficulties surrounding marriage and divorce; the question of the identity of the children of mixed marriages. But these classical categories, as we have seen, are rapidly becoming more and more confused as the rate of divorce, remarriage and intermarriage increases. Families may be made up of children of previous marriages, some to Jewish spouses, others not, and these may themselves already be constituted of second and third generations of such confusion.

A purely sociological approach to the question of the continuity of Jewish life in the Diaspora leads to further uncertainties. Some analyses and predictions, mostly derived from demographic and other studies conducted in the United States, have suggested that the intermarried couples and their offspring would simply disappear. But others conclude that they have actually remained part of a growing new ethnic Jewish culture that simply lives with such contradictions. The question is then raised about how far it will remain recognisably Jewish in subsequent generations. The time may be fast approaching when it is simply not possible to tidy up the *halakhic* confusion and reconstitute the old categories.

The worst scenarios envisage the dissolution of two thousand years of Diaspora Jewish history. Two radically different strategies have evolved within the religious movements to combat this trend, exclusivist and inclusivist: an Orthodox tendency to close ranks and seek to preserve a devoted core of Torah-true Jews; an American Reform attempt to reach out to intermarried couples and, through the patrilineal policy, integrate their children. But Rabbi Irving Greenberg, an American Orthodox rabbi and the founder of a movement for internal Jewish reconciliation, has argued recently that both of these strategies have had questionable success.

The Orthodox swing to the right, while generating an image of a more confident, aggressive Orthodoxy, has cannibalized the Orthodox center and driven off non-observant Orthodox Jews. This result foreshadows a weakening of Orthodox influence and a more polarized

Jewish people. It also calls into question the nostalgic, magical thinking that a withdrawn right-wing Orthodoxy is the guaranteed saving remnant of the Jewish people.

Another group that should be having sleepless nights is American Reform. The good news for Reform is that the study shows it taking over as the No. 1 denominational choice of American Jews, especially among young, fourth-generation American Jews. The bad news is the reasons for the surge. Poorly educated children of Conservative Jews find even the limited Hebrew in that denomination's liturgy too much for them, so they switch to a service entirely in English or with only nominal Hebrew . . .

The study shows a low conversion rate in intermarriages (5 per cent). Since earlier studies showed rates as high as one-third, the suspicion arises that Reform's patrilineal descent resolution has reduced the pressure to convert. This is bad news because a number of small studies suggest that converting sharply increases the number of children who grow up Jewish and continue to identify as such . . .

Rabbi Irving Greenberg concludes: 'No group in Jewish life should be complacent.'[15] Rabbi Greenberg's organisation in America is the National Jewish Center for Learning and Leadership (CLAL), *clal* being also a Hebrew term, part of the phrase *clal yisrael*, 'the whole of Israel', the Jewish people as a whole. It points to the quest for the unity of Jews in some form, despite the many 'denominational' differences. The question is what kind of unity is intended or desired and at what price. Certainly dialogue between the various factions can only be to the good. It is when one attempts to make policies or coalitions that the separatist tendencies emerge with all their force.

The historian David Biale, writing in the American journal *Tikkun*, puts the issue of Jewish unity in today's world rather bluntly:

The truth of the matter is that the Jewish people is *not* one people. With the breakdown of mediaeval rabbinic hegemony, the Jewish world has fragmented and returned, in a sense, to the pluralism that characterised it in the late Second Temple period, before the emergence of the rabbis as the sole Jewish authorities. Zionism has tried to overcome the fragmentation of modern Judaism by proposing a new form of national identity but, as the Who-is-a-Jew issue demonstrates, this new identity is surrounded by confusion and illusion ... One may bemoan this lack of Jewish unity or celebrate it as healthy pluralism, but the beginning of wisdom lies in recognizing this modern reality.[16]

So if unity is no longer possible in today's pluralistic Jewish world, at least in the familiar forms of the past, what does the future hold for the Jewish people? It would be a foolhardy person who would try to guess either statistically or spiritually given the unpredictability of the Jewish past. Jewish historians are aware of a famous book published in the thirties by a leading American Jewish historian in which he confidently predicted a successful future for the German Jewish community after this temporary aberration of Nazi fascism had passed! In such matters I am tempted to quote the words of the Hollywood Screenwriter William Goldman summing up the problems of making 'successful' movies: NOBODY KNOWS ANYTHING.

I recall a conversation with an Orthodox rabbi who was bemoaning the way in which Jewish young people, particularly in America, seemed to be joining cults and Eastern religions. (In a short story set in New York four groups converged on a street corner, Moonies, Hari Krishnas, Jews for Jesus and Chasidim – and they were all Jewish!) The reason for this phenomenon is partly a healthy (or unhealthy if you don't approve) Jewish curiosity about 'the other', and a fascination with the spiritual as long as it is not Jewish spirituality, which feels too claustrophobic. More practically such cults flourish on university campuses in the United States and a disproportionate number of Jewish young people, given their percentage of the population, attend university. I suggested that it could well be that the children or grandchildren of these explorers will become curious about their Jewish origins and bring back with them to Judaism some fascinating insights. He was not impressed by the argument.

Nevertheless it is possible that within these Diaspora confusions and the equally complex social changes within the State of Israel, we are actually in the middle of another period of Jewish transformation as revolutionary as that which took place at the end of the biblical period when rabbinic Judaism was created. It may be a century or two before we even know the nature of the new Judaism that is emerging, with new structures, leaders and even new scriptures to add to the accumulated body of Torah.

In the meantime we have to live with this muddle, and create such strategies as we can to encourage communication and even negotiation between the identifiable Jewish groups and institutions. With the existence of the State of Israel and well-organised Jewish Diaspora communities, we have a variety of models of community and political leadership and authority. Despite the destruction of the Nazi period we have managed as a people to reconstruct the essential civil underpinning for our survival and continuity.

Within the rich panorama of competing religious movements, Liberal, Reform, Conservative, Reconstructionist, modern Orthodox, ultra-Orthodox and Chasidic, all in their own way products of or responses to the Enlightenment and Emancipation, not to mention groups like Jewish Renewal which bring New Age ideas into Jewish practice, we have a multitude of different examples of a spiritual leadership with an emphasis on the preservation of the tradition as a living force in Jewish lives. For each of them in their way is trying to preserve the classical covenantal relationship to God through liturgical and religious forms. The question has nevertheless been posed as to whether the religious authorities alone should be the final and only arbiters of Jewish identity. That will become an increasing source of conflict as the State of Israel gains in power and asserts its right to redefine the Jewish people as a national entity.

But finally, in a secular age, where Jewish intellect and imagination and dreaming have poured into the arts, sciences and humanities creating radically new insights into the world and humanity, where is that inflow of new vision into Jewish life to be located, that unique prophetic Jewish channel of spirituality and revelation? Does it still lie in the old voices of tradition and interpretation? Or is it to be found in the new understandings that have shaped our secular culture this century? Is our present confusion evidence of dissolution or the beginnings of yet another unique Jewish synthesis of the old and the new?

Statistics do not tell us enough about the variety and nature of today's Jewish world. If we have looked at the formalities of Jewish tradition and the different communities of the past then we know something of it. But the diversity today makes it very difficult to pin down what is the essence of this strange people. It is easier to point out flawed attempts to discover this than real successes.

In 1934 there was published in Berlin the *Philo Lexikon*. In 800 pages it tried to encapsulate the great figures and movements of the Jewish past together with significant people of the present and their particular contribution. Its unspoken premise was to counter the attacks of the Nazis on Jews and Judaism by showing the extraordinary contribution of Jews to general and in particular to German culture. Under literature, starting in the eighteenth century with Moses Mendelssohn it listed 240 figures: poets such as Heinrich Heine, Richard Beer-Hoffmann, Kurt Tucholsky, Karl Wolfskehl, Else Lasker-Schüler; novelists such as Alfred Döblin, Jakob Wassermann, Stefan Zweig, Lion Feuchtwanger, Joseph Roth, Franz Werfel, Franz Kafka, Leo Perutz; philosophers such as Hermann Cohen, Franz Rosenzweig, Martin Buber; playwrights such as Arthur Schnitzler, Erich Mühsam, Ernst Toller; critics and essayists such as Karl Kraus, Alfred Kerr, Emil Ludwig, Max Brod, Ernst Bloch, Walter Benjamin, Sigmund Freud. Under separate articles were pages on artists, art historians, composers, musicians, philosophers, Nobel prizewinners, newspapers published by Jews and their journalists, actors and actresses, athletes, scientists and scholars, Yiddish poets and novelists. The lists were endless. Perhaps, with hindsight, the most poignant statistics were the ranks of Jewish soldiers who had died fighting for Germany, their Fatherland, in the First World War. But countering irrational hatred with lists of intellectual and artistic achievement, or even evidence of national achievement and loyalty, proved ineffective, except insofar as it may have given some pride to the Jews themselves as they entered that dark period.

Of those named above, how many were 'practising' Jews? Relatively few, and yet they do belong to the Jewish spiritual contribution to the twentieth century, however remote that contribution may be from classical Jewish thought.

Growing up in post-war Europe I would add my own list of Jewish people who had made their impact on my own culture and even on my spirituality as well. Most of them were children of East European immigrants to America at the turn of the century. They were hungry and ambitious and still carried memories of the food, music, wit and pain of that world, perhaps with just an echo of the Torah that had sustained their parents' generation. This is my own very partial *Philo Lexikon* of Jews who spoke and speak the language of popular culture: the songs of the Gershwin brothers, Irving Berlin, Rogers and Hart and later Hammerstein, Jerome Kern, Yip Harburg, or from a younger generation, Bob Dylan, Leonard Cohen, Paul Simon or one of a myriad other Jewish composers and balladeers, many of whom learnt their new grammar of American life from Allen Ginsberg. Then there were the extraordinary wits, humorists, comedians and entertainers who worked their way up through vaudeville to Broadway and the 'silver screen', Jack Benny, George Burns, the Marx Brothers, Al Jolson, Milton Berle, Eddie Cantor, Phil Silvers, Fanny Brice, Sophie Tucker, Danny Kaye, together with the Hollywood producers, directors, screenwriters and composers who created a fantasy world more real than much of our mundane reality. They too had their angry children, like Lennie Bruce, who took the hidden Judaism of those generations and screamed it across the nightclub floor, and helped a new generation of American Jews out of their own comfortable closet. And then the novelists and playwrights who for decades created our image of urban America in its culture and its savagery: Saul Bellow, Norman Mailer, Bernard Malamud, Arthur Miller, Clifford Odets, Philip Roth, again to name but a few. And that is to touch only a small part of that American-Jewish richness.

Incidentally, that is why the story has to be true that is told about Rabbi Dr Leo Baeck on his first visit to America after surviving the privations and horrors of Theresienstadt Concentration Camp. I no longer remember where I heard it. The then editor of *Commentary*, the celebrated intellectual Jewish magazine, approached Leo Baeck with a marvellous idea. He wanted to get together all the greatest Jewish poets and writers and compose an entirely new American-Jewish liturgy. Baeck's reply was to suggest that it would indeed be a marvellous idea, and if they all got together, and this was indeed a blessed generation, from their efforts might emerge one new Jewish prayer! The 'old world' met the 'new world'.

The list is incomplete because of all the Europeans I could add – and here I begin to feel also my limitations. For what of the worlds of North Africa, the Mediterranean and the Middle East where Jewish traditions run deep and entire worlds of culture are remote from my particular Jewish experience, but are alive and deeply significant to others. The Yiddish revival of recent years has brought to our attention the enormous power of *klezmer*, the songs and poems of those who lived in the pre-war world of Poland and died in the ghettos of Vilna and Warsaw. But other worlds, such as Ladino culture, and other Jewish languages, such as Judeo-Persian or Judeo-Arabic, all form part of a rich tapestry of Jewish creativity, traditional and modern in its form and thinking, both within and without the 'religious' world. This enormous cultural diversity, echoes of which are to be found today transplanted to Israel, are part of what Judaism, the faith and the people, are actually about.

Is it just an accident of history that those thinkers who two or three generations before would have been trained as rabbis, instead made their contributions to the world in science, art and thought? Time and again this Jewish flowering is a reminder of how impoverished the inner world of Judaism has become without the intellectual stimulus of people of the calibre of a Freud or Einstein within it, or the political challenge of an Emma Goldman or Rosa Luxemburg. If so much of contemporary Jewish religious thought feels overfamiliar, tired and curiously petty, it is because it no longer seems to be the place where the real struggle for the human soul is being fought out. That is not to say that contemporary rabbis and religious thinkers of all denominations and frameworks are not wrestling with such issues with imagination and integrity, it is just that the whole exercise feels too parochial or apologetic and addressed to too small an inner audience.

It may simply be that the Jewish people as a whole are feeling 'battle fatigue'. We have experienced more history, more tragedy, more destruction, and curiously enough more triumph in this one century than in the past two millennia, and we pay the price. In fact we rather want to be left alone, to 'tend our sheep'. It is just that with our new Jewish State under constant threat and our ears still attuned to the baying of the wolves from the war years, we cannot afford that rest we need. So we struggle on as we are, and as we always have been: divided, sometimes closed in on ourselves, sometimes absurdly open and vulnerable to the world around us. Struggling, as the name Israel means, with God, and with human beings on behalf of God, even if we are not sure any more who or what that God may be. Which leads us to the last chapter of this book.

Further Reading

On the State of the State of Israel

Daniel J. Elazar, 'Renewing the Zionist Vision', in Moshe Davis (ed.), *Zionism in Transition* (New York, Arno Press, 1980), pp. 285–300.

Mark H. Ellis, 'Justice and the Palestinians', *Manna*, no. 30 (winter 1991), Theology Supplement, p. 3 (unnumbered).

Moshe Greenberg, 'Theological Reflections – Land, People and the State', *Immanuel*, vol. 22, no. 23 (1989), pp. 25–34.

David Hartmann, 'The Challenge to Judaism', presumably The *Jerusalem Post*, date unknown.

Dow Marmur, *The Star of Return: Judaism after the Holocaust* (New York, Greenwood Press, 1991).

Jacob, Neusner, 'Israel – an Approach', *Manna*, no. 30 (winter 1991), Theology Supplement, p. 2 (unnumbered).

On the State of the Jewish Diaspora

David Biale, 'The Real Issue Behind Who-Is-A-Jew', *Tikkun*, vol. 4, no. 4 (July/August 1989), pp. 82–6, 83–4.

Irving Greenberg, 'For whom the shofar blows', *The Jerusalem Report*, 12/19th September 1991, p. 60 – based on the Council of Jewish Federations/CUNY National Jewish Population Study.

For a fascinating account of the impact of America on its immigrant Jewish community, and their impact on it, read Irwin Shaw's *The Immigrant Jews of New York*, also known as *The World of Our Fathers* (With the assistance of Kenneth Libo) (The Littman Library of Jewish Civilization, London and Boston, Routledge & Kegan Paul, 1976).

13

Thirteen are the divine qualities
The future of God

The title of this chapter comes from another example of rabbinic reworking of a biblical text. To get there requires a brief look at a passage in the Book of Exodus that became a source for religious speculation within the Bible itself as well as later. After the children of Israel have worshipped the golden calf, Moses sets about trying to rebuild the relationship with God. Having persuaded God not to destroy the people out of hand he tries to ensure that God will personally accompany the Israelites on their journey through the wilderness. In the course of this he asks God to show him the divine 'glory', the Hebrew word *kavod* meaning something like 'presence', literally God's 'weight' in the world (see chapter 1, p. 17). In the famous response God says: 'No man can see Me and live.' This may not mean that whoever sees God will immediately drop dead, for it can also be translated as: 'No man may see Me *while yet alive.*' It is about an ultimate difference between human beings and God that cannot be set aside. Instead God offers to pass before Moses and allow him to see 'My back'. This too leads to all sorts of later speculation about the nature of divine revelation – can we only trace the actions of God after the event but not at the time? As the Exodus passage continues God does pass before Moses and calls out a series of words describing the divine qualities. It is a complicated sentence that needs to be examined bit by bit (Exod. 34:6–7).

> The Eternal, the Eternal, a God of mercy and compassion, slow to anger, generous in love and truth, showing love to thousands, forgiving sin, wrong and failure, but who will surely not declare [a guilty person to be] innocent, visiting the sins of the fathers on the children and children's children to the third and fourth generation.

What seems to start out nicely by describing God as a 'God of mercy and compassion' seems to go horribly wrong by the end with visions of punishments being meted out to innocent generations into the future for the sins of their parents. Perhaps it is best to deal with this latter part first and get it out of the way before seeing what the rabbis did with this passage.

First we have to remember, as so often in the legal texts of the Bible, who is being addressed. This was a patriarchal society so the partner with God in Israel's covenant is the autonomous adult Israelite male. This 'father' 'owned' a wife, or sometimes wives and concubines, children, servants, animals, land and crops. But he was also the one who bore responsibility for the welfare of all of these who were placed in his charge. We should add one more bit of information suggested by the great philosopher and Bible scholar Martin Buber. As we noted in chapter 3 (p. 47), the biblical person thought historically in terms of three generations. Back into the past – as with 'Abraham, Isaac and Jacob', forward into the future – to the third and fourth generation. That is to say an individual could hope to see four generations of his descendants alive in his own lifetime. On this reading the warning to the 'patriarch' is that all of his existing children, grandchildren and great-grandchildren were at risk if he failed to live up to his obligations to God under the covenant. On this reading it was not a question of a punishment echoing into the future of unborn generations but a statement about responsibilities in the present moment.

In the event the 'thirteen attributes' of God that the rabbis extracted from this passage exclude this final part altogether and in fact stop in mid-sentence as we shall see. But first we have to look in more detail at the way in which God is being described.

In the biblical passage it seems that God mentions the divine name twice. We have already looked at the possible meanings of this name in chapter 1. In this case the rabbis discovered in this repetition two different attributes. The name itself they understood as referring to God's quality of love and mercy, as opposed to strict justice. So the mediaeval Jewish commentator Rashi suggests that the first use of the name means that God has mercy on the sinner before he or she sins; and the second repetition, that God has mercy on the sinner after he or she sins and repents. This led another commentator to ask the question: 'Why does God have to have mercy on someone who has not sinned at all?' To which came the answer: 'A righteous man once said to his pupils, "If you were completely without sin, I would be worried about something in you worse than sin." They asked him, "What is worse than sin?" He answered, "Pride and hypocrisy." ' Whatever the possible meanings of this repetition, they make up numbers one and two of the thirteen attributes.

The next word is *el*, another of the ancient biblical names of God, which is here linked with the following phrase *rachum v'hanun*. Just listening to these two words, and even knowing no Hebrew, one can hear from the repetition of the same vowels in each that they make a kind of pair. And indeed though each has its individual meaning they seem to be linked into a kind of combined concept. *Rachum* is from a root meaning 'womb', and generally means 'love' or 'compassion'. Perhaps it suggests the love felt by a mother for the unborn child in her womb. But the second word *hanun* means 'grace'. Before we get too theological, the Hebrew word means to give generously to another without expectation of receiving anything back in return – it is a kind of overflowing of kindness. Thus the two words together seem to mean something like an overflowing, unbounded love. This is the first clear expression of God's qualities that are being revealed to Moses.

The next phrase seems to belong to it. Literally it means 'long of nostrils'! Many biblical descriptions of emotion find their origin in physical attributes. In their view the nose registered emotions like anger, in phrases talking about the 'heat of his nose', so our phrase means something like: 'it is a long time before his nostrils indicate his anger'! This leads to translations like 'longsuffering', or simply 'patient'. Such is God's overflowing love that God is endlessly patient with people.

But the next phrase introduces a new dimension. It includes the words *hesed ve'emet*, and once again one can hear how the repetition of the same vowels in each word links them together. *Hesed* is one of those untranslatable Hebrew terms that leads to newly created English words like 'lovingkindness'. Essentially it is a word which belongs to the language of 'covenant'. Just to recap, a 'covenant' is like a contract between two people, but it goes beyond a merely legal document because it requires a kind of loyalty and faithfulness on the part of those involved (see chapter 2, pp. 28–9). Moreover it even extends beyond the normal boundaries of life. When Jonathan, the son of King Saul, realises that his friend David will eventually succeed his own father and become king, he makes a covenant with him. Normally the first thing a new king does is dispose of the surviving members of the previous royal family as potential threats to his authority. Jonathan makes David promise to show *hesed* to his children, to show a loyalty and faithfulness that continue beyond the life of Jonathan himself (1 Sam. 20:14–15).

The second word *emet*, 'truth', contains a lot of important connections. It derives from a root that is familiar to anyone who has ever attended a religious service of Jews, Christians or Muslims – *amen*. The root meaning is that something is 'fixed', 'firm', 'reliable'. So when we say 'amen' at the end of a service or following a blessing, we confirm our agreement with the sentiment just expressed. From the same Hebrew root comes the term *emunah*, that translates as 'faith' or 'belief', or better still 'trust'. Curiously English carries the same interconnection between *emunah* and *emet*, 'trust' and 'truth'. By this definition, truth is something on which you can rely.

So what happens when we put these two words together? We end up with a concept of 'faithful loyalty', a love that is reliable, one that binds people within a covenant of mutual trust.

It is at this point that we begin to see just how subtle this biblical formulation is. The love of God is seen as being at one and the same time *rachum v'hanun*, overflowing, generous and unbounded, and *hesed ve'emet*, bounded within a framework of covenant loyalty and faithfulness. To spell it out further, it tries to tackle the extraordinary religious question of how a God capable of creating the entire universe can, so to speak, restrict Himself so as to enter into a mutually responsible covenant with a limited part of that creation. God is both within and without that covenant at the same time – God's love is boundless and at the same time voluntarily restricted.

The effect of this paradox is then spelled out further. If there is a covenant with mutual obligations and responsibilities, then there must be boundaries that cannot be crossed, actions on the part of either partner that effectively break the legal conditions of the contract for which penalties need to be exacted. That is why the continuation spells out how this *hesed* can continue over a thousand generations, whereby God is prepared to forgive all kinds of wrongdoing, but some kinds of actions cannot simply be 'declared innocent' and punishment must occur to the wrongdoer.

Once again conventional translations of the things that God forgives tend to get lost in the terminology of 'sin' and 'transgression' and it is helpful to look at the Hebrew origins. The first in the list, translated above as 'sin' is *avon*, a term derived from a word meaning 'to be crooked', and it seems to mean something like habitual wrongdoing. We know that it is wrong but cannot help ourselves. The second term *pesha*, 'wrong', literally means 'rebellion' and is the strongest of the three terms. It means doing something precisely because we know that it is wrong! The third term *hatta'ah*, here translated as 'failure' is most commonly translated as 'sin'. What it actually means is to 'fail to hit the mark', 'to go astray' from a particular goal. It seems to be about failing to live up to what we could be, or going a bit off the road on the journey through life. In any event it is a state that can be remedied by the decision to return to the right path.

Lastly we come to a curious phrase which emphasises that there are limits to God's forgiveness. The key Hebrew word is *nakeh*, a verb meaning to 'declare someone innocent'. Its origins are probably legal for it means to acquit someone in a trial if they have been found not guilty of the offence. In biblical Hebrew a verb is sometimes repeated in two slightly different forms so as to emphasise the idea it contains. To assert that someone is really innocent, the phrase would literally be: 'guiltless, he would declare him guiltless'. In our case this form is used but the two words are interrupted by the word 'not' to emphasise that if someone is actually guilty, and presumably is not prepared to acknowledge that guilt and make amends, they will definitely not be acquitted by God. But it is precisely here that the rabbis make a bizarre intervention. They cut off the phrase after the first word *v'nakeh*, the positive statement that God declares someone innocent, and hence omit the negative that follows it. Whereas the Bible draws a limit on God's generosity, the rabbis extend it to infinity. So the last phrase – 'making it possible for everyone to be innocent', completes the list of thirteen attributes.

Now the rabbis have a kind of precedent for what is otherwise a breathtaking piece of surgery with a holy text. This Exodus passage was so significant that variations on it appear throughout the Bible. Moses is very quick to quote it back at God after the episode with the spies when the Israelites are condemned to wander forty years in the wilderness till that generation died off. God wanted to replace them entirely with descendants of Moses till Moses reminded God that He had described Himself as loving and merciful, citing most of our Exodus passage (Num. 14:18). One rabbi noted that in the repetition Moses omitted the word 'truth' from the list – because if God brought truth into the situation He would be quite justified in dumping the Israelites on the spot!

From then on in the various versions of this passage that appear in the Bible all omit the closing words about 'visiting the sins' and generally revise the list of attributes to make God even more generous and forgiving. For example, Psalm 103 (vv. 8–10) is quite emphatic in showing God's forbearance:

Merciful and compassionate [*rahum v'hanun*] is the Eternal,
slow to anger and full of love [*hesed*].
Not for all times does He accuse,
not forever does He keep His anger,
not according to our failings has He dealt with us,
not according to our sins has He treated us.

The final result of the rabbinic reworking of the Exodus passage is the following version recited in synagogues during festival services and the central prayer on Yom Kippur, the Day of Atonement. It is as if we tie all our hopes of forgiveness by God during that holiest of days on this one prayer, much as Moses once did so as to save the Israelites:

> The Eternal, the Eternal, a God of mercy and compassion, slow to anger, generous in love and truth, showing love to thousands, forgiving sin, wrong and failure; who pardons.

The Broken Covenant

For many this kind of formulation today, after the Shoah, is very uncomfortable. Where was that love and compassion, that faithful loyalty to the Jewish people at our time of greatest need. If a covenant binds both partners, then both have to live up to their responsibilities. So where was God? One answer, certainly as urgent, is 'Where was man?' at that time? Where was our Western civilisation and its values? Where was our simple humanity? But the theological question remains as well, and various Jewish attempts have been made if not to answer the question, at least to respond to it.

There is a story from the concentration camps that a group of pious Jews put God on trial and found Him guilty. But having reached this conclusion, they nevertheless adjourned to recite the evening prayer. Even more radical is the response of the Yiddish poet Jacob Glatstein (1896–1971):

> We received the Torah at Sinai,
> And in Lublin we gave it back.
> The dead do not praise God.
> And as surely as we all stood together
> At the Law Giving,
> So surely we all died in Lublin . . .[1]

Such formulations, and indeed the kind of trial described above, may seem shocking, but they belong to something deeply embedded in Jewish tradition, the right to call God to account for what happens in the world, and in particular to the Jewish people. It goes back to Abraham's argument with God about the fate of Sodom and Gomorrah (Gen. 18), and is expressed in the Book of Job and in the confessions of the prophet Jeremiah (11:18–12:6; 15:10–21; 17:5–18; 20:7–18). The rabbis too noted the legitimacy of such actions:

> Rabbi Phinehas the Priest bar Hama taught: Moses instituted the order of prayer for Israel when he said: The Eternal your God, is God of gods and Lord of lords, the great God, the mighty, the awesome (Deut. 10:17). 'Great' – God did great things in Egypt; 'mighty' – God brought mighty things to pass on the Sea of Reeds; 'awesome' – in the days of Moses the Tabernacle was set up, of which it is said, 'Awesome is God in Your holy place' (Ps. 68:36).
>
> But when the prophet Jeremiah prayed he only said: 'The great, the mighty God' (Jer. 32:18), but not 'the awesome God'. Why did Jeremiah say: 'God the mighty?' Because, he explained, though God saw his children put in chains and His Temple destroyed, He remained silent – so it is proper to call God 'mighty'. But Jeremiah did not say 'God the awesome' because the Temple was destroyed. Where then is the awe, if enemies came into God's house and were not awed?
>
> When Daniel prayed he said: 'O Eternal, the great and awesome God' (Dan. 9:4), but not 'God the mighty'. Why not? Because as Daniel asked, when God's children were put in chains, where was God's might?
>
> However when the Men of the Great Assembly arose, they restored the manner of praising God's greatness to its ancient form, saying: 'Now therefore, our God, the great, the mighty, and the awesome God' (Neh. 9:32). Why? Because, as they explained, God remains above all human praise.
>
> But Rabbi Jacob ben Eleazar said: As for Jeremiah and

Daniel, they knew that God loved truth and so they did not attempt to flatter Him. (Midrash Psalms 19:2)

The theologian Emil Fackenheim argues that we must even read certain biblical passages with radically new eyes after the Shoah. He cites the stories about the time when Israel left Egypt and wandered for forty years in the wilderness. In these we often read how the Children of Israel complained to Moses about their situation. They lacked food and water and were convinced that their children would die in this wilderness. Moses would bring their complaint to God and sometimes their needs would be supplied, but sometimes God would be angry with them. Fackenheim suggests that we are used to siding with Moses and God against the people in these stories. But we who have witnessed the murder of Jewish children in Nazi concentration camps cannot read these texts anymore with equanimity. We identify with this concern about their children and have to call into question the attitudes of Moses and God.

Before we can even talk today about God's 'qualities' we have to ask about faith in God at all in this post-Shoah age. Here the Orthodox theologian Eliezer Berkowits sets the problem in its painful context:

I stand in awe before the memory of the *K'doshim* [holy ones] who walked into the gas chambers with the *Ani Ma'amin* – I believe – on their lips. How dare I question, if they did not question? I believe because they believed. And I stand in awe before the *K'doshim*, before the memory of the untold suffering of innocent human beings who walked to the gas chambers without faith, because what was imposed upon them was more than man can endure . . .

The faith is holy; but so are the disbelief and the religious rebellion of the concentration camps holy. The disbelief was not intellectual, but faith crushed, shattered, pulverized. And faith murdered a millionfold is holy disbelief. Those who were not there, and yet readily accept the Holocaust as the will of God that must not be questioned, desecrate the holy disbelief of those whose faith was murdered. And those who were not there and yet join with self-assurance the rank of the disbelievers, desecrate the holy faith of the believers.[2]

He concludes: 'We are not Job and dare not speak and respond as if we were. We are only Job's brother.' In the face of a faith 'crushed, shattered, pulverized' what kind of faith, and in what kind of God, can the Jewish people affirm today and in the future?

Against Idolatry

To this question there are tentative answers by a few Jewish theologians, though all admit that no explanation rings completely true. And anyway, such views are only studied by a few. Instead, the Jewish people as a whole has opted simply to continue, to survive, to rebuild, as if the whole issue had to be put on the back-burner till a more favourable time. In effect there has been an extraordinary reversal of roles. If Jews today continue to believe in God, or at least to remain committed to Judaism as a way of life, it is despite all that happened. Such a commitment is almost absurd in its stubbornness, though few Jews would acknowledge the heroism of this loyalty. Jews have challenged God's justice and God's seeming absence during the Shoah. The death of a million children cannot be explained in terms of any sin or failure on the part of the Jewish people, the classic explanation that in the past has preserved God's honour at our own expense. If the covenant was broken it was not by us, despite the assertions of some within the Jewish world who locate such sins with great certainty in the heresies of assimilation, or Zionism or Reform Judaism. Rather, as the rabbis of the Talmud and Midrash might express it, the covenant was broken, *kivyachol*, so to speak, by God, for reasons that remain inexplicable and only time may possibly reveal. So the continuing loyalty of the Jewish people to God can only be because we too have acted with the attributes of *rachum v'hanun*, of an overflowing, un-bounded love that continues the relationship when the mutual loyalty, the *hesed ve'emet*, 'love and truth' seem no longer to operate. If that seems a radical theology, it may not even be radical enough for a horror and pain beyond comprehension or healing.

So where do we go from here? There is a verse in Ecclesiastes (3:11) that reads: 'Everything God has made beautiful in its time.' Rabbi Tanhuma (Midrash Psalms 34:1) interpreted this to mean that God had made several worlds before creating this one, but God had been dissatisfied with each and destroyed it. Apart from the uncomfortable awareness that we may well be on the way to destroying this world as well without God's help, this Midrash reminds us in a dramatic way that we are constantly living in a situation of change. Whole cultures and civilisations come and go; religious convictions of centuries can disappear almost overnight; scientific theories that transform our way of thinking are themselves overturned. If that is what happens on a large scale, it is reproduced on the smaller scale of our individual existence. In our own physical bodies cells are continually dying and being replaced, so that we literally become different people over a period of time. Everything that we see around us has its history: its creation, growth and decay. That may only seem a theoretical matter to us when we look at inanimate objects like stones or metals. But all organic matter in nature can be seen daily in its phases of change; and anyone who has responsibility for looking after a building knows only too well how quickly seemingly solid, unchanging materials can leak, rust, rot or crumble. We live in the grip of 'entropy', a marvellous word that simply means that everything eventually falls apart!

Everything changes, nothing is immutable. That is the objective reality of the world about us and the brutal truth about our own limited span of life on earth, our transience. It is spelled out in the passages from the Bible that we recite in Jewish memorial services: 'Frail men and women, their days are like grass, they blossom like a flower in the field; but the breeze passes over it and it is gone and its place knows it no more.'

Of course we cannot live comfortably with the daily awareness of that reality. It is too depressing or frightening; it would destroy all initiative or hope. In many ways we are protected from its truth by our own instincts, urges and energies, our enthusiasms and our lusts, our work ethic and power drive – we get on with living, we build and struggle, we bear children and we create. We try to establish structures and forms and institutions that will stand against the forces of change, that will survive us and thus give us some life beyond our own – in bricks and stone, or in flesh-and-blood descendants. We challenge life and defy death, and are angry or horrified when death comes to claim us.

The other way we struggle against our awareness of our own decay and death is in the powers we invest in God, or in some other absolute we create: the State, the nation, the people. *We* may be limited, but *they* are eternal, and by linking ourselves to them, we feel that we acquire something of their eternity.

That explains something of the power we invest in our religious traditions and the anxiety with which we face change. Tradition is yet another reminder in a world of constant change that some things seem to stand outside of time; that there is something unchanging, secure. This something is 'true' in the sense of the Hebrew word *emet* we have seen above, that which is firm, reliable and trustworthy. Tradition tells us that what we do was done also by our parents and grandparents and their parents before them. It goes all the way back to *torah mi-sinai*, the revelation of Torah given to us at Sinai, to use the classic rabbinic phrase for a commandment whose origins are lost in the obscurity of the past. It has been tested and proved throughout the generations. It defies time. And if it does not quite correspond to today's reality, if bits of it do not work, if we get a little impatient with it and have to struggle very hard even to understand some of it and make it fit our actual needs, well so much the better. Does that not just confirm that the world around us with its insecurities and changes is actually only an illusion; that beneath all that change are still to be located things that do not change, that are the same today as they were when revealed to our ancestors by God? In fact, is not the tradition true and eternal in the same way that the God who gave it is true and eternal?

We cling to that view of tradition at precisely the same moment that part of us becomes aware that it is not that simple. The belief in the power of tradition seems to grow in inverse proportion to the pace of change in the outer world. Tevye the milkman, of the musical *Fiddler on the Roof*, sings of 'tradition' when the winds begin to blow through Anatevka, when old certainties can no longer be taken for granted. While the tradition is alive and effective it is not seen as 'tradition' – it is simply what is and always has been. It is the way we do things here, just as we always have done. It requires no questioning and no defending. But whenever changes become too great tradition loses its quality of instinctive, everyday behaviour, its natural, unselfconscious 'rightness'. Tradition becomes instead something apart, a new kind of entity with a charter and demands of its own. Instead of being taken for granted it now expects loyalty. Instead of pointing the way for life to be lived, it becomes itself the focus of attention. Instead of being the shared, common property of all, it becomes the means of testing the degree of loyalty or 'authenticity' of a few.

And yet since tradition is real and change is inevitable, there have to be ways in which these two factors in our lives are wedded. One way lies in the formulation that begins the *Amidah* prayer: 'our God and God of our ancestors'. As one interpretation suggests, each of us inherits the God of our ancestors, but we must each encounter God for ourselves. God has to be rediscovered in each generation, but recognised at the same time as the God of generations past, manifested in a new way.

There is a tension between which of these aspects predominates in the life of any Jew who cares about such things. Indeed we find ourselves today in a very split reality where those on a personal religious quest may well undertake it outside the formal Jewish world; while for those who stay within, the personal quest seems almost to be a threat to the tradition and the collective identity of the community. Even the traditional way of accommodating change by treating it as if it was already assumed within the system does not work as before. As we have seen, according to rabbinic teaching, at Sinai God revealed not only the written Torah, but also the oral one. Whatever new laws were to be created in response to new situations were actually revealed to Moses at the time. It is all in the Torah. Our task is not to invent something new, but merely to discover or uncover what is already potentially there. 'Turn it and turn it again for everything is in it' (Sayings of the Fathers 5:25). In the famous Talmudic story (b. Menahot 29b) Moses visits the academy where the great Rabbi Akiva is teaching and cannot understand what he is saying. A student asks, 'Where do you get a warrant for that teaching?' 'From Moses on Sinai', comes Akiva's response. God has given us a system, and inspired human ingenuity will allow us to discover God's will in changing circumstances.

But as we have seen, our Jewish problem today is that the system itself has broken down, at least in the area of *Halakhah*, Jewish law. Most Jews live outside *Halakhah* or give it very little consideration, and *Halakhah* itself deals with a very limited area of concerns. The sort of change we confront today is more radical than the tradition can contain. We do not even have the comfort of pretending that nothing is really new. We see the tradition, with its power and its limitations, and we recognise the changed circumstances of our world. Our task is to accept the truth of these two realities and to hold them together as best we can. Where conflicts can be resolved we must try to do so. Where no clear decision is possible, then we have to learn to live with ambiguity, with different possibilities and the different opinions and practices of different individuals and communities. This gives us far greater responsibility to find ways of living with the insecurity it brings, to resolve the conflicts that inevitably occur and learn the tolerance and mutual respect for each other that are essential for survival in this new situation.

But if Judaism is dragged from behind by its tradition, it has also always been propelled towards the future by its messianic hopes. The tension between the two is another of those balancing forces that keeps Judaism exciting as a living faith. If today there is pressure to fall back on the past as reassurance and support in a time of healing and recovery, we also need the visions and hopes that sustain our spirit and challenge our imagination.

What are the ways forward in this situation? Perhaps the first step, as it has so often been in the past, is to identify the sources today of idolatry. If Judaism began, as the rabbis tell of Abraham, with the smashing of his father's idols, then we too have to look with rigorous clarity at today's Jewish world and the idols we create – material and spiritual that stand in the way of our encounter with God. There do seem to be enough of them around; understandable in the circumstances, as idolatry always is, but profoundly dangerous. They include uncritical versions of peoplehood, nationalism, the worship of holy places and holy relics, of ideology and ritual, and whatever puts a 'thing' before a person, an 'it' before a 'thou'.

Paradoxically, it is a Jew who is not perceived as speaking out of Jewish tradition who best expresses the price we pay for idolatry and the challenge offered to us by the religious quest. In his autobiography, *Timebends: A Life*, the American playwright Arthur Miller writes: 'An idol tells people exactly what to believe, God presents them with choices they have to make for themselves. The difference is far from insignificant; before the idol men remain dependent children, before God they are burdened and at the same time liberated to participate in the decisions of endless creation.[3]

'A People that Dwells Alone'

One of the those contemporary idols is the belief that we can, and indeed should, go it alone as the Jewish people, either politically or spiritually. Yet one of the greatest gifts to emerge from the loss of power of religion and the rise of the secular world and civil society, is the idea of 'dialogue' in all its forms – intercultural and interfaith. Moreover the radical changes in the attitude of the Church to Judaism, and hence the desire for dialogue, is one of the unexpected byproducts of the Shoah.

It is a truism that people who have experienced interfaith dialogue often feel more at home with each other, and others who have been open to the experience, than with those they left behind back home. That is not the end of the story, because the true value of dialogue is tested out in the attempt to help those 'back home' share some of the experience and at least acknowledge its legitimacy. We are not alone in our religious quest as Jews, but rarely have we been able to experience such a desire on the part of others to journey together with us. If the experience is too new to be entirely trusted, nevertheless it opens up enormous possibilities for mutual respect, understanding and love between the different faiths.

One of the central paradoxes of dialogue is that it sends us back to our tradition to discover it anew, to ask it questions from what we have learned and enjoy the way in which it responds. It also brings a measure of self-criticism that is essential for our spiritual health as a religious faith and as a people of the covenant with God. It also reminds us of something known to our own mystical tradition, that our unique task as Jews only makes sense against the background of the whole of humanity and indeed the whole of God's creation. So it is appropriate to end this book with an image drawn from the writings of a contemporary Jewish mystic, Rav Kook, the first Chief Rabbi of Palestine, a strictly Orthodox Jew who also saw in the atheistic pioneering Jews who built up the land of Israel the hands and will of God. As a mystic, he could transcend the particularism of his tradition, though his followers have all too often used his mysticism to create a narrower Judaism and a narrower nationalism. Nevertheless, his words offer a visionary hope for a Jewish future, one shared with all of humanity. For that is the essential purpose of the Jewish vocation, to be a 'kingdom of priests and a holy nation', a part of humanity and apart from humanity, as is indeed each and every individual human being.

There is one who sings the song of his own soul, and in his soul he finds everything, full spiritual satisfaction.

And there is one who sings the song of the people. For he does not find the circle of his private soul wide enough, and so goes beyond it, reaching for more powerful heights. And he unites himself with the soul of the community of Israel, sings its songs, suffers with its sorrows and is delighted by its hopes . . .

And there is one whose soul lifts beyond the limitations of Israel, to sing the song of mankind. His spirit expands to include the glory of the human image and its dreams . . .

And there is one who lifts beyond this level, until he becomes one with all creation and all creatures, and all the worlds. And with all of them he sings a song . . .

And there is one who rises together with the bundle of all these songs. All of them sing out, each gives meaning and life to the other.

And this completeness is the song of holiness, the song of God, the song of Israel . . .

Further Reading

Eliezer Berkovits, *Faith After the Holocaust* (New York, Bloch Publishing, 1975).

Eugene Borowitz, *Renewing the Covenant: A Theology for the Postmodern Jew* (Philadelphia, New York, Jerusalem, The Jewish Publication Society, 1991).

Emil Fackenheim, *The Jewish Bible After the Holocaust: A Re-reading* (Manchester, Manchester University Press, 1990).

David Hartman, *A Living Covenant: The Innovative Spirit in Traditional Judaism* (New York, The Free Press, a division of Macmillan, 1985; Woodstock, Jewish Lights, 1998).

Notes and references

Introduction

1. For a recent study of this phenomenon, see Claudine Fabre-Vassas, *The Singular Beast: Jews, Christians, and the Pig* (trans. Carol Volk, Columbia, 1997).

1 One is our God in heaven and earth

1. Throughout this book, translations of passages from the Bible are the author's own.
2. A. Marmorstein, *The Old Rabbinic Doctrine of God*, vol. 1, *The Names and Attributes of God* (Jews' College Publications, no. 10, London, Oxford University Press, 1927; republished, Westmead, Gregg International, 1969), pp. 11–12.
3. See chapter 4 for more on this subject.
4. For further discussion on this topic, see chapter 11.

2 Two are the tablets of the covenant

1. Joseph L. Baron (ed.), *A Treasury of Jewish Quotations* (South Brunswick, NJ, A.S. Barns's, New York and London, Thomas Yoseloff, 1965) cites this as a saying of 'William Norman Ewer, Eng. Journalist 1885, taken from *The Week-End Book*, 1924, p. 117.
2. This is cited by the same source as a 'Saying q. L. Roth, *Jewish*

Thought, 1954, p,. 39.

3. Lionel Blue, *To Heaven with Scribes and Pharisees* (London, Darton, Longman & Todd, in association with the Reform Synagogues of Great Britain, 1975), p. 68.

4. ibid., p. 73.

5. Judah Halevi, *The Kuzari: An Argument for the Faith of Israel.* Translated from the Arabic by Hartwig Hirschfeld, 1905. Introduction by Henry Slonimsky (New York, Schocken Books, 1964), pp. 226–77.

3   Three are the fathers of Israel

1. Michael Williams, 'Peut-on rendre less Juifs plus utiles et plus heureux en France? (Can the Jews in France be rendered more productive and happier?): The Abbé Grégoire revisited: 1787–1995', *European Judaism*, vol. 29, no. 2,(spring 1996), pp. 51–68, 65, 66.

2. W. Gunther Plaut, *The Rise of Reform Judaism: A Sourcebook of its European Origins* (New York, The World Union for Progressive Judaism, 1963), pp. 33–44.

3. ibid., p. 34.

4. Jacob J. Petuchowski, *Prayerbook Reform in Europe: The Liturgy of European Liberal and Reform Judaism* (New York, The World Union for Progressive Judaism, 1968), p. 53.

5. Howard M. Sachar, *The Course of Modern Jewish History* (London, Weidenfeld & Nicolson, 1958; rev. edn, Vintage Books, 1990), p. 148.

4   Four are the mothers of Israel

1. Blu Greenberg, 'Women and Judaism', in Arthur A. Cohen and Paul Mendes-Flohr (eds.), *Contemporary Jewish Religious Thought* (New York, The Free Press, a division of Macmillan; London, Collier Macmillan, 1987), pp. 1039–53. The article strikingly illustrates these contradictions, especially as they affect Jewish law.

2. Ellen M. Umansky and Dianne Ashton, *Four Centuries of Jewish Women's Spirituality: A Sourcebook* (Boston, Beacon Press, 1992). For further examples of such prayers, see Tracy Guren Klirs (ed.), *The Merit of our Mothers: A Bilingual Anthology of Jewish Women's Prayers* (Cincinnati, Hebrew Union College Press, 1992).

3. See the discussion of this issue in the essay by Rabbi Alexandra Wright, 'An Approach to Jewish Feminist Theology', in Sybil Sheridan (ed.), *Hear Our Voice: Women Rabbis Tell Their Stories* (London, SCM Press, 1994), pp. 152–61.

4. *Forms of Prayer for Jewish Worship*, vol. 2, *Prayers for the Pilgrim Festivals* (London, The Reform Synagogues of Great Britain, 1995), pp. 43–45.

5. E. M. Broner with Naomi Nimrod, *The Women's Haggadah* (San Francisco, HarperSanFrancisco, 1994).

6. Henrietta Szold, 'Beruriah', *The Jewish Encyclopedia*, vol. 3 (London and New York, Funk & Wagnalls, 1916), pp. 109–10.

7. See David Biale, 'The Lust for Asceticism in the Hasidic Movement', in Jonathan Magonet (ed.), *Jewish Explorations of Sexuality* (Oxford/Providence NJ, Berghahn Books, 1995), pp. 51–64.

8. Sondra Henry and Emily Taitz (eds.), *Written Out of History: Our Jewish Foremothers* (New York, Biblio Press, 1996), unnumbered page.

9. For a brief biography and discussion of the controversy surrounding her ordination and the silence soncerning her existence, see Elizabeth Sarah, 'Rabbi Regina Jonas 1902–1944: Missing Link in a Broken Chain', in Sheridan (ed.), *Hear Our Voice*, pp. 1–9.

10. Barbara Borts, 'Introduction', in Sheridan (ed.), *Hear Our Voice*, p. 150.

5 Five are the books of the Torah

1. Introduction to J. H. Hertz (ed.), *The Pentateuch and Haftorahs* (London, Soncino Press, 2nd edn, 1962), p. vii.
2. W. Gunther Plant (ed.), *The Torah: A Modern Commentary* (New York, Union of American Hebrew Congregations, 1981), p. xix.
3. Meir Zlotowitz (ed.), *The Megillah: The Book of Esther: A New Translation with Commentary Anthologized from Talmudic, Midrashic and Rabbinic Sources* (New York, ArtScroll Studios, 1976), p. x.
4. A. J. Unterman, 'Past in Present: The Jewish Way with Time', *Manna* (Journal of the Sternberg Centre for Judaism) 6 (1985), pp. 16–17.
5. *Mekilta de-Rabbi Ishmael: A critical edition on the basis of the manuscripts and early editions with an English translation, introduction and notes by Jacob Z. Lauterbach*, vol. 3 (Philadelphia, Jewish Publication Society of America, 1935), pp. 186–96.
6. I would recommend three books in particular – *The Rabbinic Anthology* of Claude Montefiore and Herbert Loewe; the encyclopaedic *Sefer Ha-Aggadah* of Bialik and Revnitsky in its English version by the late William Braude, *The Books of Legends: Sefer Ha-Aggadah*; and *The Legends of the Jews* by Louis Ginzberg. For details, see the reading list at the end of this chapter.
7. E. H. Plumptre (ed.), *Ecclesiastes* (The Cambridge Bible for Schools and Colleges, Cambridge, Cambridge University Press, 1890), pp. 75–76.
8. Abraham Joshua Heschel, 'Halakhah and Aggadah', in Fritz A. Rothschild (ed.), *Between God and Man: An Interpretation of Judaism: From the Writings of Abraham J. Heschel* (New York, The Free Press, a division of Macmillan; London, Collier Macmillan, 1959), p. 175.
9. To learn more about these figures and the development, see my book *A Rabbi's Bible* (London, SCM Press, 1991). For a brief but detailed overview of the development of Jewish Bible exegesis till today I would refer to my paper, 'How Do Jews Interpret the Bible Today?', *Journal for the Study of the Old Testament* (JSOT), 66 (1955), pp. 3–17.

10. Benedict de Spinoza, *Tractatus Theologico-Politicus*, translated from the Latin, with an Introduction by R. H. M. Elwes (London and New York, George Routledge, n.d.). This passage is a summary of materials to be found on pp. 101–103.

6 Six are the 'Orders' of the Mishnah

1. Heinrich Graetz, *History of the Jews*, vol. 2 (London, Myers, 1904), p. 639. The bibliography at the end of the this chapter offers further reading on both the historical background of the Talmud, the views of its significance in Jewish tradition, and a delightful excursus (by Hyam Maccoby) into the wit and humour of the rabbis that are also to be found within it.
2. Rabbi Alexandra Wright, 'Serving the Jewish Community', in *Leo Baeck College at Forty*, Supplement in the *Jewish Chronicle*, 8th November 1996.

7 Seven are the days of the week

1. Solomon Goldman, *The Book of Human Destiny: From Slavery to Freedom* (Abelard-Schuman, 1958), p. 676.
2. *Mekilta de-Rabbi Ishmael: A critical edition on the basis of the manuscripts and early editions with an English translation, introduction and notes by Jacob Z. Lauterbach*, vol. 3 (Philadelphia, Jewish Publication Society of America, 1935), pp. 186–96.
3. Erich Fromm, 'Meaning of the Sabbath', in Lily Edelman and Morris Adler (eds.), *Jewish Heritage Reader* (New York, A B'nai Brith Book, Tapinger Publishing, 1965), pp. 138–41, 140–41.
4. The prayer books of the Reform Synagogues of Great Britain identify these 'idols' as follows: 'When the worship of material things shall pass away from the earth, and prejudice and superstition shall at last be cut off.'

9 Nine are the months of childbirth

1. *Jewish Chronicle*, 4th December 1990, p. 24.

10 Ten are the divine commandments

1. Joseph B. Soloveitchik, 'The Lonely Man of Faith', *Tradition*, vol. 7, no. 2 (summer 1965), pp. 5–67, 8.
2. From an article 'Halakah', in *Contemporary Jewish Religious Thought*, p. 310. For further details, see end of chapter, 'Further Reading'.
3. 'Israel-Diaspora relations: the "Who is a Jew?" debate', *jpr news* (summer 1997), pp. 4–5.

11 Eleven are the stars of Joseph's dream

1. Quoted in Nahum N. Glatzer (ed.), *Hammer on the Rock: A Short Midrash Reader* (New York, Schocken Books, 1948), p. 21.
2. *London Jewish News*, 29th August 1997, p. 7.
3. The issue is discussed by Joseph Dan, the Gershom Scholem Professor of Kabbalah at the Hebrew University of Jerusalem, in a paper 'In quest of a historical definition of mysticism', *Studies in Spirituality* 3 (1993).
4. Louis Jacobs, *A Jewish Theology* (New York, Behrman House Publishers, 1973), pp. 32–33.

12 Twelve are the tribes of Israel

1. Philip José Farmer, *Tarzan Alive* (London, Granada Publishing. First published in Great Britain by Panther Books, 1974).
2. Emil Fackenheim, 'Jewish Faith and the Holocaust', *Commentary*, 1967, quoted in Fackenheim's *God's Presence in History: Jewish Affirmations and Philosophical Reflections* (New

York, New York University Press, 1970), p. 84.

3. Dow Marmur, *The Star of Return: Judaism after the Holocaust* (New York, Greenwood Press, 1991), p. 44.

4. Moshe Greenberg, 'Theological Reflections – Land, People and the State', *Immanuel*, vol. 22, no. 23 (1989), pp. 25–34, 28.

5. ibid., pp. 28–9.

6. David Hartman, 'The Challenge to Judaism', *Jerusalem Post* (date unknown).

7. Jacob Neusner, 'Israel – an Approach', *Manna*, no. 30 (winter 1991), Theology Supplement, p. 2.

8. Daniel J. Elazar, 'Renewing the Zionist Vision', in Moshe Davis (ed.), *Zionism in Transition* (New York, Arno Press, 1980), pp. 285–300, 288.

9. ibid., pp. 292–93.

10. ibid., pp. 295–97.

11. Louis Jacobs, *A Jewish Theology* (New York, Behrman House Publishers, 1973), pp. 281ff.

12. Marc H. Ellis, 'Justice and the Palestinians', *Manna*, no. 30 (winter 1991), Theology Supplement, p. 3 (unnumbered).

13. Quoted by Moshe Greenberg, 'Theological Reflections', p. 31.

14. Elazar, 'Renewing the Zionist Vision', p. 298.

15. Irving Greenberg, 'For whom the shofar blows', *The Jerusalem Report*, 12/19th September 1991, p. 60.

16. David Biale, 'The Real Issue Behind Who-Is-A-Jew', *Tikkun*, vol. 4, no. 4 (July/August 1989), pp. 82–86, 83–4.

13 Thirteen are the divine qualities

1. In Joseph Leftwich, *An Anthology of Modern Yiddish Literature* (The Hague, Mouton, 1974; International PEN Books), p. 236.

2. Eliezer Berkovits, 'Approaching the Holocaust', *Judaism*, No. 85, vol. 22, no. 1, pp. 18–20.

3. Arthur Miller, *Timebends: A Life* (London, Methuen, 1987).

Glossary

There are a number of systems for transliterating Hebrew letters. The following need particular attention. '*Kh*' is the softened form of the letter *kaf* and is pronounced as the 'ch' in the Scottish 'loch'. '*Th*' is the softened form of the letter *tav*, but can be pronounced as a normal 't'. The letter *chet* is similar in sound to the *khaf* but softer and pronounced at the back of the palate rather than in the throat. It may be transliterated by 'h' or 'ch', as in Chasidim or Hasidim.

Aggadah (lit. 'narrative'). Non-legal rabbinic writings, including biblical commentary, parables, anecdotes, etc.

Agunah. A woman whose husband has disappeared or whose death has not been confirmed, so she is 'bound' or 'chained', unable to remarry.

Aliyah (lit. 'going up'). (a) The term for being called up to read from the Torah Scroll; (b) a term for 'going up' to the land of Israel to settle.

Amidah (lit. 'standing'). The term for the central prayer in Jewish liturgy – also known as the Eighteen Benedictions.

Ashkenazi. Jews from North, Central and Eastern Europe, and their descendants.

Bat chayyil. Term for ceremony in Orthodox circles marking the coming of age of a girl.

Barmitzvah/Batmitzvah. 'Son' (from age thirteen) or 'Daughter' (from age twelve) 'of the Commandment' – from which age they are considered responsible for their actions under Jewish law.

Beth Din. Jewish court of law.

Beth Knesset ('House of Assembly'). One of the Hebrew designations for the synagogue.

Bikkur holim. The commandment of visiting the sick.

B'rit. Covenant.

Brit Milah. The ceremony of circumcision.

Chanukah. Festival celebrating the rededication of the Jerusalem Temple.

Chasid, pl. **chasidim**, **Chasidism**. A religious and social movement which developed quickly in depressed Eastern Europe following the Chmielnicki massacre and persecution. It has parallels with other popular religious movements of the same period.

Cherem. A ban of excommunication.

Chumash (lit. 'five'). The Five Books of Moses.

Conservative Judaism. American non-Orthodox religious movement that seeks to preserve Jewish tradition through developing Jewish law.

Dhimmi. Legal term to designate the protected status of Jews and Christians in Muslim lands.

Eshet chayyil ('a woman of valour'). The passage from Proverbs 31: 10–31 read to a wife on the Eve of the *Shabbat*.

Gemara. See **Talmud**.

Ger. Biblical 'temporary resident', the term used later to designate a convert to Judaism, a *ger tsedek*, 'a righteous convert'.

Get. A bill of divorce.

Haftarah. The reading from the prophets which follows the Torah reading on the *Shabbat*. It is selected so as to have some connection with the portion read from the Torah.

Haggadah (lit. 'narrative'). The book containing the liturgy for the Passover evening home service.

Halakhah. Jewish law.

Haskalah ('enlightenment'). Hebrew term for a movement at the end of the eighteenth century, encouraging assimilation to the surrounding culture and full emancipation.

Havdalah (Lit. 'separation'). Concluding service of *Shabbat* separating it from the working days of the week.

Holocaust. See **Shoah**.

Huppah. Bridal canopy.

Kabbalah. Jewish mysticism.

Kaddish (Aramaic for 'holy'). A series of praises of God that have come to be associated with memorialising the dead.

Kasher. See *Kashrut*.

Kashrut. Jewish dietary laws.

Ketubah. Marriage contract.

Kibbutz. Collective farm in Israel run on socialist principles.

Kiddush ('sanctification'). A blessing over wine (symbol of joy) and a prayer of thanksgiving marking the beginning of the *Shabbat* or a festival.

Klezmer. From two Hebrew words *klei zemer*, 'musical instrument', the name for a type of music popular in Eastern Europe, played by wandering musicians. It is currently undergoing something of a revival.

Knesset. Israel's Parliament, based in Jerusalem.

Kol Nidre (lit. 'all vows'). Aramaic formula for annulling vows recited at the beginning of the service on the eve of the Day of Atonement, and hence the name of that service.

Kosher. See **Kashrut**.

Ladino. Judeo-Spanish dialect, spoken by Sefardim.

Liberal Judaism. A term that denotes both the pre-war German non-Orthodox, but 'traditional', movement, and the more radical British Liberal (and Progressive) movement founded by Israel Mattuck, Lily Montagu and Claude Montefiore.

Machzor. The prayer book used for Jewish festivals.

Mamzer. The child of a forbidden sexual union, traditionally forbidden to marry anyone except another *mamzer*. The concept was abolished by non-Orthodox Jewish movements.

Matzah, pl. *Matzot*. Unleavened bread eaten during the Festival of Passover.

Mechitzah. A screen or other barrier separating the sections for men and women in traditional synagogues.

Megillah, pl. **Megillot**. One of five 'scrolls' (Song of Songs, Ruth, Lamentations, Ecclesiastes, Esther) in the third part of the Hebrew Bible, each one read during a particular Jewish festival.

Midrash. The search for deeper meanings of biblical texts in addition to the plain sense. Sometimes Midrash is expressed as law (*Halakhah*), at other times as myths, legends, ethics, parables, homilies, etc. (*Aggadah*).

Mikveh. Ritual bath.

Milah. See B'rit.

Minyan. A quorum of ten men traditionally required for a Jewish religious service to take place. Non-Orthodox movements have either abolished the requirement of ten, or else included women to make up the numbers.

Mishnah. Legal codification of the 'Oral Law', traditionally said to have accompanied the 'Written Law' given to Moses by God at Sinai. As a discrete body of law it was compiled by Rabbi Judah Ha-Nasi at the end of the second century CE.

Mishneh Torah. Literally the 'second' or 'repetition of' the Torah. A codification of Jewish law by Moses Maimonides (1135–1204).

Mitzvah ('commandment' or 'precept'). A legal or social obligation incumbent on Jews. From this it acquires the more general meaning of a 'good deed'.

Mohel. The person who performs ritual circumcision.

Moreh Nevuchim (*Guide for the Perplexed*). A book written by Moses Maimonides (1135–1204) in Egypt in which he tried to reconcile the challenging philosophical ideas of his time with traditional Jewish ideas and interpretations of Scripture.

Orthodox Judaism. A term for post-Emancipation movements that try to preserve relatively unchanged, Jewish tradition, ritual and law. They include 'modern' or 'central' Orthodox, more fundamentalist (ultra-Orthodox) and Chasidic groups.

Pentateuch. The five Books of Moses that open the Hebrew

Bible: Genesis (Heb. *b'reshit*, 'in the beginning'); Exodus (Heb. *shemot*, 'names'); Leviticus (Heb. *vayiqra*, 'and He (God) called'); Numbers (Heb. *b'midbar*, 'in the wilderness'); Deuteronomy (Heb. *d'varim*, 'words').

Pesach (lit. 'to spring over'). The Festival of Passover commemorating the exodus from Egypt.

Progressive Judaism. See **Liberal Judaism**.

Purim. A festival celebrating the miraculous deliverance of the Jews by Queen Esther and Mordechai from the plot to kill them by Haman, Grand Vizier to Ahasuerus, king of Persia. Recorded in the biblical book of Esther.

Rabbi/Rav ('my master', 'my teacher'). A title applied to scholars and later the spiritual leaders of Jewish communities.

Reconstructionist Judaism. American movement, a breakaway from the Conservative movement, founded by Mordechai Kaplan, that sees Judaism as a religious civilisation.

Reform Judaism. A term covering different non-Orthodox Jewish religious movements around the world since the nineteenth century, from radical (American Reform) to conservative (British Reform).

Rosh chodesh ('head of the month'). The New Moon.

Rosh Hashanah ('head of the year'). The two-day festival that commemorates the beginning of the Jewish New Year in the autumn.

Seder ('order'). The term for the 'order of service' of the domestic celebration on the Passover evening.

Sephardi. Jews from Spain and Portugal and their descendants.

Shabbat ('sabbath'). The day of rest.

Shavuot. The Festival of Weeks, Pentecost, celebrating the revelation at Mt Sinai.

Shekhina. Rabbinic term expressing the tangible presence of God in the world.

Shema. One of the central parts of Jewish prayer affirming the Oneness of God. It comprises three paragraphs: Deut. 6:4–9; 11:13–21; Num. 15:37–41. Reciting the first paragraph the speaker accepts the 'yoke of the kingdom of heaven'; with the second paragraph, the 'yoke of the commandments'.

Shoah (Heb. 'destruction'). A term for the murder of six million Jews during the Second World War by the Nazis. More commonly known as 'Holocaust'.

Shofar. Ram's horn, blown in biblical times to warn of approaching enemy danger. Associated with the New Year period where it is said to 'wake up' the sleepers and encourage them to do repentance.

Shul. Yiddish term for synagogue, literally 'school'.

Siddur ('order'). The term for the prayer book used for daily and *Shabbat* services.

Simchat Torah ('rejoicing in the Torah'). Festival marking the completion of the annual cycle of weekly Bible readings.

Sofer. A scribe, someone who writes with special Hebrew lettering a Torah scroll or other religious document.

Sukkot. Festival of Tabernacles.

Synagogue. Traditionally the 'House of Prayer, House of Study and House of Meeting' of the Jewish community.

Tallit. Prayer shawl worn at all morning services. Though customarily, though not exclusively, worn by men only in the past, it is increasingly being worn by women, particularly in non-Orthodox movements.

Talmud ('teaching'). A compilation made up of the *Mishnah* with its *Gemara* (commentaries and additions), which together make up the Talmud. It covers both religious and civil matters. A mixture of laws, customs, discussion, stories and *obiter dicta*, it become the foundation of Jewish practice and study throughout the world. Two versions of Talmud: one compiled in Palestine (the *Yerushalmi* or Palestinian), completed about 400 CE, and the other in Babylon (the *Bavli* or Babylonian), completed between a hundred to three hundred years later, the latter being authoritative.

Tefillin ('phylacteries'). Boxes containing biblical verses worn on the head and arm during morning prayers.

Tisha B'Av. Ninth day of the month of Av, a fast-day commemorating the destruction of both Temples and other Jewish disasters.

Glossary

Torah ('teaching'). The Written Torah consists of the five books of Moses (the Pentateuch) The Oral Law Torah, initially conceived as being given to Moses to accompany the Written Torah, is regarded as incorporating the totality of Jewish religious tradition.

Yiddish. A language derived principally from Middle High German and Hebrew, written in Hebrew characters. It assimilated elements from the various countries in which it was the *lingua franca* of the Jewish population, principally Eastern Europe.

Yom Kippur. Day of Atonement.

Festival calendar

The Jewish calendar is lunisolar: the months are calculated according to the moon, and the years according to the sun. Since there are eleven days left over after each twelve months, an additional month (a second month of Adar) is added every four years to ensure that the annual cycle of festivals keep their original relationship to the harvest seasons.

Of the pilgrim festivals, *Pesach* and *Sukkot* are seven-day festivals in the Bible, with the first and last days considered as full days of rest and celebration. *Shavuot* is only a single day festival. In the rabbinic period, because of problems in determining the exact dates of the festivals outside the land of Israel, each festival day was kept for two days in the Diaspora, a practice still maintained by Orthodox communities but not by Liberal and Reform ones.

Tishri	September/October	30 days
1	New Year's Day I	
2	New Year's Day II	
3	*Tzom Gedaliah* (Fast)	
10	Day of Atonement	
15	*Sukkot* I	
16	*Sukkot* II	
17–21	*Hol Ha-Moed* (intermediate days)	
21	*Hoshana Rabba*	
22	*Shemini Atzeret*	
23	*Simchat Torah*	

Festival calendar

Marcheshvan	October/November	29 days
Kislev	November/December	30 days
25	*Hanukkah*	
Tevet	December/January	29 days
10	*Asarah be-Tevet* (Fast)	
Shevat	January/February	30 days
15	*Tu Bishvat* (New Year for Trees)	
Adar	February/March	29 days
13	*Ta 'anit Ester* (The Fast of Esther)	
14	*Purim*	
Nisan	March/April	30 days
14	Eve of Passover (*Seder* evening)	
15	Passover I	
16	Passover II	
17–21	*Hol Ha-Moed* (intermediate days)	
21	Passover VII	
22	Passover VIII	
27	*Yom Ha-Shoah* (Holocaust Memorial Day)	
Iyar	April/May	29 days
5	Israel Independence Day	
18	*Lag ba-Omer* (33rd day of Counting the Omer)	
Sivan	May/June	30 days
6	*Shavuot* I	
7	*Shavuot* II	
Tammus	June/July	29 days
17	*Shiv'ah Asar be-Tammus* (Fast)	
Av	July/August	30 days
9	*Tisha B'Av* (Fast)	
Elul	August/September	29 days

Historical time-line

Before the Common Era (BCE)

Thirteenth century: exodus from Egypt.

Thirteenth/twelfth century: conquest of the land of Canaan.

Twelfth/eleventh century: period of the Judges.

c. 1000 David appointed King.

c. 960 Solomon, his son, succeeds King David. The building of the First Temple in Jerusalem.

c. 920 The Kingdom divides after Solomon's death: the Northern Kingdom of Israel, the Southern Kingdom of Judah.

722 Destruction of the Northern Kingdom by the Assyrians, and deportation of population.

586 Destruction of the Southern Kingdom, Jerusalem and the Temple by Nebuchadnezzar. Mass deportation to Babylon.

538 Return of exiles under Cyrus.

332 Alexander the Great conquers Palestine.

198 Antiochus the Third rules over Judah.

167 The Maccabean Revolt.

164 Rededication of the Temple – the Feast of *Hanukkah* instituted.

63 Pompey conquers Palestine.

c. 20 BCE –*c.* 50 CE Philo. Jewish philosopher living in Alexandria who sought to harmonise Greek philosophy with Judaism.

After the Common Era (CE)

c. 37–*c.* 100 Flavius Josephus. Soldier and historian. In Rome he recorded Jewish history (*The Jewish War, The Antiquities of the Jews*).

50–135 Akiva ben Joseph. Most prominent among the *Tannaim*, the rabbis recorded in the Mishnah. He supported the Bar Kokhba revolution against Rome and died as a martyr.

66–70 The Jewish Revolt against Rome. Destruction of Jerusalem and the Temple.

73 The fall of Masada, Herod's royal citadel, to the Romans. According to Josephus the 960 defenders, men, women and children, committed mass suicide.

c. 70–85 Jochanan ben Zakkai establishes an academy at Yavneh.

117–38 Reign of Emperor Hadrian.

132–35 Bar Kokhba revolt.

c. 200 Completion of the editing of the Mishnah by Judah Ha-Nasi.

219 Establishing of the Babylonian Academies of Sura and Pumbedita.

321 First recorded reference to Jews resident in Germany, in the region of Cologne.

c. 425 Completion of Jerusalem Talmud.

Sixth/seventh century: completion of Babylonian Talmud.

638 Muslim conquest of Jerusalem.

Seventh–tenth centuries: the Khazars, a national group of Turkish type, who established an independent kingdom in the Volga-Caucasus region and adopted Judaism.

711 Muslim conquest of Spain.

Ninth–eleventh centuries: growth of Jewish communities in the Rhineland.

Ninth–twelfth centuries: growth of Jewish communities in North Africa and Spain under Islam.

882–942 Saadia Gaon. Leader of the struggle against the Karaite movement.

c. 960–*c.* 1028 Rabbenu Gershom, *Me'or Ha'Golah*, 'The Light of the Exile'.

1013–1103 Isaac ben Jacob Alfasi, Rif. Author of *Sefer Ha-Halakhot*, a compendium of the Talmud.

1040–1105 Rabbi Solomon ben Isaac, Rashi. Leading French commentator on Bible and Talmud.

1066 Jews settle in England after the Norman conquest.

c. 1075–1141 Judah Halevi. Spanish Hebrew poet and philosopher. Author of religious and secular poetry. His major philosophical work is the *Kuzari*, based on a disputation before the King of Khazars between a Jew, a Christian and a Muslim.

c. 1085–*c.* 1175 Rabbi Samuel ben Meir (Rashbam). French commentator on Bible and Talmud. Grandson of Rashi.

1089–1140 Rabbi Abraham Ibn Ezra. Leading Spanish Bible commentator and philosopher.

1096–99 Destruction of Jewish communities in Rhineland during the First Crusade.

1135–1204 Moses ben Maimon, Maimonides, Rambam. Philosopher and Codifier of Jewish law. Author of the *Mishneh Torah* and *The Guide for the Perplexed*.

1144 First ritual murder libel at Norwich.

c. 1159 Benjamin of Tudela travelled through Spain, France, Italy, Greece, Turkey, the Aegean, Cyprus and Asia Minor to Palestine, recording Jewish life and communities in his *Book of Travels.*

c. 1160–*c.* 1235 Rabbi David Kimhi (Radak). French grammarian and Bible commentator.

c. 1165–*c.* 1230 Rabbi Eleazar ben Judah of Worms (Eleazar Rokeah). German Talmudist, Kabbalist and author of liturgical poetry.

1190 York Massacre: 150 Jews attacked by a mob took refuge in Clifford's Tower. On the advice of Rabbi Yom Tov of Joigny, head of the community, they committed mass suicide, rather than surrender.

1194–1270 Moses ben Nahman, Nahmanides, Ramban. Spanish mystic and Bible commentator.

Twelfth–thirteenth centuries: Chasidei Ashkenaz movement, a pietistic circle in mediaeval German Jewry.

1215 Fourth Lateran Council ordered Jews to wear a special badge. Enforced in France in 1269.

1242 Following a disputation in 1240, the Talmud and other Jewish books were burned in Paris.

1244 Emperor Frederick II gave special privileges to Jews in Austria, a model followed elsewhere.

1247 Papal Bull condemning the blood libel – the accusation that Jews used Christian blood to bake their Passover unleavened bread.

1249–1316 Rabbi Menahem ben Solomon Meiri of Perpignan. French Talmudist.

1263 Opening of the Disputation in Barcelona.

c. 1270–c. 1343 Jacob ben Asher (Tur). Spanish codifier of the Talmud, author of *Arbaah Turim*.

1288–1344 Rabbi Levi ben Gershon (Gersonides; Ralbag). French philosopher, Bible and Talmud commentator.

1290 Edict of expulsion from England, Jews having arrived with William the Conqueror in 1066.

1293 Death in prison of the great Talmudic authority Rabbi Meir of Rothenburg who refused to allow an extravagant ransom to be paid for his release.

End of thirteenth century: publication of the Zohar ('Splendour'), major work of Jewish mysticism, an esoteric commentary on the Torah, compiled and edited by Moses ben Shem Tov Leon, though traditionally ascribed to second-century Shimon bar Yohai.

1305 following inner Jewish disputes on the legitimacy of studying philosophy, a partial ban was imposed by Solomon ben Abraham ibn Adreth (Rashba).

1306 Expulsion of the Jews from France.

1336 The opening paragraph of the *Alenu* prayer was prohibited in Castile because of alleged anti-Christian sentiments.

1336 'Judenschläger' massacres began in Germany and lasted three years despite protection afforded to the Jews by the Count of Nuremberg.

1348 Black Death massacres throughout Europe following rumours that Jews were responsible for the plague. A protective Bull issued by Pope Clement VI was ineffective.

1391 Riots against Jews in Spain. Forced conversions; start of the 'marrano' problem.

1394 Final expulsion from France.

1413 Disputation opens in Tortosa.

1437–1508 Isaac ben Judah Abravanel, Portuguese Bible commentator, philosopher and statesman.

1438 The first Mellah, the area where Jews were supposed to live, established in Fez and Morocco. In Muslim countries the Jewish Quarter was never as bad as the Ghetto.

c. 1470–c. 1550 Obadiah ben Jacob Sforno, Italian Bible commentator and philosopher. He taught Hebrew to Johannes Reuchlin, Christian Hebraist who defended the Talmud.

1475 The printing of the first Hebrew book completed – an edition of the commentary of Rashi on the Pentateuch.

1481 The first *auto-da-fé* in Seville.

1488–1575 Rabbi Joseph Karo. Spanish Talmudist and mystic. Author of the *Shulhan Arukh.*

1492 Expulsion of Jews from Spain – 160,000 left.

1493 Expulsion of Jews from Sicily.

1497 Expulsion of Jews from Portugal and forced baptism of Jewish children.

Sixteenth century: Jews expelled from Spain settle in the Ottoman Empire and Holland.

1511–c. 1578 Azariah De Rossi. Greatest scholar of Hebrew letters during the Italian Renaissance. His chief work *Me'or Einayim* ('Enlightenment of the Eyes') included a revolutionary study of the development of the Bible and Jewish history.

1516 Establishment of the first ghetto in Venice.

1522–70 Rabbi Moses ben Jacob Cordovero (Ramak). Palestinian Kabbalist, author of *Pardes Rimmonim.*

c. 1525–1609 Rabbi Judah Löw ben Bezalel (Maharal). Bohemian Rabbi, Talmudist and moralist. Legendary creator of the Golem of Prague.

1527 Expulsion of Jews from Florence.

c. 1525–72 Rabbi Moses Isserles (Rema). Polish codifier. His glosses to Joseph Karo's *Shulhan Arukh* giving Ashkenazi variants to Karo's Sephardi version of the *Halakhah* made it the authoritative Code of Jewish law.

1534–72 Isaac ben Solomon Luria (Ari). Palestinian Kabbalist in Safed who profoundly influenced the development of Jewish mysticism.

1542 Martin Luther's *Of the Jews and their Lies* advocated

destroying Jewish synagogues and schools, confiscating their sacred books and forbidding rabbis to teach.

1553 Talmud burned in Rome.

1554 Jewish Synod in Ferrara established internal Jewish censorship of printed books to ensure no materials would appear that could be interpreted as anti-Christian – the cause of attacks on Hebrew literature.

1555 Bull *Cum nimis absurdum* renewed all mediaeval repressive anti-Jewish legislation. Jewish doctors could not treat Christians. Jews forced to wear the Yellow Hat and to live in ghettos. Though temporarily alleviated in 1586 (Bull *Christiana Pietas*), Pope Clement VIII (Bull *Caeca et obdurata* 'Blind and obdurate') confirmed the worst repressions.

1556 Protest by the Sultan, Suleiman the Magnificent, against the Pope's treatment of the Jews.

1564 Printing of the Talmud permitted.

1577–84 Jews in Rome forced to visit churches to hear conversionist sermons.

1580 Council of the Four Lands (provinces of Poland) formed, an autonomous Jewish body which provided leadership for Jews of Poland for almost two hundred years.

1604–57 Manasseh ben Israel, Dutch rabbi of Marrano origin. A public figure, founder of the first Hebrew printing press in Amsterdam.

1626–76 Sabbatai Zevi, the false Messiah who converted to Islam in 1666 in Constantinople.

1632–77 Benedict Spinoza, Dutch philosopher, initiator of modern biblical commentary with his *Theologico-Political Treatise.*

1648/49 Bogdan Chmielnicki's uprising against Polish rule in Ukraine led to massacres of 100,000–300,000 Jews and destruction of hundreds of Jewish communities.

1654 First Jew sails for New Amsterdam from Holland, Jacob son of Samson. He was later joined by a party of Jewish refugees from Brazil.

1655 Manasseh ben Israel petitions Oliver Cromwell for the readmission of Jews into England.

1656 Excommunication of Benedict Spinoza in Amsterdam.

1671 Jews allowed to settle in Brandenburg, the beginnings of the important Jewish community of Berlin.

1698–1738 Joseph Süss Oppenheimer (Jew Süss). German-Jewish financier. Accused of stealing State moneys he was hanged, refusing to accept baptism. His story is told in Lion Feuchtwanger's *Jud Süss.*

1700–60 Israel ben Eliezer, Baal Shem Tov ('Good Master of the Name' (of God)), Besht. Polish religious leader and creator of the Chasidic movement.

1704–72 Dov Baer of Mezhirech, the Maggid. Responsible for the spread of the Chasidic movement.

1707–46 Rabbi Moses Hayyim Luzzatto (Ramhal). Italian Kabbalist and writer of ethical works (*Mesillat Yesharim* – 'The Path of the Upright'), Hebrew poetry and verse dramas. Forced to leave Italy for his messianic ideas, he settled in Amsterdam and died in Palestine.

1720–97 Elijah ben Solomon Zalman, the Vilna Gaon. Lithuanian Talmudist and commentator on Bible, Midrash and Zohar. The leading opponent of the Chasidim.

1722 Opening of the Ashkenazi 'Great Synagogue' in Duke's Place, London.

1729–86 Moses Mendelssohn. German philosopher. A friend of Lessing who modelled the hero of his verse drama *Nathan the Wise* (1779) on him. An exponent of Enlightenment values, encouraging Jews to learn German, he was also a defender of Judaism. In 1780 to 1783 he published a German translation of the Bible with a Hebrew commentary (the *Biur*).

c. 1740–1810 Levi Yitzhak of Berdichev. Polish Chasidic master who helped expand and consolidate the movement.

1742 Expulsion of Jews from most of 'Little Russia' by Empress Elizabeth.

1744–1812 Meyer Amschel Rothschild. Founder of the Rothschild banking dynasty.

1744/45 Expulsion of Jews from Prague by Empress Maria Theresa, to be allowed to return three years later.

1757 Burning of the Talmud in towns in Poland and Russia.

1760 Establishment of the British Board of Deputies, the representative body of British Jewry.

1764 The Council of Four Lands dissolved by the government

of Poland, so as to end Jewish autonomy.

1768 'Haidamacks', roving bands of peasants and Cossacks, massacred Jews in Polish/Ukrainian towns. In Uman thousands were killed in synagogues which were burned down.

1772 First partition of Poland.

1772, 1781 Bans of excommunication published in Vilna against the Chasidim by their opponents, the Mitnagdim. Signatories included the Vilna Gaon.

1772–1811 Rabbi Nahman of Bratslav. Ukrainian Chasidic leader, great-grandson of the Baal Shem Tov. His teachings are incorporated in a series of stories. He left no successor.

1782 Patent of Toleration of Emperor Joseph II lifted ecclesiastical and other social restrictions against Jews, opening up their entry into wider society.

1784–1855 Sir Moses Montefiore, the British communal leader, intervened with governments worldwide on behalf of Jewish communities.

1787 The Constitution of the United States of America gave Jews full equality with other citizens.

1788 Shneur Zalman of Lyady. Author of the *Tanya*, founds *Chabad*, a movement within Chasidism stressing intellectuality – the name is derived from the first letters of the terms: *Chokhmah* ('Wisdom'); *Binah* ('Understanding') and *Da'at* ('Knowledge').

1791 Jews, who had slowly returned to France after the expulsion of 1394, were given Emancipation, the long-term consequence of the Declaration of the Rights of Man.

1791 Establishment of the Pale of Settlement, territory within the borders of czarist Russia where Jews had the right of residence. Permission was needed to live outside the Pale.

1794–1886 Leopold Zunz, German historian, one of the founders of the movement for the scientific study of Jewish history and Judaism in the nineteenth century.

c. 1797–1856 Heinrich Heine. German poet and essayist. In 1825 he converted to Christianity but later regretted it. He worked in Paris as a journalist and poet.

1800–65 Samuel David Luzzatto (Shadal). Italian scholar, philosopher, grammarian, Bible commentator, lecturer at the rabbinical college of Padua from 1829.

1807 Napoleon convenes the 'Sanhedrin' made up of rabbis and lay leaders. The ninth article read: 'That the Jew is required to consider the land of his birth or adoption as his fatherland.'

1808–88 Samson Raphael Hirsch. German rabbi, biblical commentator and writer, leading figure in the creation of neo-Orthodoxy and the struggle against Reform.

1810–83 Israel Salanter. Lithuanian scholar and founder of the Musar, ethical, movement in Lithuania and Russia.

1810 Opening of the first Reform Synagogue by Israel Jacobson (1768–1828) in his boarding school in Seesen, Germany.

1810–74 Abraham Geiger. German rabbi and scholar, the leader of Reform Judaism. In Berlin, from 1870, he helped found the Hochschule (Lehranstalt) für die Wissenschaft des Judentums, the seminary for the training of Reform and Liberal rabbis.

1819 Foundation of the Verein für Kultur und Wissenschaft der Juden in Berlin, the forerunner of the 'Science of Judaism' movement that brought modern scholarly methods to the study of Judaism.

1819–1900 Isaac Meyer Wise. German-born rabbi, pioneer of Reform Judaism in America and founder of the Hebrew Union College (Reform rabbinic seminary 1975).

1827 Russia began conscripting Jewish children, between twelve and twenty-five, into the army for a twenty-five year service. Even younger children were kidnapped for this purpose.

1840 The Damascus Affair. Jews were accused of murdering a missing friar. Only the intervention of leading Jews of France and England prevented a massacre and secured the release of wrongfully imprisoned Jews.

1842 Foundation of the West London Synagogue for British Jews (Reform).

1844 Appointment of Nathan Marcus Adler (1803–91) as British Chief Rabbi. He helped establish Jews' College in 1855 and the United Synagogue (Orthodox) in 1870.

1844–46 Synods of Reform rabbis in Braunschweig, Frankfurt and Breslau.

1847–1915 Solomon Schechter. Rabbinic scholar who discovered the Cairo Genizah. He became a leader of Conservative

Judaism in America and major builder of the Jewish Theological Seminary (Conservative rabbinic seminary).

1851 Founding of the *Monatschrift fur die Geschichte und Wissenschaft des Judentums,* a journal dedicated to the scientific study of Jewish history, by Zacharias Frankel (1801–75).

1854 Foundation of the first modern rabbinic seminary, the Jüdisch-Theologische Seminar (Jewish Theological Seminary) in Breslau (Conservative).

1855 Foundation of Jews' College, London (Orthodox rabbinic seminary).

1856–1927 Ahad ha-Am (Asher Ginsberg). Ukrainian Hebrew essayist, advocate of spiritual dimension to Zionism.

1858–1922 Eliezer Ben-Yehudah (Perelmann). Lithuanian-born Hebrew writer and lexicographer. The 'father' of Hebrew as a modern spoken language and editor of a seventeen-volume comprehensive Hebrew dictionary.

1858–1938 Claude Montefiore. English scholar and theologian. Cofounder of Liberal Judaism in Britain. Founder of the *Jewish Quarterly Review* in 1888.

1860–1945 Henrietta Szold. American Zionist, creator of Hadassah, the Women's Zionist Movement of America.

1859–1917 Ludwig Lazarus Zamenhof. Polish linguist, creator of Esperanto.

1860 Foundation of the Alliance Israelite Universelle to defend Jewish civil liberties, provide vocational and other training for backward Jewish communities and defend Jews from attack and help them in disaster.

1865–1935 Abraham Isaac Kook. Rabbinic scholar, mystic and Zionist, he became the first Chief Rabbi of Palestine.

1869–1904 Theodor Herzl. Austrian journalist and writer. Founder of political Zionism.

1872 Foundation of the Berlin Hochschule für die Wissenschaft des Judentums (Liberal rabbinic seminary).

1873 Foundation of the Rabbinerseminar für das orthodoxe Judentum in Berlin, by Rabbi Azriel Hildesheimer (1820–99).

1873–1956 Leo Baeck. German rabbi, theologian and religious leader. In Berlin he lectured on midrash and homiletics at the Hochschule für die Wissenschaft des Judentums. From 1933 he was the President of the representative body of German Jewry. Deported to Theresienstadt Concentration Camp he survived the war, lived in Britain and taught at the Hebrew Union College, Cincinnati.

1875 Foundation of Hebrew Union College, Cincinnati (Reform rabbinic seminary).

1877 Foundation of Neolog (Conservative) rabbinic seminary, Budapest.

1878 Agricultural settlement of Petach Tikvah established. The first such Jewish settlement in the land of Israel for almost two thousand years.

1878–1965 Martin Buber. Vienna-born philosopher, Bible scholar and religious thinker, best known for his books on Chasidism and his philosopy of dialogue. Settled in Palestine in 1938. He was a passionate advocate of Jewish–Arab understanding.

1879–1942 Janusz Korczak (Henryk Goldszmidt). Polish author, social worker and pioneer in children's education. He accompanied children in his care to the death-camp in Treblinka.

1880 Foundation in Russia of ORT (Obshchestvo Rasprostraneniya Trudasredi Yevreyev (Society for Manual Work among Jews)), organisation for promoting vocational training for skilled trades and agriculture among Jews. From 1920 World ORT became an international organisation. ORT schools now operate in Africa, Asia and South America in collaboration with local governments.

1881–1983 Mordecai Kaplan. American rabbi and founder of the Reconstructionist movement.

1881/82 Following pogroms in Russia the beginning of a massive emigration, particularly to the United States.

1885 Nathaniel Meyer, first Lord Rothschild, takes his seat in the House of Lords.

1885 Pittsburgh Platform. Document reflecting the position of the more radical camp of American Reform Judaism. The Columbus Platform of 1937 represented a return to a more traditional position. The San Francisco Platform of 1976 continued this trend, while reflecting greater stress on Jewish peoplehood in the wake of the Holocaust.

1886 Foundation of the Jewish Theological Seminary, New York

(Conservative rabbinic seminary).

1886 Foundation of Yeshiva University, New York (Orthodox).

1886–1929 Franz Rosenzweig. German philosopher, Bible-scholar, educator and theologian. He instituted the Lehrhaus, for Jewish studies, in Frankfurt and translated the Bible into German together with Martin Buber.

1894–1906 'Dreyfus Affair'. A French-Jewish army captain, Alfred Dreyfus, falsely convicted of spying, which led to rising expressions of anti-Semitism in France, was eventually released.

1897 First Zionist Congress in Basel.

1897 Foundation in Vilnius of the Bund, a Jewish non-Zionist, socialist party and trade union.

1905 First publication of the *Protocols of the Elders of Zion*, an anti-Semitic forgery claiming to the record of a Jewish conspiracy for world domination. Published first in Russia, and exposed as a fraud by *The Times*, it has nevertheless been reprinted countless times and used for anti-Jewish propaganda.

1914–18 Over one million Jews fought for their respective countries during the First World War, and 140,000 died.

1917 Balfour Declaration. A letter from the British foreign secretary supporting the establishment of a Jewish national home in Palestine.

1922 The League of Nations placed Palestine under the British Mandate, till the British withdrew on 15th May 1948.

1926 Foundation in London of the World Union for Progressive Judaism.

1929–45 Anne Frank. Dutch girl whose diary records her experience in hiding in Amsterdam till captured by the Nazis and murdered in Bergen Belsen extermination camp.

1932 Youth Aliyah. An organisation for settling and educating Jewish children in Palestine, created by Recha Freyer in Berlin. Subsequently led by Henrietta Szold.

1933 Hitler comes to power in Germany and immediately begins anti-Jewish actions.

1935 The Nuremberg Laws deprive Jews of their civil rights in Germany.

1935 Fräulein Rabbiner Regina Jonas (1902–44), the first woman rabbi, ordained in Berlin. She served as a rabbi in Berlin, was deported to Theresienstadt Concentration Camp and died in Auschwitz.

1938 Breslau Rabbinic Seminary closed.

1938 9–10th November, 'Kristallnacht', the 'night of broken glass'. Jewish communities attacked and synagogues burnt throughout Germany.

1942 Wannsee Conference, 20th January, where the Nazi leaders planned the 'Final Solution', the extermination of the Jews under their control.

1942 Berlin Hochschule für die Wissenschaft des Judentums closed.

1943 19th April, the beginning of the Warsaw Ghetto Uprising.

1945 At the end of the Second World War, six million Jews, one third of the world Jewish population, had been killed by the Nazis in the Shoah.

1947 29th November, the United Nations votes for the division of Palestine between Jews and Arabs.

1948 14th May, David Ben Gurion proclaims the creation of the State of Israel, followed immediately by the War of Independence.

1955 Foundation of the Academy for Jewish Religion, New York, a pluralistic rabbinic seminary.

1956 The Suez Crisis.

1956 Foundation of the Leo Baeck College, London, the postwar rabbinic seminary (Reform and Liberal) created to be the European successor of the Hochschule für die Wissenschaft des Judentums.

1967 The Six Day War.

1967 Foundation of the Reconstructionist Rabbinical College, Philadelphia.

1973 The October War.

1979 Peace Treaty between Israel and Egypt.

1982 Lebanon War.

1987 Beginning of the Intifada.

1987 Following relaxation of controls over countries within the Soviet Union, Jewish emigration and Jewish educational and cultural activities were allowed. Some seven hundred thousand Jews left the former Soviet Union for Israel by 1998.

Historical time-line

1994 Prime Minister Rabin and Yasser Arafat sign the Gaza-Jericho Accords.

1995 Murder of Prime Minister Rabin at a Peace demonstration in Tel Aviv.

Subject Index

Subject Index

Beruriah 87, 88, 90, 93

Besht, *see* Baal Shem Tov

Beth Din 77, 207, 208, 308

Beth Jacob Schools 89

Biale, David 275

Bikkur holim 160, 308

Black Death 54, 319

Bloch, Ernst 279

Blood libel 33

Blue, Rabbi Lionel 36, 37, 133, 227, 239

'Book of Life' 184

Breslau 67, 133

Brice, Fanny 279

B'rit 28, 308

Brod, Max 278

Bruce, Lennie 279

Buber, Martin 14, 114, 248, 278

Burns, George 279

Cantor 79, 211

Cantor, Eddie 279

Catholic Church 41, 42

Chanukah 10, 308, 315, 316

Chasid, Chasidism 7, 63, 138, 223, 238, 240, 244, 247, 248, 249, 251, 276, 277

Chazan, see Cantor

Cherem 60, 113, 308

Chmelnitzki 55, 57, 321

Christian, Christianity 4, 5, 6, 7, 13, 17, 23, 37, 39, 40, 41, 42, 43, 45, 54, 57, 62, 88, 98, 101, 106, 113, 114, 142, 160, 162, 164, 198, 206, 218, 219, 237, 238, 240, 241, 243, 254, 259, 272, 286, 297

Chronicles, Book of 50

Chumash (Pentateuch) 96, 97, 98, 101, 105, 113, 119, 156, 163

Circumcision 28, 39, 66, 170, 171, 172, 173, 174

Codes (of Jewish Law) 104, 243

Cohen, Hermann 278

Cohen, Leonard 279

Columbus Platform 68

Conservative Judaism 7, 66, 68, 70, 91, 212, 214, 217, 220, 221, 223, 270, 275, 277, 308

Conversion (to Judaism) 39, 40, 224, 226, 260

Cossack 55, 56

Covenant 28, 29, 33, 39, 46, 76, 106, 170, 209, 211, 221, 222, 268, 270, 271, 277, 286, 287, 289, 292

Crusade, Crusaders 6, 54, 189, 237

Cyrus 53

Da'at miqra 100

Daniel 50, 290, 291

David, King 29, 50, 52, 76, 108, 109, 173, 235, 286

Day of Atonement, *see* Yom Kippur

De Leon, Moses 244

Deuteronomy, Book of 50, 51, 105

Dhimmi 57

Dialogue, interfaith 219, 297

Diaspora 53, 61, 220, 225, 226, 230, 268, 269, 270, 273, 274, 277

Dienemann, Rabbi Max 91

Dina d'malkhuta dina 57

Disputations 41

Döblin, Alfred 278

Documentary Hypothesis 14

Dorfler, Aryeh 91

Dreyfus 58, 327

Dylan, Bob (Robert, Zimmerman) 279

Ecclesiastes 50, 104, 109, 110, 234

Edom 34, 50, 110

Egypt, Egyptians 12, 15, 32, 33, 34, 45, 52, 61, 144, 161, 175, 176, 179, 180, 228, 291

Einstein, Albert 7, 280

Subject Index

The Explorer's Guide to Judaism

Subject Index

174, 196, 199, 200, 203, 207,
208, 212, 213, 214, 215, 216,
217, 218, 219, 220, 221, 222,
224, 225, 226, 227, 228, 229,
230, 241, 248, 253, 270, 274,
275, 276, 277, 291, 298, 310
Ottoman Empire 54, 57
Ozick, Cynthia 92

Palestine 6, 59, 60, 68, 68
Palestinians 9, 219, 271, 272
Passover 10, 32, 33, 34, 35, 61, 86,
103, 172, 176, 179, 181, 183,
219, 239, 250, 254, 311, 315
Patriarchs 48, 49, 51, 82, 284
Patrilineal Descent 224
Paul 106
Pentateuch, see Chumash
Pentecost, see Shavuot
Perutz, Leo 278
Pesach, see Passover
Petuchowski, Jacob 48
Pharisees 17, 39, 119, 122, 150 241
Pharaoh 32, 33, 36, 76, 180
Philo Lexikon 260, 278
Pittsburgh Platform 67
Plaskow, Judith 92
Plaut, Rabbi Gunther 98, 99
Plumptre, E. H. 109, 110, 111
Poland 2, 57, 89, 239
Progressive Judaism 218, 221, 227,
273, 311
Progressive Revelation 67
Prophets 142
Proselyte 39
Proverbs 50, 89
Psalms, Book of 44, 50, 104, 156
Pshat 106
Purim 35, 103, 311, 315

Rabbi, Rabbinic 3, 5, 12, 15, 17,
18, 19, 20, 22, 23, 32, 44, 49,
50, 61, 63, 76, 77, 88, 92, 97,
101, 104, 105, 106, 107, 108,
111, 112, 113, 114, 119, 121,

122, 123, 125, 131, 132, 133,
134, 135, 136, 137, 138, 139,
140, 150, 155, 156, 158, 160,
194, 196, 203, 207, 211, 213,
218, 222, 224, 227, 228, 229,
230, 231, 235, 249, 250, 260,
261, 275, 277, 280, 284, 288,
289, 295, 311
Rabbi Meir 86, 87, 88
Rachel 78, 235
Rashi 88, 96, 97, 98, 101, 113 217,
285
Rebeccah 78
Reconstructionist Judaism 68,
220, 221, 230, 270, 277, 311
Redemption 29
Reform Judaism 40, 62, 63, 64,
65, 66, 67, 68, 69, 70, 89, 91,
99, 133, 161, 164, 195, 198,
199, 207, 212, 213, 214, 215,
217, 218, 220, 221, 224, 229,
270, 275, 277, 292, 311
Reform Synagogues of Great
Britain 198
Responsa 104, 131
Ritual Murder 55, 318
Rogers, Richard 279
Rome, Roman 4, 34, 50, 103, 110,
123, 237
Rosenzweig, Franz 14, 43, 114,
278, 327
Rosh chodesh, see New Moon
Rosh Hashanah 103, 147, 184, 250,
311, 314
Roth, Joseph 278
Roth, Philip 279
Russia 58
Ruth 38, 50, 76, 103

Sabbatai Zevi, Sabbatianism 238,
248
Sadducees 119, 150, 241
Safed 130, 245
Samuel 50, 76, 127
Sandak (Sandek) 173, 174

335

Subject Index

Index of biblical verses

Index of biblical verses

WITHDRAWN

Index of rabbinic texts